SEMINAR STUDIES IN HISTORY

The Origins of the Cold War, 1941–1949

3rd Edition

Martin McCauley

PEARSON
Longman

London • New York • Toronto • Sydney • Tokyo • Singapore
Hong Kong • Cape Town • Madrid • Paris • Amsterdam • Munich • Milan

PEARSON EDUCATION LIMITED

Head Office:
Edinburgh Gate
Harlow CM20 2JE
Tel: +44 (0)1279 623623
Fax: +44 (0)1279 431059

London Office:
128 Long Acre
London WC2E 9AN
Tel: +44 (0)20 7447 2000
Fax: +44 (0)20 7447 2170
Website: www.history-minds.com

First published in Great Britain in 2003

ISBN 0 582 77284 2

British Library Cataloguing in Publication Data
A CIP catalogue record for this book can be obtained from the British Library

Library of Congress Cataloging in Publication Data
A CIP catalog record for this book can be obtained from the Library of Congress

10 9 8 7 6 5 4 3 2 1

Typeset in 10/12.5pt Sabon by Graphicraft Limited, Hong Kong
Printed and bound in Malaysia, LSP

The Publishers' policy is to use paper manufactured from sustainable forests.

CONTENTS

INTRODUCTION TO THE SERIES

Such is the pace of historical enquiry in the modern world that there is an ever-widening gap between the specialist article or monograph, incorporating the results of current research, and general surveys, which inevitably become out of date. *Seminar Studies in History* is designed to bridge this gap. The series was founded by Patrick Richardson in 1966 and his aim was to cover major themes in British, European and world history. Between 1980 and 1996 Roger Lockyer continued his work, before handing the editorship over to Clive Emsley and Gordon Martel. Clive Emsley is Professor of History at the Open University, while Gordon Martel is Professor of International History at the University of Northern British Columbia, Canada, and Senior Research Fellow at De Montfort University.

All the books are written by experts in their field who are not only familiar with the latest research but have often contributed to it. They are frequently revised, in order to take account of new information and interpretations. They provide a selection of documents to illustrate major themes and provoke discussion, and also a guide to further reading. The aim of *Seminar Studies in History* is to clarify complex issues without over-simplifying them, and to stimulate readers into deepening their knowledge and understanding of major themes and topics.

ACKNOWLEDGEMENTS

The publishers would like to thank the following for permission to reproduce copyright material: Little, Brown and Company for two extracts from George F. Kennan's *Memoirs 1925–50*, copyright © 1967 by George F. Kennan; Harcourt Brace & Company and Milovan Djilas for two extracts from Milovan Djilas, *Conversations with Stalin*; Curtis Brown Ltd, London (copyright the Estate of Sir Winston S. Churchill) for three extracts from Winston Churchill's *Triumph and Tragedy*; Arthur Schlesinger, Jr. for an extract from his article 'Origins of the Cold War' from *Foreign Affairs* vol. xlvi (1967).

Although every effort has been made we have been unable to trace the copyright holders of *The Tragedy of American Diplomacy* (Revised Edition, 1962) edited by William Appleman Williams and *The Eden Memoirs, the Reckoning* (1965) by Anthony Eden, and would appreciate any information that would enable us to do so.

FOREWORD TO THE THIRD EDITION

The bipolar world is no more. Gone is the world divided into two camps, armed to the teeth with nuclear weapons, threatening one another and the rest of humankind. The extraordinary ideological battle, between two visions of the European Enlightenment, has died away. The younger generation today find it difficult to understand the tension and conflict. In the eyes of the downtrodden, deprived and despised, globalisation has assumed the mantle of evil. In the past, they looked to communism to champion their cause. Will a new ideology emerge to replace Marxism? If it does, a new Cold War will be in prospect. Then there is the conflict between radical Islam and the West. It appears that humankind is incapable of coming to rest and living in harmony. There are salutary lessons to be learnt from the confrontation between America and Russia. If conflict is not managed with skill, the result can be disastrous, even the end of the world. This study concerns itself with the origins of that conflict but, it must be admitted, there are hugely divergent views on the subject. As scholars say, more research is needed.

MARTIN McCAULEY
NOVEMBER 2002

CHRONOLOGY

1939

23 August	Molotov and von Ribbentrop, German Foreign Minister, sign in Moscow the German-Soviet Non-Aggression Pact, having already signed a trade and credit agreement (19 August). In a secret protocol the two sides divide up east central Europe. The Soviet Union acquires Finland, the Baltic States (except Lithuania), eastern Poland and Bessarabia. On 28 September 1939 another agreement gave Moscow Lithuania. (The existence of this secret protocol was denied by Moscow until the late Gorbachev era.)
1 September	Germany attacks Poland and penetrates up to the line agreed in the secret protocol and the Second World War begins.
3 September	Britain and France declare war on Germany.
17 September	Soviet troops begin their march into eastern Poland (as agreed by the secret protocol). Lvov falls to them on 21–22 September.
28 September	Molotov and von Ribbentrop sign in Moscow a new German-Soviet border and friendship treaty which lays down a new demarcation line on Bug on the river Vistula. Lithuania becomes part of the Soviet zone of influence.
30 November–12 March 1940	The Soviet-Finnish (or Winter) war begins with an air raid over Helsinki and the march of Soviet troops into Karelia. A Finnish People's Government, composed of Finnish émigré communists, headed by Otto Kuusinen, is announced by Molotov. Had Finland fallen, this government would have taken over the country.
14 December	The League of Nations rules that the Soviet Union was the aggressor in the war with Finland and excludes it from the League.

1940

11–12 March	Finland concedes Soviet demands at peace negotiations in Moscow. Finland gives up Vyborg and a part of Karelia. Hangö is rented as a military base to the Soviet Union for 30 years.

26 June	The Soviet government demands that Romania secede Bessarabia and northern Bukovina to it. When Romania does not concur, Red Army units occupy both regions on 28 June.
21 July	Field Marshal von Brauchitsch, commander-in-chief of the army, is ordered by Hitler to begin preparing for war against the Soviet Union. Hitler envisages a five-month campaign in the spring of 1941.
12–13 November	Molotov arrives in Berlin for negotiations concerning the division of the world. Moscow wants Finland, Romania and Bulgaria.
18 December	Hitler signs instruction no. 21, Operation *Barbarossa*, which envisages all preparations for an attack on the Soviet Union to be finished by 15 May 1941.

1941

11 March	The United States begins Lend-Lease economic and military aid to Britain (to USSR on 7 November).
13 April	The Japanese ambassador in Berlin, Matsuoka, returning to Tokyo, breaks his journey in Moscow (8 April) and signs a neutrality treaty with the Soviet Union which recognises existing territory and borders and in the case of war with third parties the signatories will remain neutral. Japan also recognises the independence of the Mongolian People's Republic.
30 April	Operation *Barbarossa* is postponed from 15 May to 22 June (the same date Napoleon launched his attack on Russia in 1812).

The Great Patriotic War, 1941–5

22 June	German units attack the Soviet Union across a broad front without a declaration of war. Churchill offers Stalin help as does Roosevelt (23 June); Molotov, not Stalin, announces to the Soviet people that Germany has invaded.
23 June	Hungary breaks off diplomatic relations with the Soviet Union and Slovakia declares war on Moscow and provides Germany with two divisions.
26 June	Finland declares war on the Soviet Union.
27 June	Hungary declares war on the Soviet Union.
30 June	The State Committee for Defence (GKO) is set up and Stalin becomes its head (1 July).
3 July	Stalin, in a radio broadcast, proclaims the Great Patriotic (Fatherland) War and orders that no territory shall be conceded to the enemy.

12 July	Great Britain and the Soviet Union sign an agreement on mutual aid against Germany. Unilateral peace negotiations or armistices are ruled out.
29 July–1 August	Roosevelt sends Harry Hopkins to Moscow to assess the political and military situation in the Soviet Union.
August–September	British and Soviet forces occupy Iran, required by the Western Allies as a supply route to the Soviet Union.
11 August	After meeting at sea off the coast of Newfoundland, Roosevelt and Churchill agree on the Atlantic Charter, promising the restoration of independence to occupied states.
30 September–20 April 1942	Battle for Moscow; Hitler calls it Operation *Typhoon* and it is code-named Moscow *Cannae* (the battle in 216 BC in south-eastern Italy where the Roman legions were destroyed by Hannibal). The German offensive comes to a stop in December and on 5 December a Soviet counter-offensive forces the Germans back.
7 December	Japanese forces attack Pearl Harbor, Hawaii, bringing the US into the war.
15–18 December	Anthony Eden (later Lord Avon) visits Moscow to meet Stalin and is informed that the Soviet Union wishes to retain its territorial gains of 1939–40.

1942

1 January	In Washington, 26 states, including the Soviet Union, sign the United Nations Pact (also called the Washington Pact), which recognises the Atlantic Charter as the joint programme of objectives and principles.
11 April	Roosevelt cables Stalin that the Americans are planning an offensive to relieve the Russians.
26 May	In London, Molotov signs an Anglo-Soviet alliance and friendship treaty for 20 years.
29 May–1 June	Molotov holds talks in Washington on a second front in west Europe (Britain had already agreed to this on 26 May) and economic aid.
11 June	The foreign ministers of the USSR and the United States sign, in Washington, a treaty on the principles of mutual aid in the struggle against German aggression and on cooperation in the post-war world.
12–15 August	Churchill and Averell Harriman, for Roosevelt, hold talks in Moscow with Stalin on measures against Germany and its allies.
12 December	Soviet-Czechoslovak alliance signed in Moscow, indicating desire of Czechoslovaks to collaborate with the Russians after the war.

1943

31 January–2 February	The southern part of the German army at Stalingrad surrenders on 31 January (Field Marshal Paulus) and the northern part on 2 February (General Strecker). The Russians lose 1.1 million men and the Germans 800,000.
14 April	Stalin's son, Yakov, a prisoner-of-war in the German Sachsenhausen concentration camp, deliberately seeks death by entering a prohibited zone and is shot dead. (The Germans apparently offered to exchange him for Field Marshal Paulus but Stalin refused.)
25 April	The Soviet Union breaks diplomatic relations with the Polish government-in-exile over the latter's demand for an international inquiry into the Katyn affair.
6 May	The communist Union of Polish Patriots (a forerunner of the Lublin committee), set up on 1 March but only reported on 8 May, requests that Stalin permit the establishment of a Polish division in the Soviet Union to be called the Tadeusz Kosciusko division. Stalin grants permission on 9 May.
15 May	Stalin dissolves the Cominform to demonstrate that the Soviet Union has no expansionary aims; the functions of the Cominform are taken over by the Central Committee Secretariat and a department of international affairs is set up.
19–30 October	Moscow Conference of Foreign Ministers (Molotov, Eden and Cordell Hull (United States) agree, inter alia, that Austria be reconstituted in its 1937 frontiers and that East Prussia be removed from Germany.
28 November–1 December	At Tehran Stalin, Churchill and Roosevelt agree, in principle, on the partition of Germany. The Curzon line is to be the Polish-Soviet frontier. Stalin requests Königsberg, the capital of East Prussia.

1944

6 June	D-Day landing of Allied troops in Normandy, code-named Operation *Overlord*.
1–22 July	Bretton Woods conference of 44 states on finance and economic affairs after the war. It agrees to establish the International Monetary Fund (IMF) to be concerned with macro-economic problems such as currency rates and fiscal and monetary policy, and to set up the World Bank to be concerned with micro-economic affairs such as funding of capital projects. The Soviet Union declines to join.
21 July	The Polish committee for national liberation is set up in Cholm after its liberation by Soviet troops. It then moves to Lublin on 25 July (the Lublin committee).

26 July	A treaty of friendship and alliance is signed by the Soviet government and the Lublin committee in Moscow. Diplomatic relations are established on 2 September.
1 August–10 October	Warsaw uprising, led by General Bor-Komorowski. Soviet troops refuse to come to their aid and the Poles surrender on 10 October.
23 August	Romania changes sides and declares war on Germany.
4 September	Finnish troops cease hostilities and a Finnish delegation is sent on 6 September to Moscow to negotiate a peace treaty.
5 September	The Soviet Union declares war on Bulgaria and invades it on 8 September.
8–9 September	*Coup d'état* in Bulgaria by the communists and officers to establish a democratic government of the patriotic front, led by Georgiev (pro-Soviet). Moscow declares the war over on 9 September.
12 September	London protocol, signed by the United States, the Soviet Union and Great Britain, on future occupation zones in Germany and the administration of Greater Berlin.
19 September	A ceasefire is agreed by the Soviet Union, Great Britain and Finland in Moscow. Finland is to withdraw to the 1940 frontiers. It concedes Petsamo to the Soviet Union and has to pay reparations.
7 October	At Dumbarton Oaks, the United States, Great Britain, the Soviet Union and China agree to establish the United Nations (and a draft UN charter) as the successor organisation to the League of Nations.
9–18 October	Stalin and Churchill meet in Moscow and negotiate on a post-war settlement, especially on eastern and south-eastern Europe. Stalin agrees in principle to Churchill's 'percentages' deal, apportioning zones of influence in the Balkans.
10 December	General de Gaulle signs a Soviet-French alliance treaty against Germany for 20 years. De Gaulle declines to recognise the Lublin committee and Stalin the separation of the Rhineland and Ruhr from Germany.

1945

1 January	The Lublin committee is renamed the Provisional Government of the Republic of Poland and the Soviet government establishes diplomatic relations with it on 5 January. The United States and Britain refuse to recognise it.
20 January	Hungary, a German ally, signs an armistice with the Soviet Union.

4–11 February	Stalin, Churchill and Roosevelt discuss future military operations and the post-war world at Yalta.
3 March	Under Soviet pressure Finland declares war on Germany (effective from 19 September 1944).
11 April	Soviet-Yugoslav treaty of mutual assistance signed. Similar treaties are signed with the other east and south-east European states.
12 April	Roosevelt dies and Vice President Harry Truman becomes President.
23 April	President Truman warns Molotov, the Soviet Foreign Minister, in a brusque fashion, that Moscow must keep to the Yalta agreements. Molotov ripostes that he has never been spoken to in this manner in his life.
25 April	Soviet and US troops meet on Torgau, on the Elbe.
2 May	Berlin capitulates to the Red Army.
7 May	The general capitulation of the Wehrmacht is signed by Colonel General Jodl in the headquarters of General Eisenhower in Reims, France. It is to be effective at 0.10 on 9 May.
8 May	General Field Marshal Keitel, Admiral von Friedeburg and Colonel General Stumpff sign the unconditional surrender of German forces at the Soviet headquarters at Berlin Karlshorst. The document is dated 8 May but it is signed at 0.16 on 9 May.
12 May	Churchill uses the term 'iron curtain' for the first time, in a telegram to President Truman.
24 May	At a victory reception in the Georgevsky Hall, in the Kremlin, for over a thousand officers, Stalin lauds the Russian nation and places it above all other nations in the Soviet Union.
26 June	In San Francisco, the charter of the United Nations is signed by 50 states.
4 July	An allied commission for Austria is agreed by the Soviet Union, the United States, Great Britain and France.
16 July	The US tests successfully the first atomic bomb at Alamogordo, New Mexico.
17 July–2 August	The United States, the Soviet Union and Great Britain agree on the political and economic goals of their occupation policy in Germany at the Potsdam Conference.
6 August	The United States drops atomic bomb on Hiroshima, Japan.
8 August	The Soviet Union declares war on Japan.

9 August	The United States drops an atomic bomb on Nagasaki, Japan.
14 August	The Soviet Union and China (Chiang Kai-shek) sign a treaty of friendship and alliance which confirms Soviet use of Port Arthur and Dairen, the confirmation of the status quo in the Mongolian People's Republic and Soviet influence in northern Manchuria. The East Chinese railway, sold to the government of Manchukuo in 1935, reverts to joint Soviet-Chinese administration.
15 August	Japan surrenders on the understanding that Hirohito will remain emperor.
21 August	Japanese troops capitulate to the Red Army, including over 600,000 prisoners.
23 August	The United States ends the Lend-Lease programme.
2 September	Japan surrenders to the Allies on board *USS Missouri* (V-J Day).
11 September–2 October	London conference of the foreign ministers of the Soviet Union, the United States, Great Britain, France and China finds agreement difficult. Discussions on peace treaties for defeated states and reparations for the Soviet Union.
24 October	The Soviet Union, Belorussia and Ukraine join the UN as founding members.
16–26 December	Foreign ministers conference in Moscow sets up a Far East Commission and Molotov and Byrnes (US) discuss the withdrawal of Soviet troops from China and non-intervention in the domestic affairs of China. On Korea, Molotov proposes a Soviet-American commission to unite the two parts of Korea, politically and economically. The commission adjourns in May 1946 without achieving anything.
29 December	Soviet-French trade treaty but little agreement on compensation for French property in Soviet-occupied regions.

1946

22 January	Carpatho-Ukraine is separated from Czechoslovakia and becomes the Transcarpathian oblast, in the Ukrainian Soviet Socialist Republic.
25 February	The Red Army is renamed the Soviet Army.
5 March	Churchill's speech at Fulton, Missouri, speaks of an 'iron curtain' descending in Europe from Stettin (Szczecin) in the north to Trieste in the south. He calls for an Anglo-American alliance. Stalin sharply criticises the speech on 13 March.
15 March	USSR Sovnarkom becomes the USSR Council of Ministers. People's Commissariats are renamed Ministries.

25 April–15 May; 15 June–12 July	The second conference of the four powers (the USSR, the United States, Great Britain and France) discusses European security and Germany, the Trieste problem and a peace treaty with Austria.
4 November–12 December	At the third conference of foreign ministers, Molotov refuses to accept proposals on Germany and Austria.

1947

10 February	The foreign ministers of the victorious powers sign peace treaties with Italy, Romania, Bulgaria, Hungary and Finland.
10 March–24 April	Molotov, at the fourth foreign ministers conference, in Moscow, rejects Western proposals for a federal Germany and also the Marshall Plan. Reparations are agreed at $20 billion, with the Soviet Union receiving half.
12 March	President Truman proclaims the Truman Doctrine which promises US help to countries threatened by communism.
5 June	General George Marshall, US Secretary of State, announces the Marshall Plan, the European recovery programme.
27 June–1 July	At the foreign ministers conference in Paris, Molotov rejects the supra-national organisation necessary to implement the Marshall Plan.
22–27 September	An information bureau of communist and workers' parties (Cominform) is set up in Szklarska Poręba, Poland, by communist and workers' parties from the Soviet Union, Hungary, Romania, Bulgaria, Poland, Czechoslovakia, France, Italy and Yugoslavia (until 1948). Its headquarters are in Belgrade, and in Bucharest from 1948.
25 November–16 December	Council of Foreign Ministers meets in London but again fails to make progress on German and Austrian peace treaties. The United States, Britain and France begin considering the establishment of a west German state.

1948

19–25 February	The communists take power in Czechoslovakia.
23 February	The United States, Britain and France begin discussions in London to establish the future Federal Republic of Germany.
20 March	The Allied Control Commission in Berlin is paralysed by the withdrawal of Marshal Sokolovsky.
2 April	The US Congress approves Marshall Aid and an economic cooperation administration is set up to run it.
6 April	In Moscow, a treaty of friendship and mutual aid for 10 years is signed by Finland and the Soviet Union.

23 June	After the introduction of the Deutsche Mark in the Western zones of Germany and West Berlin (20 June), a currency reform is also announced for the Soviet Occupied Zone and all Berlin. The Western allies refuse to accept the Soviet reform, and the Soviet military administration (SMAD) then blockades completely the three Western sectors of Berlin (the Berlin Blockade).
24 June–12 May 1949	Berlin Blockade: all land and waterways to West Berlin and East Germany are blocked. Berlin is supplied by air lift from 26 June 1948 to 29 June 1949.
28 June	The Communist party of Yugoslavia is expelled from the Cominform at a conference in Bucharest and Cominform's headquarters are moved to Bucharest.

1949

25 January	The Council for Mutual Economic Assistance (Comecon or CMEA) is set up by the Soviet Union, Bulgaria, Hungary, Poland, Romania and Czechoslovakia.
4 April	NATO is set up in Washington.
4 May	Four-power agreement in New York on the ending of the Berlin Blockade to be effective on 12 May.
23 May–20 June	Foreign ministers conference in Paris fails to reach agreement as the Soviet Union rejects the Basic Law (Grundgesetz) announced for the three Western zones on 23 May.
25 September	Tass reports on the explosion of the first Soviet atomic bomb.
1 October	Soviet note on the German question. The Western powers are held solely responsible for the division of Germany after the formation of the Federal Republic of Germany on 20 September 1949.
1–2 October	The Soviet Union is the first state to recognise the People's Republic of China.
7 October	The German Democratic Republic (DDR) is established.

Map 1 Soviet territorial gains in Europe 1939–49

Allied Control Zone of Germany and Austria
Ceded to USSR by Britain and America
Annexed by USSR in 1945
States which became Communist between 1945 and 1948
Yugoslav gains from Italy 1945
Cities divided into 4 Occupation Sectors
1937 frontiers
The Iron Curtain from 1948
Germany since 1945
FINLAND
Viborg
Leningrad
ESTONIA
Pskov
LATVIA
Riga
LITHUANIA
Memel
Königsberg
Vilna
USSR
Minsk
SWEDEN
DENMARK
Szczecin (Stettin)
Danzig
EAST PRUSSIA
Annexed by Poland
American
Bremen
Soviet
Berlin
Annexed by Poland
Pozban
Warsaw
Pinsk
British
POLAND
Erfurt
Wroclaw (Breslau)
Prague
Cracow
Lvov
French
Nuremberg (Trials 1945-6)
CZECHOSLOVAKIA
Uzhgorod
Czernowitz
FRANCE
French
American
Soviet
Vienna
USA
AUSTRIA
Kishinev
Budapest
French
SWITZERLAND
British
HUNGARY
ROMANIA
Monarchy abolished 1947
Trieste (British and US occupation 1945-55)
Bucharest
Belgrade
YUGOSLAVIA
Monarchy abolished 1945
Monarchy abolished after Plebiscite June 1946
BULGARIA
Monarchy abolished 1946
Communist activity 1946-9
Sofia
BULGARIA
ITALY
Monarchy abolished 1946
ALBANIA
GREECE
TURKEY
0
800 km
Monarchy restored after Plebiscite Sept. 1946

Map 2 Europe 1945–8

PART ONE THE BACKGROUND

CHAPTER ONE

SETTING THE SCENE

The intervention of the United States in April 1917 tipped the scales in favour of the Entente Powers in the First World War. Americans, first and foremost President Woodrow Wilson, wished to ensure that such mutual self-destruction never occurred again. His vision of a world free from the awful threat of war involved national self-determination for all peoples, representative government, the promotion of political changes through constitutional gradualist means and not by revolutions, and the fostering of enlightened public opinion. Wilson perceived in the guiding principles of pre-1914 diplomacy – namely, spheres of influence and the balance of power – the seeds of inevitable doom. He wished to render these principles obsolete by the establishment of an organisation, universal in its reach, which would group all independent states in a league of nations. It would ensure that the legitimate security needs of all states were recognised and respected. Crises could be defused through negotiation and the moral authority of the league. A major plank in the platform of Wilsonianism was an 'open door' world economy. This implied that tariff barriers, imperial preference and all other state-erected obstacles to the free flow of capital and goods world-wide must be dismantled. In short, Wilson had a gleaming liberal capitalist vision of the future, and his political assumptions were based on civil liberties and freedom for every individual to develop his talents and abilities not only in the United States but throughout the whole world. Wilsonianism, then, was the expression of faith of a confident, strong nation. American values, it was confidently assumed, would in due course become universal values.

The Bolshevik revolution of October 1917 was the first decisive rejection of President Wilson's views. The communist state represented the opposite pole of political thinking. It was collectivist in that through democratic centralism it subordinated party members to the leaders and the rest of the population to the party. It sought to establish a socialist economy, in which the market economy would be abolished. It placed the interests of Soviet Russia ahead of those of any person or group of persons; hence national self-determination, despite its espousal by Lenin, was unlikely to be high among its priorities. The

Soviet state was based on rule by one class, the working class (tactically allied to the poorer strata of the peasantry in the short run), to the exclusion of other classes, and the bourgeoisie and the capitalist ethic were vilified. It announced its unremitting hostility to the world capitalist system and international economy, foretelling doom for them both.

If Wilsonian idealists were appalled by the October revolution, so too was the American business community. Both groups comforted themselves with the belief that such an un-American system of government and economy could not survive very long.

There was another group which took a jaundiced view of the turn of events in Petrograd and Moscow; namely, the American diplomats who specialised in Russia and eastern Europe. Some of them had known and relished service in Imperial Russia and one of them, Joseph Grew, found the fact that Western diplomats negotiated with their 'red' counterparts at Genoa and Rapallo in 1922 'profoundly disgusting'. The United States declined to recognise the new Soviet state, but in order to acquaint itself with its thinking a Division of Russian Affairs was established in the State Department. A key centre for research on the Soviet Union was Riga, capital of Latvia, which had been part of Russia until the October revolution, but was now an independent republic and a haven for many middle- and upper-class Russian exiles. The views and attitudes developed in Riga had a profound influence on the policy formulations drawn up by the Division of Russian Affairs in Washington, which Yergin dubs the 'Riga axioms' [Yergin 1980: 17]. Great stress was laid, in these, on the world revolutionary goals and practices of Soviet leaders, and the advice emanating from Riga took the Soviet 'threat' very seriously and warned the United States to be on its guard. Charles Bohlen and George Kennan were two of the brightest stars in the Riga firmament. Immersed in Russian language and cultural studies, they consciously and unconsciously acquired the thought patterns of the highly civilised, non-radical elite of Imperial Russia, now in exile. Kennan, not surprisingly, had very explicit views about the value of an alliance with the USSR. 'Never,' he declared, 'neither then nor at any later date did I consider the Soviet Union a fit ally or associate, actual or potential, for this country.'

As the 1920s passed it became palpably clear that the Soviet Union had come to stay, and with the Great Depression undermining confidence in the capacity of the market economy to regulate itself and the Soviet Union bounding ahead industrially, the latter became more attractive. The American business community, led by Henry Ford, began to contribute to Soviet industrialisation. American diplomatic attitudes began to change after Japan's invasion of Manchuria in 1931, which boded ill for China, an area of special concern to the United States. The realisation that the Soviet Union might be of some use in restraining Japanese imperialism led to formal diplomatic recognition in 1933, with the USSR promising not to interfere in internal American politics and the United States talking about a loan if Moscow acknowledged the debts run up by the Provisional Government. President Franklin D. Roosevelt chose William Bullitt as the first US ambassador to Moscow. He was no stranger to the Soviet capital, for in 1919 he had negotiated a *modus vivendi* between Soviet Russia and the West which had subsequently been rejected by the British and US governments.

The new honeymoon lasted just under a year. Even George Kennan was caught up in the general enthusiasm, as a special relationship with the Soviet Union appeared to be within reach. However, internal Soviet events had a decisive impact on relations. The murder of Sergei Kirov, in December 1934, marked a major step forward in Stalin's mastery over the party, government and political police. This was to be completed in 1936. The Soviet Union turned more and more inward as it paid off its external debts, cut back on industrial imports from the capitalist world and made a determined bid for autarky. The reasons behind the purges are still not clear, but they affected mainly those in middle and senior positions in the party and state bureaucracies, industrial management, the military, and the creative and technical intelligentsia. It was as if the Stalin leadership wanted to proletarianise the bureaucracy and other key positions in the state. This change in the political climate chilled the Americans to the bone. They were appalled by the trials and the execution of many Soviet officials whom they had known personally. Gradually almost all those whom they knew disappeared, leaving them with a profound sense of loss; the Soviet world they knew was fast vanishing and they had great difficulty in comprehending the new one coming into being. Their sense of isolation was increased by vituperative abuse which was hurled at them from all sides. Kennan thought that the Soviets were out to create the impression that they, the Americans, were devils, evil and dangerous. As such, no Soviet citizen would voluntarily approach them. Bullitt became disillusioned and longed to escape from the place. When he left in mid-1936 he had become a 'hardliner', who believed that the advance of Bolshevism in Europe had to be stopped and that a *rapprochement* between France and Germany might be one way in which to do this. The brief Moscow spring of 1933–4 had raised such high hopes that the dashing of them led to the opposite extreme – an almost unquestioning acceptance of the 'Riga axioms'. These events were to have a lasting impact on the formation of US policy towards the Soviet Union, for many of the key Americans involved in policy-making in the 1940s had earlier seen service in Moscow and Riga.

The Soviet state presented the Western analyst with peculiar problems. To what extent did ideology determine Soviet foreign policy? Marxism-Leninism claimed universal validity, and regarded the final victory of socialism as inevitable. On the one hand this seemed to imply that the Soviet Union did not need to conduct an aggressive foreign policy since events were bound to move in its favour. But it could also be argued that Soviet intervention might speed up the revolutionary transformation of the world. Just what was the relationship between Soviet internal and external policy? Would Stalin's aggressive domestic policy inevitably produce a thrustful foreign policy? Would Stalin follow in Hitler's footsteps? The conventional wisdom of American specialists on the Soviet Union was that Marxism-Leninism made the USSR potentially and actually an expansionist, aggressive force. Hence the United States must always be on its guard and maintain a state of constant vigilance. Someone who did not share this view, much to the chagrin of the professionals, was Joseph Davies, US ambassador in Moscow in 1937–8. He was not a career diplomat, but had been awarded the Moscow embassy for his part in securing the re-election of President Roosevelt. His task was to improve US-Soviet relations and to win Stalin's confidence, if possible. His first-hand experience of Stalinism led him to believe that the inherent contradictions of communism doomed it to oblivion and that the Soviet planned economy represented state socialism. He perceived a re-emphasis of the profit motive in the USSR and the emergence of a new upper class, and he regarded these as further indications that the Soviet Union was returning to economic orthodoxy. The progressive social policy of the Soviet state had done much to improve the lot of the ordinary person. As for the international communist organisation, the Comintern, this was not to be feared, for it was long on rhetoric and short on influence, especially in America. In any case, the Soviet Union's participation was needed if Europe was to be stabilised.

These views, so diametrically opposed to the prevailing wisdom, did not endear Davies to his staff. Nevertheless, he underlined the gulf between the perceptions of the professional Soviet-watchers and the domestic politicians in the United States – one which was to appear many times in the succeeding years. Davies later wrote a highly successful book, *Mission to Moscow* (1941), which was turned into a film, in 1943, and achieved great popular acclaim. This demonstrated the US public's predilection for a rosy analysis of Soviet reality. Yet Davies's successor, Laurence Steinhardt, reverted to the traditional line. In his experience, he stated, the Soviets only responded to force, and, if force could not be applied, 'oriental bartering or trading methods' were in order.

The Soviet-German Non-Aggression Pact of 23 August 1939 did not surprise the US 'professionals' as much as it did British and French diplomats. The events which followed – the joint Soviet-German attack on Poland, resulting in another partition; the Winter War with Finland; the incorporation of the Baltic States and Bessarabia into the USSR – strengthened the conviction that the Soviet state was expansionist and aggressive. Besides the 'hardliners' or, as they saw themselves, the 'realists' in the State Department – Bohlen, Loy Henderson and Kennan in particular – there were other voices in the United States which also articulated the 'Riga axioms'. One of these was that of Joseph C. Kennedy, US ambassador to the Court of St James, whose anti-Soviet views led him to support British appeasement of Germany. Another was the Republican leader Robert Taft, a strong isolationist and opponent of US involvement in the war. There were also vociferous east European pressure groups, especially the Poles, with the Roman Catholic Church often prominent.

Great Britain's relations with the Soviet Union before 1941 went through various phases. The Anglo-Soviet treaty of 1921 regulated commercial relations but diplomatic relations remained coldly formal. Great store was placed on the British working class by the Comintern (Communist International), and in September 1925 an Anglo-Russian committee was set up at the Trades Union Congress. The failure of the General Strike of May 1926, however, led to the demise of the committee in 1927. In the same year Great Britain broke off diplomatic relations and cancelled the 1921 trade treaty. Stalin claimed that the 'British Tory government' had definitely undertaken to start a war against the Soviet Union. One of the early show trials involved British Metro-Vickers engineers and this soured relations. The united front tactics adopted at the VIIth Comintern Congress in 1935 had little impact in Britain. The Communist party of Great Britain remained small and, on the whole, working-class loyalties belonged to the Labour party whose leadership was unimpressed by Soviet achievements. Labour leaders had been a traditional target of communist abuse and this had hardened their attitude towards Moscow. Marxism was unattractive as an ideology and was little studied. (Clement Attlee, Labour Prime Minister, 1945–51, once remarked that the Labour party owed more to Methodism than Marxism.) The USSR attracted support from some intellectuals, but again many of these radicals, some to be found in the left wing of the Labour party, were not Marxists. Just as direct contact with the Soviet Union disillusioned some Americans so it did Sir Stafford Cripps. His fervent advocacy of the popular front in 1938 had led to his expulsion from the Labour party, but in May 1940 he became British ambassador in Moscow. He quickly changed his mind about the Soviet Union, even though he remained as ambassador there until January 1942.

On the right, politicians such as Winston Churchill – an active supporter of intervention in Soviet Russia between 1918 and 1920 – were never in two minds about the eventual goals of the USSR. However, Churchill was a realist and perceived early that Germany posed the more immediate threat to European security.

The abortive Anglo-French negotiations with the Soviet Union in 1939 took place against the background of Stalin's decimation of the Red Army's officer corps, which was thought to have gravely damaged the defences of the Soviet Union. There now seemed to be little military advantage in an alliance with the USSR. Indeed, it looked increasingly likely that Britain and France, far from supporting the Soviet Union, would go to the aid of its victims, and this was one of the reasons why Stalin brought the Winter War against Finland to a rapid conclusion in the spring of 1940.

The German invasion of the Soviet Union on 22 June 1941 was a major turning-point in European and world history. Now it was war to the death, and the victor would inevitably be the dominant power on the European continent and a competitor with the United States for supreme influence over world affairs. Should Great Britain and the United States hold aloof and allow Germany to tear the USSR apart? (Just after Hitler attacked the Soviet Union the future Vice President and President, Harry Truman, expressed himself very forcibly: 'If we see that Germany is winning the war we ought to help Russia, and if Russia is winning we should help Germany and in that way let them kill as many as possible.' However, Truman added, he did not want Hitler to be victorious under any circumstances.) This presumed that Germany was the stronger power. What if the Red Army and the Wehrmacht were more or less equal? Would it not be advisable to stay on the side lines and watch as the dictatorships destroyed one another, to the common benefit of mankind? Churchill was in no doubt about which policy to adopt. 'We shall give whatever help we can to Russia and the Russian people,' he declared in a radio broadcast at 9 o'clock on the evening of the invasion. 'This is not a class war, but a war in which the whole British Empire and Commonwealth of Nations is engaged, without distinction of race, creed or party.' Churchill's loathing and fear of Hitler was summed up in a famous quotation: 'If Hitler invaded Hell I would make at least a favourable reference to the Devil in the House of Commons.' Roosevelt expressed himself in like vein to Joseph Davies: 'I can't take communism nor can you, but to cross this bridge I would hold hands with the Devil.' (In theological terms the Devil is a cunning, powerful adversary, someone with whom one avoids confrontation. Roosevelt was notoriously unwilling to confront Stalin.) Roosevelt sent his associate Harry Hopkins to see Stalin in July 1941 to discuss American aid for the Soviet war effort. Both powers thus decided to tip the balance against Germany, which was seen as the greater evil. This was to have momentous consequences. Once the Third Reich had been swept away a power vacuum would be created in eastern and south-eastern Europe, and much depended on who filled it. But little thought was devoted to this problem in London and Washington in 1941. The primary goal of the British and Americans was to win the war; all other questions were of secondary importance. Roosevelt possessed an infinitely complex mind. He was clearly aware that the Soviet Union was a dictatorship and that the differences between Soviet and American culture, ideology and economic systems were immense. Hence he saw eye to eye with some of the propositions advanced by the Soviet specialists in the State Department. However, he differed from them in some significant respects. He made a distinction between the Soviet dictatorship and national socialism (Nazism). The latter, he believed, was much more concerned with expansion than the former, and this implied that if the Soviet Union's legitimate security needs were met it might be possible to wean Moscow away from supporting communist movements abroad. The end of the war would, most likely, find the Soviet Union economically weak and confronted with the enormous task of rebuilding the shattered country. In this situation if it were possible to overcome Soviet suspiciousness about Western capitalist intentions, Soviet energies could be deflected from expanding communist influence through the Comintern to concentrating on the reconstruction of the homeland. If this came about the West would benefit considerably. The success of Hopkins' mission led Roosevelt to hope that if negotiations were conducted at the highest level – in other words with Stalin personally, thereby avoiding entanglements in the all-embracing Soviet bureaucracy – an agreement could be reached. The United States was economically much stronger than the USSR and this would make peacetime collaboration all the more attractive to a Soviet Union seeking industrial imports. The Manhattan Project, the construction of the atomic bomb, would provide the Americans with another card to play. The only alternative to a *rapprochement* with the USSR was the division of the world into blocs, increasing military arsenals and probably war. Such an eventuality was unthinkable and quite unacceptable.

Informal discussions about the post-war world at heads-of-government level took place at the first meeting of the Big Three at Tehran in November 1943 and appeared to presage success for Roosevelt's grand design. Stalin's request for the Soviet western frontier of 1941 was granted; this involved placing the Baltic States, eastern Poland and Bessarabia in the Soviet Union, as well as northern Bukovina which had historically never been part of Imperial Russia. The Polish frontier was moved westwards – and it was agreed that no confederation of central European or Balkan states should be allowed to come into existence whose goals were inimical to Soviet security interests. Stalin said that it was not easy to force communist regimes on other people, and in any case, as he pointed out, he had other problems to deal with. The mood of Roosevelt and his advisers was one of great optimism. They thought that a new day had dawned, as Harry Hopkins later put it. Stalin's behaviour had demonstrated that he was reasonable and far-sighted; there seemed no reason to doubt that a long-term agreement could now be negotiated with the USSR. The east and south-east Europeans would learn to live with the Soviet Union, and anyway they were not going to be bolshevised. The Soviet Union, in the United Nations, would play a major role in keeping peace throughout the world. This rosy view lasted until the next meeting of the Big Three, at Yalta, in February 1945. Doubts then began to set in [*Doc. 11*]. The wartime honeymoon meant that the 'Riga axioms' had been forced into the background. The view that a constructive relationship could be achieved with the Soviet Union if obligations were scrupulously carried out became known as the 'Yalta axioms'. As long as cooperation lasted and bore fruit they would stay there, but if the high hopes entertained were not fulfilled it was inevitable that the 'Riga axioms' would make a comeback. This happened increasingly in 1945, and by 1947 an open breach had appeared between Moscow and Washington. The conflict associated with this turn of events, primarily involving the United States and the USSR, is known as the Cold War. (The phrase 'Cold War' was first used by the fourteenth-century Spanish writer Don Juan Manuel who was analysing the conflict between Christendom and Islam. A hot war either ended in death or peace but a cold war 'brings neither peace nor honour to those who wage it'. The phrase was popularised by Walter Lippmann, a critic of it, in 1947.) Who was responsible for it? Was it inevitable? Was Stalin genuinely interested in a post-war agreement? Was a great opportunity lost by the world powers, one which could have brought immense benefits to both sides as well as to the rest of the world?

There are several major explanations for the Cold War:

1 the orthodox or traditional;
2 the revisionist;
3 the post-revisionist (mark 1);
4 the post-revisionist (mark 2).

1 The orthodox or traditional interpretation was trenchantly formulated by George F. Kennan in his famous 'long telegram' of 22 February 1946 [*Doc. 18*] and in his anonymous (Mr X) article 'The Sources of Soviet Conduct' in the July 1947 issue of *Foreign Affairs* [*Doc. 26*]. By the end of 1948 the overwhelming majority of American and west European politicians had adopted his analysis. It was articulated in academic works, among which the books of William H. McNeill [McNeill 1953] and Herbert Feis [Feis 1957] were particularly influential.

According to these writers [*Doc. 1*], the wellsprings of the Cold War are to be found in Marxism-Leninism with its doctrine of class struggle leading to revolution on a world scale; in the bitter struggle for survival of the young Soviet regime between 1918 and 1920; and in the Soviet leadership's need to mobilise the population against a perceived external threat, thereby increasing its internal control. Orthodox historians regard the policies of the Soviet government *vis-à-vis* capitalist states as fundamentally hostile, merely tempered by cooperation when deemed necessary. They take it for granted that the Soviets always sought ways of undermining the authority of non-communist powers so as to expand the communist world. During the Second World War Stalin hoped that the capitalist states would engage in mutual self-destruction, allowing the USSR to intervene when deemed advantageous. The German attack forced the Soviet Union into a tactical alliance with the Western powers, but Stalin always sought to expand his influence by using indigenous communists and the Red Army. Not content with eastern and south-eastern Europe, the USSR attempted to draw the whole of Germany into the Soviet orbit and, by fomenting strikes and social unrest in western and southern Europe and in Asia, sought to expand communist influence in those regions as well.

According to the orthodox view, President Roosevelt and his Secretary of State Cordell Hull (to April 1945) and afterwards President Truman and his Secretary of State James F. Byrnes, misjudged the ambivalent and potentially expansionist nature of Soviet foreign policy. Harbouring vain hopes about the democratisation of the Soviet regime and fearing that the American public would not countenance a long-term commitment in Europe, they acceded to Stalin's request for pro-Soviet states in eastern and south-eastern Europe as representing the legitimate security needs of the Soviet Union. At the same time they hoped to integrate the USSR in a liberal democratic world order.

Because the American leaders had no clear vision of what the post-war world would be like, they were prepared to make political concessions in return for short-term military gains – despite the warnings of the British. In order to secure Stalin's cooperation they approved a strategy which resulted in the Red Army penetrating right to the centre of Europe. They accorded the Soviet Union a major say in the future of Germany and did not utilise the potential resistance to the sovietisation of eastern and south-eastern Europe. For instance, in May 1945 they recognised the Polish Provisional Government after a few London Poles had been added; at Potsdam they accepted the moving of the Polish frontier westwards; and they tolerated the economic exploitation of the Soviet zone of Germany. At the Moscow meeting of the council of foreign ministers in December 1945 they acknowledged Bulgaria and Romania as communist states; and by accepting the peace treaties with Bulgaria, Romania, Hungary and Finland at the end of 1946 they abandoned all hope of influencing events in those regions.

Despite increasing exasperation at Soviet intransigence in the United Nations, and at their inability to pierce the 'iron curtain', the Truman administration continued to seek cooperation with the USSR. The Baruch Plan, in June 1946 [*Doc. 17*], proposed joint US-USSR control over the production of atomic weapons. The Americans were also prepared, in July 1946, to sign an agreement with the Soviets which would have resulted in foreign troops leaving Germany, on the understanding that both the United States and the USSR would be entitled to intervene if German policies came to be seen as a threat to their security. In June 1947, the United States even invited the Soviet Union and its eastern and south-eastern European supporters to participate in the reconstruction of Europe – the Marshall Plan.

The division of Europe into blocs became inevitable when the Soviet Union refused all these offers of cooperation. The major American priority now became the containment of communist expansionism, and in order to prevent the economic collapse of the non-communist European states the US leadership in 1947 decided to embark on a huge aid and investment programme. The three Western occupation zones in Germany were to be included in this recovery programme, and as a consequence the division of Germany had to be regretfully accepted. The reaction of the Soviet government was to step up the bolshevisation of its zone of occupation in Germany and in eastern and south-eastern Europe and to seize power in a coup in Czechoslovakia in February 1948. Coercion, chicanery and the brutal use of force accompanied Soviet actions. Moscow attempted to disrupt western and southern Europe by means of a communist-led wave of strikes from November 1947 onwards, and to force the Western powers out of Berlin by blockading all the road, rail and water routes to the German capital. The Soviet offer, in March 1952, to discuss the formation of a united, demilitarised, neutral and democratic Germany was another move in the same direction. European states west of the iron curtain felt themselves threatened by Soviet political and military power and sought American protection. This led to the formation of the Organisation of European Economic Cooperation in 1948, to the setting up of the North Atlantic Treaty Organisation in 1949, and to the re-arming of West Germany and its integration into NATO as a result of communist aggression in Korea between 1950 and 1953. As a consequence Soviet expansion in Europe was halted, but the desire to expand had by no means been eliminated.

The revisionist interpretation [*Doc. 2*] rejects the traditional analysis as Western-orientated, as a self-serving capitalist exposé based on a profound misconception of Soviet internal reality and external goals. The early revisionists are to be found among the critics of Truman's foreign policy, such as the former vice-presidential candidate Henry A. Wallace, and among European opponents of Western integration, in the 'neutral' movement (between the United States and the USSR) of the late 1940s. The works of the historian William A. Williams, whose first major publication appeared in 1959, had a seminal influence, and the research to which the protest movements against the Vietnam War gave rise, especially those of the 'New Left' in the late 1960s and early 1970s, completed the process. Books by ex-students of Williams figured prominently among the works of the revisionists, especially those by Gabriel Kolko [Kolko and Kolko 1972]. Other important studies were penned by Gar Alperowitz [Alperowitz 1967], Barton J. Bernstein and Lloyd C. Gardner [1970]. The revisionist school afforded an enormous stimulus to the study of the Cold War and led to the opening up of the archives, if only to disprove their theses.

The revisionist school of thought believes that the Soviet Union cannot be held responsible for the Cold War. It only narrowly escaped defeat during the Second World War, and its enormous human and material losses meant that by 1945 it was near economic ruin. It was confronted by a prosperous United States, whose gross national product had more than doubled during the war, and which furthermore enjoyed a monopoly of atomic weapons. Under Stalin the USSR had concentrated primarily on building up its economy and had devoted little attention to world revolutionary goals. Its security needs led it to seek governments in contiguous states which were not anti-Soviet and to ensure that no military threat ever emanated again from German soil. These goals did not inevitably mean that eastern and south-eastern Europe would be sovietised. Communist behaviour west of the Soviet sphere of influence was calculated not to cause offence to the United States. Indeed, the socialist movement in Scandinavia and western and southern Europe at the end of the war was held in check by Moscow and thereby contributed to the survival of capitalism long before the Marshall Plan was drafted.

The reasons for the confrontation, according to the revisionists, are to be found in the American economic and political system. The liberal capitalist US economy needed ever-increasing trade and investment opportunities to overcome its endemic weaknesses; this in turn implied the expansion of American political influence. This produced the 'open door' policy which required that the United States be afforded 'equal opportunity' in all foreign markets, leading to free trade and the elimination of tariffs and preferential systems. Because the United States was the leading economic power, this policy of equal opportunity could only lead to increasing American domination, both economically and politically, of the world. Wartime propaganda in favour of 'one world' or the 'open world' in which the United States and the USSR would join hands to the mutual benefit of mankind was not eyewash; it was the conscious policy of the American leadership which had grasped the realities of American development. The goal was a *Pax Americana* over the whole world, with American power ensuring global peace.

As the revisionists see it, the decisive factor which led to US involvement in the war against Japan and Germany was the desire to maintain and to expand where possible the US share in the world economy, since Japan and Germany were in the process of establishing autarkic empires. The same policy was conducted against Great Britain. During the whole war the struggle against the sterling area and imperial preference was of primary importance to US diplomacy. The long-drawn-out negotiations on the Lend-Lease agreement, on the founding of the World Bank and the International Monetary Fund – concluded at Bretton Woods in 1944 – and the loan extended to Great Britain by the United States in November 1945 [*Doc. 15*] resulted in Great Britain being forced to open up its traditional markets to US competition. The United States seized the opportunity of replacing the British in Latin America and of stepping up competition against British Middle East oil interests. As for American–Soviet relations, the struggle with the USSR over the future of eastern and south-eastern Europe acquired greater significance in and after 1945. This area had traditionally been of little consequence to the United States, but now the 'open door' policy was applied here, to ensure the viability of liberal capitalism and American influence.

The Soviet leadership, from this revisionist viewpoint, could not tolerate such a threat to its security interests in eastern and south-eastern Europe, particularly as American trade and investment were frequently accompanied by militant anti-communism. The USSR countered by affording revolutionary movements a free hand and concluding bilateral treaties in an attempt to protect its sphere of influence against American penetration. The Truman administration responded by applying further pressure to force the 'open door' policy on eastern and south-eastern Europe; the Soviet request in January 1945 for a large credit was deliberately ignored; Lend-Lease deliveries abruptly ceased at the end of hostilities in Europe; at Potsdam the Americans refused to agree to the level of German reparations necessary to ensure the rapid recovery of the Soviet economy; and in May 1946 all reparation deliveries from the US zone were terminated. Washington also tried to use its atomic monopoly to force the USSR to become more amenable. It postponed the Potsdam conference until the atomic bomb was ready for use, and it attempted by means of the Baruch Plan [*Doc. 17*] to ensure an American atomic monopoly for decades and to gain control over the Soviet economy. The Marshall Plan was designed to implant an informal American empire in Europe – including eastern and south-eastern Europe – and thereby to extend American political influence over the USSR itself.

When the Soviet will to resist could not be broken, the Americans, according to the revisionists, settled for their sphere of influence. A policy leading to the division of Germany and of Europe was consciously conducted from early 1946 onwards. American isolationism and European capitalist and socialist opposition were overcome by creating a myth about Soviet expansion on a world scale. The Truman Doctrine in 1947 was the political corollary of the Marshall Plan; the establishment of NATO was decided during the Berlin blockade, and during the Korean War the constellation of political forces in the United States and Allied countries was pushed to the right. American pressure and the Western decision to form blocs resulted in the Soviet Union seeking greater political conformity in eastern and south-eastern Europe. It was this that led to the emergence of people's democracies, often by brute force. This widened the gulf between East and West, but the Soviet Union always harboured the hope that a *rapprochement* with the West might come about.

Post-revisionist interpretations seek to avoid the polarities of blame-it-all-on-the-Soviets or blame-it-all-on-the-Americans. They see the situation as so infinitely complex that no generalisation about who was to blame will suffice. The weaknesses of the orthodox and revisionist analyses are evident: the former pays little attention to the legitimate security needs of the USSR, while the latter ignores Soviet behaviour which gave rise to shifts in American policy. Neither analysis had had access to Soviet sources. Neither could make up its mind whether the Cold War should be seen as an almost inevitable consequence of the collision of two diametrically opposed socio-political systems or whether the whole episode could have been avoided if the signals from each side had been read correctly and acted upon. The mishandling of the information available to the US government on Japanese intentions before Pearl Harbor does not inspire confidence in American intelligence, and American incompetence was certainly paralleled on the Soviet side. It is asking too much to expect two states which had very little experience of dealing with each other before 1941 to learn to 'read' each other correctly so quickly.

Dissatisfaction with the orthodox and revisionist analyses, allied to the increased access to official documents, has produced a flood of post-revisionist studies which attempt to stand back from the battle, avoid blatant partisanship and, at the remove of a generation or more, to pass a cold, critical eye over the 'sins' of all participants.

The founding text of post-revisionist (mark 2) interpretation is by John Lewis Gaddis who developed a sophisticated analysis based on containment before and after Kennan [Gaddis 1972, reprinted 2000]. The United States and Britain needed Stalinist Russia as an ally to defeat Germany and Japan. Given the extent of the fighting, victory was secured quickly and with remarkably few American and British casualties. However, the price that had to be paid for this strategy was the emergence of an even more powerful and less understandable totalitarian state. Containment, the term generally used to describe US policy towards the USSR after 1945, may be regarded as a series of attempts to deal with the consequences of the bargain struck during the Second World War. The object of this policy was to restrain the Soviets from re-shaping the international order in a way that would have been as dangerous to Western interests as that which would have been implemented by Germany and Japan had they won the war. The term 'containment' was coined by Kennan in July 1947, when he appealed publicly for a 'long-term, patient but firm and vigilant containment of Russian expansive tendencies' [*Doc.* 26]. During the war Roosevelt, Truman and their advisers were aware of the problem of Soviet expansionism. What they attempted, and failed, to do was to square the circle of helping the Soviet Union defeat Germany while at the same time ensuring that Moscow abided by the ideals for which the war was being fought, expressed in the Atlantic Charter [*Doc.* 4].

One way of resolving the dilemma would have been to come up with military operations which would have contained the Russians while attracting their support to the extent necessary to defeat Germany and Japan. The concept was already there, articulated by Truman, but at that time he was not in government. The orthodox view of the Cold War regards US policy as flawed since it did not take sufficiently into consideration the effects of the crushing Soviet victory in 1945. In other words, the United States concentrated too much on military policy and neglected military-political policy. William C. Bullitt expressed this view succinctly in 1948 when he averred that America had won the war but lost the peace.

Bullitt had proposed an alternative policy in a series of memoranda to President Roosevelt in 1943. He argued that Stalin's war goals were not those of the West. Those who claimed that participation in the anti-fascist coalition had purged the Soviet dictator of his autocratic and expansionist tendencies were assuming, on the basis of no evidence whatsoever, that he had undergone a conversion similar to that of Saul on the road to Damascus (when the scourge of the Christians had, in a blinding flash, realised that Christ was the Son of God, and thereafter became Paul the Apostle). A Europe run from Moscow would be just as dangerous as a Europe run from Berlin. The problem was to prevent the domination of Europe by the Moscow dictatorship without losing the participation of the Red Army in the war against the Nazi dictatorship. The policy Bullitt put forward was reminiscent of that advocated by Churchill later – namely, that of introducing Allied troops into eastern Europe and the Balkans. The goal would be twofold: to defeat Germany, and to prevent the Red Army from overrunning Europe. Bullitt echoed Stalin's (and Clausewitz's) sentiments when he pointed out to Roosevelt in August 1943 that war was an attempt to achieve political objectives by fighting, and political objectives had to be kept in mind when planning operations. Roosevelt did reveal some interest in Anglo-American military operations in the Balkans (much to the dismay of the US military). Apparently Churchill did not formally propose to Roosevelt the deployment of Anglo-American forces in order to contain the Soviets until after the Yalta Conference in early 1945. However, Roosevelt never adopted the dual policy of deploying troops so as to secure victory and contain the Soviets.

There were various reasons for this. One was the President's understanding of the balance of power. American security was best served by preventing various hostile states coming together. The diplomatic recognition of the USSR in 1933 was partly to counter and keep Germany and Japan apart. The Nazi-Soviet Pact was a body-blow to this policy and potentially very dangerous. After the German invasion of the Soviet Union in June 1941 Roosevelt attempted quickly to repair relations with Moscow. After Pearl Harbor (December 1941) the President was always concerned to prevent a German-Soviet *rapprochement* and to enlist Moscow's help in defeating Japan.

Another reason was the effect left on the President by the First World War, which he had experienced at first hand. According to Averell Harriman – US ambassador to the Soviet Union from 1943 – [Harriman 1975: 34], Roosevelt

> had a horror of American troops landing again on the continent and becoming involved again in the kind of warfare he had seen before – trench warfare with all its appalling losses. I believe that he has in mind that if the great armies of Russia could stand up to the Germans, this might well make it possible for us to limit our participation largely to naval and air power.

The United States never committed more than 90 divisions, instead of the 215 thought necessary, for the defeat of Germany and Japan. General Marshall admitted that this had only been possible because of Soviet manpower. Consequently, Roosevelt viewed the United States as a base for military technology which would provide the war matériel while others provided the manpower to do the actual fighting.

The United States was obliged to bear most of the burden of the war against Japan. Although the defeat of Germany was always given priority, the US public would not long have tolerated heavy defeats at the hands of Japan while the United States was committing large forces to the war against Germany. The war against Japan was conceived of as a long operation, one that would require Soviet help after the defeat of Germany. In the event, it was remarkable that the two wars came to an end almost simultaneously without heavy US casualties. No one could have envisaged that the atomic bomb would be available in 1945 to be used to hasten the end of hostilities against Tokyo. Roosevelt could argue that he had taken into account political as well as military objectives. Had the war against Japan been over in 1943 or 1944, then US policy towards Moscow might have been different.

Roosevelt sought to build a stable post-war world by offering the Russians a prominent role in it – Russia would be one of the world's four policemen, alongside the United States, Britain and China, to impose world order, bombing recalcitrants into submission whenever necessary. The President appeared to believe that Soviet hostility emanated from insecurity, which was spawned by external threats. These were the challenge of Germany and Japan, the West's unremitting hostility to communism and the refusal of the international community to afford Russia its rightful place in the world. Roosevelt regarded Russians as friendly people who did not have any foolish ideas of conquest, and so forth: and now that they had got to know the Americans, they were much more willing to accept them. Hence he expected Stalin's suspicions of US intentions gradually to fade away.

Roosevelt did not regard Marxism-Leninism as a great threat. It had limited appeal to the American working class. Communism, which concentrated on subversion and propaganda, was not as dangerous as fascism, which deployed force and coercion. He perceived that Russian national interest was more significant than ideology in fashioning Stalin's policies.

Roosevelt believed in collective security and an open world, and this involved breaking down the barriers which existed. He was most effective in his goal of breaking up the British Empire and opening its markets by astute political and economic pressure. He never got round to doing the same *vis-à-vis* the Soviet Union but he did regard German reparations and a large post-war reconstruction loan for Russia as weapons in his armoury. Interestingly enough, he refused to inform the Soviets officially about the atomic bomb even though he was aware they knew about it. Did he envisage using it as a bargaining chip?

Roosevelt was mindful of the need to avoid a post-war settlement which contained the seeds of future conflict. Given Stalin's powerful position in the Soviet Union, a better relationship, based on mutual respect, had to start at the top. In view of his arch-suspiciousness of the motives of others, it is astounding that Stalin had ever trusted Hitler, but after having his fingers burned there he was unlikely to fall into the same relationship with an American President. Nevertheless, one cannot blame Roosevelt for trying. Yet despite all his efforts he could not overcome the suspicion in Stalin's mind that the delay in launching the second front was aimed at bleeding Russia white and sparing American lives. The D-Day landings, in June 1944, did not dispel his doubts. As late as April 1945 Stalin was warning subordinates that the United States and Britain might forge an alliance with the Germans to fight Moscow. The same month the Red Army began constructing defensive installations in eastern Europe. It appeared that Roosevelt's policy of banking on Stalin was unravelling. The President was also aware that he had to convince the American public that an eastern Europe dominated by Moscow was a good deal. That would not be easy and, had he lived, it is likely that he would have introduced policy linkages (military, political and economic) aimed at encouraging the Russians to follow his agenda.

The tide of war turned for the Red Army at Stalingrad (February 1943), and in 1944 Soviet forces began to penetrate eastern and south-eastern Europe. It was now a matter merely of *when* Germany would be defeated. Stalin seized the initiative and made demand after demand for equipment. By late 1944 American officials, who had felt the sharp edge of Russian tongues, were quite hostile to Roosevelt's policy of turning the other cheek. Professional Soviet watchers were also of like mind and their unease was accentuated by Roosevelt's exclusion of the State Department from important dealings with Moscow. They were acutely aware of the growing gap between Stalin's war aims and the ideals of the Atlantic Charter.

Averell Harriman and General John R. Deane, head of the US military mission in Moscow, articulated these views most forcefully. Both began as believers in Roosevelt's policy of winning friends and influencing people by extending aid without strings attached. Inside a year they had been disillusioned by Soviet behaviour. In September 1944 Harriman expressed his convictions clearly – unless the US took issue with the present policy there was every indication the Soviet Union would become a world bully wherever its interests were involved [Harriman 1975]. To Deane each transaction was negotiated on its own merits, irrespective of past favours. Harriman and Deane were not as pessimistic as George Kennan about establishing a *modus vivendi* and a *modus operandi* with the Russians. Kennan could not foresee any agreement with Moscow other than conceding separate spheres of influence. Harriman, Deane and Bohlen, then in Washington, did not believe that the American public would countenance the concession to the Soviets of eastern and south-eastern

Europe as their sphere of influence where they could impose any policy they desired. Harriman suggested that the best solution would be to strengthen the hand of those around Stalin who wanted to play the game along US lines and to show Stalin that the advice of the counsellors of a tough policy was leading him into difficulties. The United States should adopt a firm but friendly *quid pro quo* attitude. Roosevelt wanted to win the war first and then turn the screw. Harriman and the others regarded this as misguided since Lend-Lease could be more effectively used during wartime than after the war. If the United States waited until after victory, the issues it would wish to take up might already have been resolved in Moscow's favour.

President Truman, excluded by Roosevelt from decision making, was woefully ignorant of foreign affairs. He immediately turned to the former President's key advisers and they grasped the opportunity to push the give-and-take policies which Roosevelt had failed to adopt. Now there had to be a *quid* for every *quo*. Truman gave Molotov a dressing down (the Soviet Foreign Minister spluttered that he had never been talked to like that before – in itself a white lie). Truman thought he was implementing Roosevelt's policy, but to Moscow he had reversed it. His Secretary of State, James F. Byrnes, had as little experience of foreign affairs as he had. Nevertheless Truman was very keen to reach an accommodation with Moscow. He did not accede to Churchill's wish to deploy troops in Germany in such a way as to restrict the Red Army to as little of that country as possible, and in May 1945 he sent the terminally ill Harry Hopkins to Moscow in the hope of cutting a deal.

The Americans overestimated Russia's dependency on them. Washington thought that Moscow could be made amenable by its anticipated need of large loans for post-war reconstruction; world public opinion could be mobilised against it and there was the ultimate weapon, the atomic bomb. Things never worked out like this. Moscow would do its own re-building, albeit more slowly, and anyway a huge Soviet loan would never have got through Congress, where many would have demanded free speech in the Soviet Union and the removal of Moscow from eastern Europe. Adverse publicity was no problem to Stalin. What else could one expect of the capitalist press? Stalin's spies in London and Washington assured him that the atomic bomb could not actually be used. Anyway, domestic pressures forced Truman to accept the principle of international control of atomic weapons before Secretary Byrnes had had an opportunity to attempt to prise concessions out of Moscow.

By the time of the Moscow foreign ministers' conference in December 1945 Byrnes had come to the same conclusion as Roosevelt a year earlier about the impossibility of reconciling the goals of the Atlantic Charter and the Soviet need for security. The only solution was to paper over Russian hegemony in eastern Europe as best one could. Moscow made some concessions on Bulgaria and Romania and the United States on Japan, but these met with a hostile reception in America where the Secretary of State was regarded as gaining little and giving away a lot.

The *quid pro quo* tactics were unsuccessful because the United States was unwilling to use the ultimate weapon, the threat of war, to extract concessions. Once in control of eastern and south-eastern Europe and part of Germany, Russia could strip these countries to benefit Soviet industrial reconstruction. Moscow would have benefited from Western loans but was not willing to pay the American price. An example of this was the Bretton Woods agreement, in 1944, which set up the International Monetary Fund (IMF) and the World Bank. As late as December 1945 Molotov was forwarding positive memoranda to Stalin on joining these organisations. What turned the tide was the need to declare gold and foreign currency reserves and adhere to strict criteria (including IMF inspections to check on implementation) to qualify for loans.

Stalin and his close advisers lacked the sophistication to realise the damage they were causing the Soviet Union by implementing a no-concession policy towards the United States. Others, such as Maxim Litvinov, dismissed as Foreign Minister in 1939, and who favoured a cooperative policy with the West, did perceive the cost but lacked access to Stalin. However, Stalin might not have listened to him.

Frustration at American inability to influence significantly Soviet actions by demonstrating trust or exerting pressure found expression in George Kennan's 8,000-word 'long telegram' of February 1946 [*Doc. 18*]. The State Department had been puzzled by the increasing torrent of anti-Western references in the speeches of Soviet policy-makers and had requested Kennan to provide an explanation. He did so with gusto, and stated simply that US foreign policy towards the Soviet Union during and after the Second World War had been based on fallacies. One was that Stalin's trust could be won by being completely open with him, and another was that his respect could be gained by a *quid pro quo* policy. Yet another was that if Washington chose the right option Moscow would be amenable. Kennan regarded Soviet foreign policy as being conditioned by Soviet domestic policy and not by what the West did or did not do. He thought that a hostile international environment was the breath of life for the prevailing internal system in this country. The disappearance of Germany and Japan meant that the United States and the United Kingdom would have to be dressed up to replace them. There could be no permanent resolution of differences with a government which relied on a fictitious external threat to maintain domestic legitimacy. In March Kennan noted:

> We are thus up against the fact that suspicion in one degree or another is an integral part of the Soviet system, and will not yield entirely to any form of rational persuasion or assurance. . . . To this climate, and not to wishful preconceptions, we must adjust our diplomacy.

Kennan was astonished by the impact his analysis of Soviet behaviour had in Washington. After all, he was not proposing a new policy but explaining Soviet behaviour. The consequences for policy were quickly drafted. In the future, conflicts with Moscow would be aired openly – though not in a provocative manner – and there would be no more concessions to the Soviet Union. A line would be drawn beyond which Soviet expansionism would be resisted, but there would be no attempt to liberate occupied areas; Allies could call on the United States for military and economic aid to resist communism. Negotiations with Moscow would continue, but only to ensure that the Russians accepted American positions, or to demonstrate Soviet intransigence so as to win allies abroad and support at home. The goal of the new policy, based on patience and firmness, was to encourage the Soviets to negotiate and compromise. In September 1946, Clark Clifford, the President's respected counsel, expressed the hope that the Russians would change their minds and work out with the US a fair and equitable settlement when they realised that the Americans were too strong to be beaten and too determined to be frightened.

The new policy bore immediate fruit. The Soviets were induced to remove their troops from Iran and to abandon hopes of forcing Turkey to make boundary concessions and grant bases. In Greece, aid was to be extended to those fighting communist insurgents, and the US Sixth Fleet was to be permanently based in the eastern Mediterranean. The United States refused to concede the Soviet Union a significant role in the occupation of Japan and made clear it would not permit a Soviet takeover of the whole of Korea. In Germany, reparations from the US zone were stopped and plans set in motion to merge the western zones. At the same time, Moscow was offered a four-power treaty guaranteeing the disarmament of Germany for 25 years. Soviet efforts to acquire former Italian territory in the Mediterranean basin were rejected, but the United States continued to seek agreement on peace treaties with Germany's wartime allies. The most dramatic *démarche* was the Truman Doctrine [*Doc. 24*], couched in the terms of a commitment to Greece and Turkey but containing the seeds of a world-wide commitment to resist Soviet expansionism. Truman's declaration that it 'must be the policy of the United States to support free peoples who are resisting attempted subjugation by armed minorities or by outside pressures' [*Doc. 24*] has been seen by most observers as the beginning of the Cold War in earnest.

Ironically, President Truman enunciated this policy at a time when US defence spending was falling rapidly. The number of troops had declined to 3 million in July 1946 and to 1.6 million a year later. Defence expenditure in the fiscal year 1946 had dropped to $44.7 billion and $13.1 billion in 1947. The stark reality was that the United States was incapable of taking on communism on a global scale. What had to be done was to distinguish between core and peripheral interests and then to find the resources to defend the former.

Kennan used the term 'containment' for the first time in his famous Mr X article [*Doc. 26*]. It was not intended as a detailed analysis of national strategy, and contains some passages which appear to contradict Kennan's own government's policies. In this and other utterances Kennan made clear that the goal of universal harmony, a world without wars and conflicts, was a myth. The United States should pursue its own national interest instead of trying to restructure the world order – he referred to this as universalism – and concentrate on the particularist approach of trying to maintain equilibrium within it, so that no single country, or group of countries, could dominate the world. Hence some parts of the world were more important to the United States than others. Of prime importance was the need to identify those countries which were absolutely vital to the United States, countries in which regimes should be friendly towards Washington. This list ranged from western Europe to Canada, Iceland, Greenland, Scandinavia, the British Isles, the Iberian peninsula, Morocco, the west coast of Africa, South America, the Mediterranean countries and the Middle East as far as Iran, and Japan and the Philippines. He refined his thinking shortly afterwards, and stated that there were only five centres of military and economic power in the world which were important for US national security: the United States, Great Britain, Germany and Central Europe, the USSR and Japan. These centres had the requisite resources to ensure an amphibious attack on the United States. Of these, only one, the USSR, was in hostile hands. The goal of US policy should be to ensure that none of the others fell into unfriendly hands. The United States needed to establish a list of priorities which would permit it to react quickly or slowly in given circumstances, bearing in mind its limited resources. The United States should refrain from intervening in the domestic affairs of other states wherever possible.

Kennan had supported the alliance against Hitler, but the consequence of Germany's defeat was to place the Soviet Union in a position where it might gain control of two or more power centres inimical to the United States and its allies. Russian traditional habits of thought blended well with Marxist-Leninist ideology. The latter helped to legitimise an illegitimate government. However, ideology was not a reliable guide to Soviet behaviour. This was because it was amorphous and permitted the Soviet leadership to enunciate any particular thesis it found tactically useful. Hence truth was not a constant but was actually created by the Soviet leaders themselves. Ideology served the function of justifying action already decided upon. Stalin might not feel secure until he dominated the world. His march to world domination would not be in response to the need to establish a world classless society but the fruit of his own insecurity. Therefore the goal of containment should be to limit Soviet expansionism; communism was only a threat inasmuch as it served as the instrument of that expansionism. Kennan did not believe that Moscow would resort to war to achieve its aims. Stalin was no Hitler, with a timetable of aggression. He would prefer to make gains by political rather than military means.

The threat to the political centres of western Europe and Japan was real, but it was psychological rather than military. It was possible that the demoralised peoples of these regions would succumb to communism either through a coup or free elections. It was vital for the United States that these centres did not fall under the sway of communism – and by extension Soviet domination – because if this happened it would reduce Americans to a 'position of helplessness and loneliness and ignominy among the nations of mankind'. Since Kennan saw the Soviet challenge as essentially psychological his policies to counter it were also partly psychological. Restore self-confidence in states under the threat of Soviet expansionism, exploit the differences between communist states and between them and Moscow, and modify the Soviet concept of international behaviour in order to secure a negotiated settlement of outstanding issues. The announcement of American economic aid to western Europe would boost confidence there and would encourage European integration. This in turn would reintegrate Germany into Europe. Aid to eastern Europe would help to detach the region from Moscow (this was never a serious plan). Kennan was thinking of a future European federation as the optimal way of protecting large and small states against Soviet attempts at domination. The Soviet threat meant that thoughts of punishing Germany, Italy and their allies had now to recede. The same was true in Japan. Occupation should give way to rehabilitation. Without military forces the United States could not successfully pursue such a policy. There had to be a soldier behind the diplomat. However, there was a limit to military power. Since the Soviet threat was not military but political, it could not be overcome solely by military force. Kennan therefore did not propose a military alliance for western Europe, but rather its political and economic recovery.

In Asia, he advocated that the US secure island bases in the western Pacific, such as Okinawa and the Philippines, and not become entangled on the mainland. The expansion of communism as such was not significant; it all depended where. China, for instance, was not important to US security interests, and should not be mentioned in the same breath as Greece and Turkey. Kennan looked to the emergence of independent power centres in Europe and Asia, not the transformation of the world into American and Soviet zones of influence. These new independent power centres, by definition, would be friendly towards the United States.

Besides promoting these policies, the United States should also, argued Kennan, seek to restrict the capacity of the Soviet Union to exert influence beyond its borders. This could be done by encouraging and exploiting tensions within the world communist movement. The history of the Comintern demonstrated that Moscow could not tolerate diversity, and its attempts to impose its will would lead, over time, to a steady stream of disillusioned former followers. This would present the United States and Europe with a range of opportunities to challenge communist hegemony. Kennan perceptively regarded China as posing a greater threat to Soviet security and its control of the international communist movement than to the United States, since it lacked the industrial base to construct the air and amphibious power necessary to invade America. Soviet communism – in reality, imperialism – contained the seeds of its own destruction. It would crumble just like the Roman Empire which found it impossible to control faraway provinces.

The most effective method of modifying Soviet behaviour lay in a combination of deterrents and inducements, called 'counter-pressure' by Kennan. Soviet leaders

> are prepared to recognize *situations*, if not arguments. If, therefore, situations can be created in which it is clearly not to the advantage of their power to emphasize the elements of conflict in their relations with the outside world, then their actions, and even the tenor of their propaganda to their own people, *can* be modified. [Harriman 1975: 115]

The way to bring this about was for Americans to be themselves. The United States 'must demonstrate by its own self-confidence and patience, but particularly by the integrity and dignity of its example, that the true glory of Russian national effort can find its expression only in peaceful and friendly association with other peoples and not in attempts to subjugate and dominate those peoples'. He likened American–Soviet relations to a long-range fencing contest in which the

> weapons are not only the development of military power but the loyalties and convictions of hundreds of millions of people and the control or influence over their forms of political organization. . . . It may be the strength and health of our respective systems which is decisive and which will determine the issue. This may be done – and probably will be done – without a war. [Harriman 1975: 129]

Containment as a strategy meant the abandonment of universalism. The dream of reshaping the world through a fundamental restructuring of the world order, which included the disarmament of past and potential adversaries, the application of the principle of national self-determination, the opening up of the world economy by reducing barriers to trade and the flow of capital, and – most important of all – the creation of an international organisation to implement such a programme, lingered on. These two strands of US foreign policy, the particularist and the universalist, coexisted uneasily during these years and later. Hence there has always been a duality to US foreign policy. In 1947, the United States had to face the reality that there was an adversary which also had a universalist dream for mankind, and that the two could not be reconciled. There were now two worlds, and it would be futile to pretend that one world could be created out of them.

There was general agreement that the Soviet Union must not be permitted to expand into key political centres. However, the resources of the United States were limited. It was quite incapable of taking on the security of the whole world, so the policy adopted was to identify core centres of interest to defend. Kennan accepted that there were areas which could fall under Soviet control without endangering American security. These included the mainland of Asia, from Afghanistan to Korea. If communist regimes took over in the non-industrialised Asian mainland this did not require the United States to intervene, since hostility was no threat but only became so when allied to industrial power.

An effective way of enhancing US security was to extend economic and technological aid to key political centres. A major advantage of this was to obviate the necessity to station US troops there to maintain the balance of power. Hence President Truman, in 1947, decided to concentrate on the economic recovery of western Europe and Japan. This involved cutting back on US defence expenditure. In December 1947, James Forrestal, Secretary for Defence, put American objectives succinctly. They were: economic stability, political stability and military stability, in about that order. This policy was based on the assumption that the Soviet Union was not preparing for war. After all, Washington had the atomic bomb. The Americans believed that the emergence of self-confident, prosperous centres of political power would enhance US security rather than establish spheres of influence. The policy in Europe, as one State Department official put it, was to 'create a third force . . . strong enough to say no both to the Soviet Union and the United States, if our actions should seem so to require'.

The Truman administration implemented the first part of Kennan's containment strategy very conscientiously. The second part of his strategy was to promote the fracturing of the world communist movement. Because the administration had no intention of resisting communism world-wide, it began to adopt the term 'totalitarian' rather than 'communist'. The Russians could not complain that they were the target, since if they had done so they would have admitted they were totalitarian. There was also the important point that anti-communism was negative and that a positive policy was always preferable – such as the defence of free peoples everywhere. Offering Marshall Plan aid to the USSR and its east European allies would force Moscow to choose – almost certainly against – but this would place the blame for splitting Europe economically on the Russians' shoulders. Should an east European communist state accept the aid, this would be used to lessen that state's economic reliance on the Soviet Union. Such an opportunity did occur in 1948 when Yugoslavia was expelled from the Cominform.

The third plank in Kennan's strategy had been to engineer changes in the Soviet perception of international relations, in order to persuade Russian leaders that they would be better served by learning to live with a diverse world than by trying to remould it in their image. Neither war nor appeasement was effective by itself. Both positive and negative policies were needed, and this involved negotiating wherever there was a good chance of results.

Yet Kennan regarded many of the US administration's moves between 1948 and 1950 – the formation of NATO, the establishment of a West German state, the decision to keep US troops in Japan after occupation ended, and the decision to build the hydrogen bomb – as guaranteed to increase Soviet suspiciousness and insecurity and consequently to reduce the opportunities for successful negotiations.

Kennan left as head of the Policy Planning Staff in late 1949 because he found that the soil was no longer as receptive as previously to his ideas. Nevertheless, US policy bore the indelible mark of his imprint and would do so for decades to come.

Halliday, in a post-revisionist interpretation, suggests various theoretical approaches to explain the origins of the Cold War [Halliday 1983]. First, Soviet threat theorists place the blame on the policies of the USSR. Crises were the result of Soviet expansionism and aggressiveness. Whether Soviet behaviour was the result of Marxist-Leninist theory or of the traditional values of pre-1914 Russian society is of secondary importance. The fact that Soviet actions were responsible for crises in world politics is self-evident, irrespective of whichever explanation one favours.

Secondly, US imperialism theorists produce, in essence, a mirror image of the Soviet threat view. Again the responsibility is focused on the policies of one state, and the actions of the other, innocent, one are not regarded as having contributed to the impasse. These theorists locate the aggressiveness and belligerence of the West in the social system of capitalism, which they regard as needing confrontation and military production to survive.

Thirdly, the super-power theorists place the blame on the two major powers, arguing that the United States and the USSR jointly subordinated the world to their common interests and remaining differences. Popularised by China in the 1960s, the super-power theory identifies the two major powers as 'colluding and contending' in their efforts to dominate the world. This view was popular among those who wanted a third alternative to the super-powers, whether they were European conservatives, anti-Soviet Marxists or Third World nationalists.

Fourthly, arms-race theorists identify the stockpiling of weapons, particularly of nuclear weapons, as the central factor in world politics. The danger of the destruction of the economic, social and cultural fabric of the world by nuclear weapons, and the apparent lack of control of the arms race, were regarded as so significant as to explain the course of world politics. The political and social impact of the arms race was regarded as broadly similar in East and West.

Fifthly, north–south theorists locate the driving force of world politics essentially in the conflict between rich and poor states, between imperial and colonial, dominant and dominated states. The great importance this issue has assumed since 1945 and the immiseration of millions in the Third World have contributed to a situation where these issues override the East–West conflict and generate these and other conflicts. The production of weapons and the conflicts between rich states are, in reality, means of consolidating their influence over weaker and poorer states.

Sixthly, the West–West theorists see world politics dominated by conflicts between the richer capitalist states, reminiscent of the period before 1914. From this perspective, the US conflict with the USSR is a mask to hide the real conflict with its major capitalist rivals – western Europe and Japan. The Soviet threat is the only ideological instrument available to unite the major capitalist states. Turmoil in the Third World is the consequence of these intercapitalist rivalries.

Seventhly, the intra-state theorists identify the primary causes in the inner workings of the major world powers. International relations are an extension of domestic affairs. Changes in foreign policy are the result of shifts in internal power relations, or of weaknesses and changes in the economy and/or social composition of the countries concerned. Those in charge of foreign policy may pretend that they are responding to forces and states abroad, but, in reality, are attempting to resolve domestic policy disputes.

Lastly, class-conflict theorists perceive international politics to be determined by the flow of social revolution and the conflict between capitalism and communism, on a world scale. They believe that it is the simultaneous unity and diversity of the world as transformed by capitalism which explains the turmoils of the post-war world. Sometimes it is expressed in rivalry between the major states of the capitalist and communist blocs.

The opening of the Soviet archives, as well as those of eastern and southeastern Europe, has fuelled fierce debate. Gaddis has moved from stressing American national security needs to an emphasis on ideas and patterns in Stalinist thought. The debate about whether there was a Soviet domestic policy and a separate Soviet foreign policy is neatly solved by saying that Stalin's mind did not make this distinction. Molotov's memoirs [Molotov 1993] appear to reinforce the view that the Cold War was well nigh inevitable. He does concede that Stalin was too self-confident and overreached himself at times in 1945, especially concerning Turkey.

This study is an attempt at post-revisionism. Its aim is not to apportion blame but to attempt to unravel some of the complexities of the issues which gave rise to the Cold War and to consider whether the whole episode could have been avoided.

PART TWO DESCRIPTIVE ANALYSIS

CHAPTER TWO

MOSCOW'S VIEW OF THE WORLD

The Roman Empire almost united Europe. Rome was an imperialist power and it viewed the rest of Europe, indeed any territory, as potential booty. Once subdued, Roman law and institutions were introduced to civilise the natives. An important element was to foster the concept that a pan-European family of peoples existed. Eventually the project failed because the locals rebelled against the heavy tax burden and colluded with the empire's opponents. The Romans hardly penetrated into eastern Europe. However a successor empire did emerge: the Russian Empire. The Russian state began in Kiev, in present day Ukraine, then suffered the Mongol yoke (1240–1480), during which time Moscow became the power centre. By the end of the sixteenth century, Russia had expanded as far as it could in the east, to the Pacific Ocean. In the nineteenth century, Moscow's power expanded to include the Caucasus and Central Asia.

The rest of Europe only became alarmed at the spread of Russian power in the middle of the nineteenth century. Russia played a major, perhaps even a crucial role, in defeating Napoleon and vitiating the French dream of conquering Europe. His Roman dream ended at Waterloo. In 1815, Tsar Alexander I was a hero and his troops were in Paris (they are credited with coining the word 'bistro', which in Russian means 'quickly', in 1814). The Russians had earned the right to be treated as equal partners in rebuilding Europe. However if the Russians sat at the same table, they did not share the same beliefs as the other European powers when it came to running a state. Russia was an autocracy but the rest of Europe was moving towards a wider distribution of power, fuelled by the industrial revolution. If the Tsar did not take to the new ideas, many members of his aristocracy did. One result was the Decembrist Revolt, an attempt to remove Tsar Nicholas I. The new tsar quickly perceived that the flood of new fangled ideas from western Europe could prove fatal for the Romanov dynasty. Censorship became much stricter and even Russia's national poet, Alexander Pushkin, was sent into exile in the south.

Tsar Alexander's love affair with all things French ended abruptly but he was not the only one to turn away from the West and look more deeply at

Russia's heritage. An important segment of the educated elite and nobility dropped French and began speaking their native tongue, Russian. They had rediscovered their Russianness. They now agonised over eternal questions: what is Russia?; what does it mean to be Russian?; how should Russia develop?; should it borrow from the West or feed entirely on Russian institutions and tradition? A split developed between those who wanted to look outward for inspiration, the westernisers, and those who wanted to look inward, the Slavophiles.

This debate crystallised towards the end of the nineteenth century in a conflict between Marxists and Social Revolutionaries. Russia's vast territories and harsh climate favoured communal, collective responsibility for life and labour. When the new doctrine of socialism appeared, Russia was natural socialist territory. The Marxists were urban, industrial socialists and the Social Revolutionaries were (non-Marxist) agrarian socialists. Given that Russian industrialisation only got under way in the 1890s, it appeared that the Marxists would have to wait a long time before being in a position to bid for power.

The First World War (1914–18) accelerated events. The war burden was too great for the Russian state and it collapsed in February 1917. Marxism was in crisis as (Marxist) social democratic parties had voted, in 1914, to support their governments when war broke out. Lenin, the leader of the Bolshevik wing of Russian social democracy, was appalled. He called for the imperialist war to be transformed into a class war. He was met with a deafening silence. The split between Lenin's Marxists and the Marxists in the rest of Europe underlined a further divide. Marxists in the rest of Europe thought in terms of nation states and placed their nation and state ahead of everything else. Russia, on the other hand, was not a nation state but an empire. Hence the Bolsheviks could promote the defeat of their state in the war because they believed that it would usher in an international revolution. They found the commitment of other Marxists to their nation state baffling. If a socialist revolution occurred, it would be limited to a particular nation state.

When the Bolsheviks took power they inherited an empire. Lenin eventually chose to call the new state the Union of Soviet Socialist Republics. However some nation states remained outside: Finland, Estonia, Latvia and Lithuania, for example. The new Soviet state was a federal state but contained within its borders some nation states, such as Georgia and Ukraine. Russia was labelled the Russian Soviet Federal Socialist Republic (RSFSR) and was, by far, the largest republic. It was not a nation state as it included over a hundred nationalities, some with their own designated territory. Stalin, a Georgian, wanted to subordinate all republics to Moscow, but Lenin overruled him. Lenin was sensitive to the imperial Russian legacy and wanted to demonstrate that the new Soviet state was much more than a successor state to the Russian empire. Arguably this was his greatest mistake. He had a very limited understanding of nationalism as he was the product of an empire. He even promoted new nations within the Soviet Union. A federal state of constitutionally equal republics, of which Russia was only one, was a time bomb. Stalin never took the concept of equal Soviet republics very seriously. He was an imperialist, seeking to rule from Moscow. Curiously, in the Soviet constitution of 1936, he retained the format of constitutionally equal republics.

A major goal for Stalin during the Great Fatherland War (1941–5) was to gather in all the lands which had formed part of the Tsarist Russian empire. He identified with Russian tsars such as Ivan the Terrible (1533–84) and Alexander I (1799–1825). The former had brought vast swathes of new territory under Moscow's control and the latter had been a victor over Napoleon and was the first Russian Tsar to enjoy pan-European influence. There was another dimension to Russia, its state religion, Russian Orthodoxy. To be a Russian meant being an Orthodox Christian. Messianism was an important element of this religion. Almost effortlessly, the new communist state slipped into the clothes of the old one. The new religion was Marxism and it was also universalist, promising – no, guaranteeing – a paradise on earth. Russia, again, saw itself as the saviour of mankind.

Stalin, in 1945, saw himself as the real victor. Capitalism, surely, could never again be the dominant force it had been before 1941. Stalin was aware of the terrible price the Soviet Union had paid for victory. It had carried the major burden of war and had ensured the survival of bourgeois (non-Marxist) democracy in the rest of Europe. He expected to be rewarded for Russia's heroic sacrifices. Playing the role of Alexander I in the twentieth century would be a start.

Stalin enjoyed jousting with Churchill and Roosevelt during the war. They afforded him great respect and he turned out eventually to be a better tactician than either of them. His major concern was to ensure that they did not gang up against him and he sought, with considerable skill, to play one off against the other. Neither quite fathomed how vain the Russian dictator was. He was a paradox. He craved adulation but when it was extended he became uncomfortable. According to one story, Stalin had wanted to lead the victory parade in Red Square himself on 24 June 1945, on horseback. He tried to mount the white stallion but failed. Marshal Zhukov was then given the job. After the parade, Stalin toasted the Russian (not the Soviet) people and their role in victory. On 27 June he appropriated the title of Generalissimo (the superlative of the Italian word *generale*). He would not share his martial glory with any of his commanders. He exacted revenge on Zhukov, in 1946, when he was framed and packed off to the Odessa military district.

THINKING ABOUT COOPERATION

Andrei Gromyko, Soviet ambassador in Washington, 1943–5, and later Foreign Minister, believed that Stalin was thinking in terms of long-term collaboration with the West, especially the United States (Zubok and Pleshakov 1996: 27). This cooperation did not extend to joining the International Monetary Fund, set up in September 1944, and later the World Bank. Arguably this was a tactical mistake as once in, Moscow could have claimed large loans from the other members, first and foremost from the United States. Khrushchev thought that Stalin imagined himself playing the role of Alexander I, able to dictate the rules of the game to the other powers. Stalin was mindful of the fact that the Tsar's troops had ended up in Paris. His had only got to Berlin.

Stalin, in 1943, commissioned Ivan Maisky and Maxim Litvinov, both seasoned diplomats of the pre-Stalin school, to write memoranda on the future of the world. In January 1944, Maisky, in a long document to Molotov, summarised some of the conclusions that he had reached with Litvinov. The number one priority for the Soviet Union was peace. The country would need at least 10 years to recover completely. Europe would need up to 50 years to go socialist. This would remove the security threat from that part of the world. The borders of 1941, those achieved by conquest, had to be retained while other territories, such as southern Sakhalin and the Kurile islands, were taken from Japan. Military bases were needed in Finland, Romania and the Dardanelles, and access to the Persian Gulf obtained. Germany had to become a military dwarf and the resurrection of France prevented. Popular front governments (coalitions of socialists and non-socialists) in major countries were advisable. The Soviet Union would become the fulcrum of democracy in Europe. All this was to be achieved in collaboration with the United States and Great Britain (Zubok and Pleshakov 1996: 28–9). This implied a firm commitment to a working relationship with the two main Western powers. The Soviet sages thought that Moscow could play London off against Washington as the Americans would inevitably seek to muscle into Britain's imperial interests. A step forward would be agreements on spheres of interest. Churchill, recognising the limits of British power, offered Stalin the percentages agreement in south-eastern Europe. The only country which would not be communist would be Greece. The Yalta agreement recognised eastern, south-eastern Europe as Soviet spheres of interest. The United States would have no role to play in Europe.

The above reads like nineteenth-century British *Realpolitik*. Ideology is absent as it was thought that it would antagonise the West, especially the United States. This was all the more important as Russia badly needed credits to rebuild its economy. If the impression could be created that the Soviet Union was like any other great power, interested in stability in a world facing chaos, then the money might flow. Maisky, especially, placed great significance on good relations. He envisaged problems for Russia if it fell out with the rich United States. The Americans would then attempt to resuscitate Germany and Japan. How prescient he proved to be. Stalin devoted considerable attention to the formation of the United Nations, being very keen to ensure that the

Americans played an important role. The Kremlin dictator envisaged Russia, America and Britain running the world. He did not favour Geneva or any other European site for the UN. It had to be New York since that would ensure continuing US interest. On 9 February 1946, in the Bolshoi Theatre, Stalin delivered his state of the union message to his functionaries and the world. Gone were the hopes of credits and technology from the West. Instead the Soviet Union would have to resurrect its economy itself. The necessary capital would come from cutting consumption. Rearmament was again on the agenda as the country would have to achieve security by becoming so strong that no power would threaten it. Russia was to look inward for strength in the coming struggle.

THE COST OF WAR

The Soviets paid a fearful price for victory but to Stalin every sacrifice had been worth it. Russia contributed most to the defeat of national socialist Germany. It lost almost 8.7 million men and women in combat and a further 18 million civilians, a total of 19 per cent of the pre-war population. Soviet losses accounted for almost half of total fatalities during the Second World War and 90 Soviets died for every American. About 70,000 villages, 65,000 kilometres of railway track, half of all the railway bridges in occupied territory and over half of urban living space there had been destroyed.

Agriculture, after suffering disorganisation during collectivisation, had again been thrown into disarray, and the total area of sown land in 1945 was only 75 per cent of that of 1940. The grain harvest was 47.3 million tonnes, compared with 87 million tonnes in 1940. (Global agricultural production was 60 per cent of that of 1940.) Although global industrial production was stated to be 90 per cent of the 1940 figure, steel output only reached 12.3 million tonnes compared with 18.3 million tonnes in 1940. The Red Army counted about 11 million men and women whereas the US forces alone came to about 12 million. Rapid demobilisation of Soviet forces led to troop levels dropping to 2.8 million by 1948, according to Khrushchev. Top priority had to be given to restoring the shattered economy and in this regard reparations from ex-enemy countries were valuable. Reparations were held to be of key importance by the Soviets whereas they were of no significance to the US economy and of little value to Great Britain. Such a situation dictated that the USSR should conduct a prudent foreign policy, one which secured maximum advantage without involving the country in any new conflict.

Internally, the war had loosened the hold of Stalinism on the Soviet population. The initial response to the German invasion in Belorussia and Ukraine and in non-Slav areas in the Caucasus was one of indifference and defeatism; sometimes the advancing Wehrmacht was even welcomed by the local population. Many non-Russian Soviet prisoners-of-war stated that they wished to be afforded the opportunity of fighting the Red Army but the Germans did not trust their intentions. Among the Soviet population patriotism and religion were used to rally support for the struggle against Germany. The majority of Red Army soldiers were peasants, and they, as well as their counterparts who had toiled on the home front, expected tangible rewards at the end of hostilities. The Communist party, which had retreated into the background during the early part of the war, began to reassert its authority in 1944 and the Stalinist system was gradually reimposed. The NKVD reported to Stalin that many returning soldiers were critical of the gulf in living standards they had witnessed. Some were no longer afraid of the political police. Stalin had every returnee screened. Some were shot but most ended up in labour camps (the gulag). This was the Stalinist way of dealing with dissent. Partisan groups offered some resistance in the Baltic States and Ukraine, but the ease with which the old system was reimposed – even though it involved cutting the Soviet military leaders down to size by transferring them to less important posts – revealed the strength of Stalinism. It was in Stalin's interest to seek an accommodation with other powers, but had a war broken out he would have had at his disposal a formidable military machine and the ability to exact even more sacrifices from the Russian population and, to a lesser extent, from the non-Russian Soviet population. How long the USSR could have sustained a total war, however, is quite a different question.

The First World War had given rise to high hopes that capitalism was on its last legs, and Lenin was very optimistic that the socialist dawn was ready to break over the whole world. These hopes had proved unfounded, for capitalism had shown more vitality than expected. How would it emerge from the Second World War? No Soviet economist would dare advise Stalin that capitalism would prove so strong that its demise was out of the question. Soviet thinking proceeded on the assumption that the war had either mortally wounded capitalism or that it had given it only a temporary access of strength, and that the renewal of the struggle for markets would lead inevitably to its self-destruction. The fact that the American gross national product had more than doubled during the war pointed to the strength of capitalism there, but what of continental Europe, where the war had exhausted the market economies? Eugene Varga, a Hungarian who had become a leading Soviet economist, published his findings in 1945 and they were widely discussed in the Soviet economic literature. One conclusion was that the old Soviet methods of analysis were no longer adequate. In the capitalist economies, the war had necessitated the development of large-scale state administrative structures, and it was unlikely that these would be completely dismantled when peace returned. Hence the 'anarchy of the market' would be contained to a certain extent. The huge expansion of the wartime American economy would lead, it was thought, to overproduction after the war. On the other hand, European states would suffer from unemployment and underproduction. It was likely that the conjunction of these two factors would lead to the export of American capital and goods to Europe and elsewhere. The result would be a world-wide expansion of US economic power, a corollary of which would be increased American political influence. The constellation of forces within capitalism would thus change, but Soviet analysts predicted that this change contained within itself the seeds of its own destruction, since it could only produce fratricidal strife as each state sought to defend its own markets.

The Soviet state was hopeful of obtaining some of the available US capital for its own economic development. To this end various requests involving huge amounts of credit were made to the US government – without, of course, conceding that the Soviet government would tolerate any linking of these loans to Soviet political behaviour in Europe or elsewhere. Moscow presumed that Washington would be genuinely interested in capital exports. Along with the desire for American credits went the fear that American penetration of Europe – which could also include the desired Soviet sphere of influence in eastern and south-eastern Europe – could take on an imperialist character. If this occurred in Europe it could also occur in Asia and elsewhere. The inevitable result would be that anti-Soviet forces would be immeasurably strengthened. The Americans would not need to station troops in order to acquire influence; the mighty, not to say the almighty, dollar would perform the same function.

Looking back, one can list Soviet foreign policy tactics under three headings: (1) all resources and forces had to be mobilised to halt and turn back the march of American capitalism but to stop short at endangering the security of the Soviet Union. The support of communists, socialists, radicals and capitalists who were also nationalists was to be enlisted; (2) Soviet sources of strength, such as the Red Army and Soviet control of foreign communist parties, were to be utilised to the very limit so as to defend Soviet security interests and, wherever possible, expand Soviet influence; (3) great care was to be taken, given the different levels of influence the Soviet Union enjoyed in eastern and south-eastern Europe, Germany and western and southern Europe, not to provoke the United States unnecessarily.

One effect of the war had been to give the Soviet Union, under the leadership of 'Uncle Joe' Stalin, a much better image in the world as a whole, and the abolition of the Comintern in May 1943 seemed to indicate that the Soviet Union was no longer expansionist. Moscow appealed to all peace-loving, democratically minded and anti-fascist forces to unite under the banner of democracy, a new type of democracy. Just what this implied was never spelled out, for by leaving it undefined it could be all things to all men. It involved communist parties declaring that their immediate goal in the Soviet sphere of influence was the democratic revolution and that socialism was a long way off. In line with this approach revolutionary rhetoric was placed in cold storage. The emphasis was now on cooperation with the Western Allies. The nature of this cooperation varied from country to country, depending on the strength of pro- or anti-Soviet forces. The Soviets themselves had no clear vision of where the new-type democracy and socialist internationalism would lead. However, they were clear about one thing; it had to serve Soviet security needs. Hence the shape it took would be determined to a considerable extent by the American reaction to it. Three different approaches were pursued in chasing this goal: (1) in eastern and south-eastern Europe, and in north Korea, every effort was made to secure a decisive role in government for the Communist party and to hasten the social transformation of the area in order to ensure a permanent pro-Soviet commitment there; (2) in western and southern Europe and in China – the obvious areas of expansion for American capitalism – an effort was to be made to stabilise the political and economic order even when this meant restricting the activities of communist parties; (3) in countries such as Germany and Austria, where the Soviet Union had to cooperate with the Western Allies, its aim was to win the goodwill of the inhabitants in order to ensure that eventual Soviet withdrawal would not lead to these countries slipping into the capitalist orbit. Germany was the more serious problem, and here the aim was to obtain guarantees which would banish the prospect of Germany adopting anti-Soviet policies. On the other hand, the Soviets had to ensure that German industrial potential did not serve the interests of Anglo-American capitalism. Besides these three approaches there were others which corresponded to the peculiarities of the local situation. In Finland, for example, the Soviets could have imposed a people's democracy but did not bother to do so. Hence Soviet tactics in respective countries were very flexible and varied and this confused American analysts; which in turn created mistrust.

EASTERN AND SOUTH-EASTERN EUROPE

In the immediate aftermath of the October revolution the precise boundaries of Soviet Russia were not of great significance to Lenin and the other Bolshevik leaders. Even the one-sided Treaty of Brest-Litovsk, which the new government concluded with Imperial Germany in March 1918, was viewed with equanimity by Lenin, since he took it for granted that after the inevitable socialist revolution in Germany it would melt away like snow in the midday sun. Following the defeat before Warsaw, in 1920, immediate Soviet expansion was out of the question, but in negotiating the Treaty of Riga in March 1921 the young Soviet state actually offered the Polish republic more territory than it was willing to swallow. Moscow reasoned that the more non-Poles there were in Poland the more unstable that state would be. The defeat of left-wing German attempts at revolution in 1923 finally ended Bolshevik hopes for a socialist Europe in the foreseeable future.

With this change of heart went a change in diplomatic practice. Soviet Russia now began to stake out its frontiers with all contiguous states and to arrange bilateral treaties of friendship. The first goal was to seek to recover the frontiers of Imperial Russia, and then to venture further afield in eastern and south-eastern Europe. This was deemed necessary as a result of inter-war developments in the region. The peace treaties at the end of the First World War had sought to establish a cordon sanitaire to hold back permanently the advance of Bolshevism. Poland had spurned all Soviet efforts to construct a pact in eastern Europe to resist German expansion. Czechoslovakia, the only state to retain a bourgeois democratic form of government in the area, had gone under, due partly to the activities of Slovak fascists. Hungary, Romania and Bulgaria had all sided with national socialist Germany and the first two had not only declared war on the USSR but had provided fighting troops as well. To the Soviets it seemed self-evident that the only way to prevent a recurrence of such events was to establish Soviet hegemony there.

The Soviet Union had already taken the first step in this direction by the secret protocol to the Soviet-German Non-Aggression Pact of August 1939 which had established mutual spheres of influence. As a result, Finland, the Baltic States, eastern Poland and Bessarabia came within the Soviet orbit. By late August 1940 Estonia, Latvia, Lithuania, eastern Poland, Bessarabia and northern Bukovina had been incorporated in the USSR through military occupation and 'arranged' plebiscites. The Treaty of Moscow, in March 1940, which ended the Winter War – not ratified by Finland at the time – meant that large tracts of Finnish territory bordering the Soviet Union were acquired. When Stalin's Foreign Minister, Molotov, visited Berlin in November 1940 he asked for German acceptance of Soviet domination of Finland, and the incorporation of southern Bukovina into the USSR. He also declared that Bulgaria, Yugoslavia, Greece and even a part of Poland then occupied by the Germans should be regarded as falling within the Soviet zone of influence. Furthermore, Molotov requested military bases in the Straits (the Bosphorus, the Sea of Marmora and the Dardanelles) and a Soviet–Danish condominium over the Skaggerak and Kattegat. Even after the German invasion of the Soviet Union Stalin made several attempts to conclude a peace treaty with Hitler on the basis of the above spheres of influence.

After the failure to agree spheres of influence with Germany in Europe Stalin turned his attention to Great Britain as a potential partner. When Anthony Eden, the British Foreign Secretary, visited beleaguered Moscow in December 1941 Stalin asked that the territorial gains made by the Soviet Union under the Non-Aggression Pact with Hitler be recognised by the British government [*Doc. 5*]. He insisted on the USSR's need for an area around Memel, Tilsit, the Petsamo area in Finland and military bases in Finland and Romania. In return he stated that the USSR would not object if Britain established bases in Norway, Denmark, Belgium, the Netherlands and France. However, these proposals were not as far-reaching as the agreement with Germany which had divided Europe into two spheres of influence, one German and the other Soviet. Germany, of course, was to be the great loser. Poland could be compensated for its loss of territory in the east by being given most of east Prussia and other German territory, possibly up to the river Oder. East Prussia north of the Neman river was to become part of Lithuania. Czechoslovakia was to be re-established in its pre-Munich frontiers and to receive some Hungarian territory. Yugoslavia was to reappear and be enlarged at the expense of Hungary and Italy. Albanian independence was to be restored at the expense of Italy. Turkey could receive the Dodecanese Islands and possibly some Bulgarian territory. Separatist movements in the Rhineland and Bavaria were to be supported. Stalin also raised the question of German reparations and suggested an armed council of the victorious powers to keep the peace after Germany's defeat.

The British reaction to such talk about spheres of influence was not entirely negative. Churchill drafted plans for federations in east central Europe and in the Balkans, with the aim of restricting the expansion of German influence in those areas. However, a by-product of these plans would have been the erection of barriers to the expansion of Soviet influence also. Churchill even thought of launching a second front in the Balkans instead of in France or Belgium since it held out better hopes of military success. Churchill was ready to include territorial concessions in the Anglo-Soviet Treaty of May 1942, but in the end the view of President Roosevelt prevailed that there should be no binding frontier agreements made before the end of hostilities. At Tehran, in November–December 1943, Churchill conceded the Curzon line as Poland's eastern frontier with the USSR and accepted the Soviet Union's other territorial gains of the period 1939–41. When he went to Moscow in October 1944 the British Prime Minister proposed spheres of influence in south-eastern Europe [*Doc.* 7]: the Soviet Union was to be accorded 90 per cent influence in Romania, the British 10 per cent; in Greece the percentages were to be reversed; Bulgaria was to be divided 75:25 in favour of the Soviet Union, with Hungary and Yugoslavia 50:50. Stalin put a large tick against these numbers but the following day Molotov asked for a revision; he wanted Hungary to be 75:25 (in favour of the USSR) and Bulgaria 90:10 instead of 75:25. No firm agreement was reached, but it appeared that Great Britain and the Soviet Union had agreed on spheres of influence. The British claimed that the agreement was only temporary, to last until the end of hostilities, but they must have been aware that the penetration of these countries by the Red Army would have more than temporary consequences.

The German invasion of the Soviet Union marked the turning-point in the war for Great Britain. Another turning-point of equal impact was the landing of American troops in north Africa in November 1942; from then onwards it was the United States which would have the major say about military operations in Europe. This implied that any agreement about spheres of influence between Stalin and Churchill would have to be counter-signed by the stronger Western power, the United States. While Great Britain was inferior to the Soviet Union in Europe it was also clear that the USSR was weaker than the

United States. Stalin therefore gave priority to the attainment of hegemony over eastern and south-eastern Europe, since he regarded this as absolutely essential to Soviet security needs. American penetration of the area had to be prevented, even if this meant souring relations with the United States.

A key element in restructuring eastern and south-eastern Europe was finding a solution to the problem of national minorities. Moscow solved the problem either by force or by acting unilaterally. The Germans were expelled from Pomerania and Upper and Lower Silesia, this benefiting the Poles. They were also expelled from east Prussia, where once again the Poles were the chief beneficiaries, and from the Sudetenland, where they were replaced by Czechs and Slovaks. Transylvania was transferred to Romania and most of the Hungarian minority was expelled from Slovakia. Land reform was enacted everywhere and resulted in landowners, one of the main props of support of bourgeois rule, being socially and politically emasculated. Enterprises which had been under German control were seized by the Soviets, thus sapping much of the political and economic vitality capitalists might have exercised. Anti-fascist democratic mass organisations were established and communists and communist nominees obtained key posts in government. Those states which had gained territorially and financially, mainly at the expense of the Germans, needed a strong ally to ensure that the gains were permanent. The USSR was ideally suited to play this role. A network of treaties of friendship and cooperation was gradually built up and the Soviet aim was to conclude agreements touching on every aspect of life. The presence of Soviet forces, or the threat of their intervention, was a powerful conditioning factor. The progress of the region towards people's democracies was varied, however, not only because of differing local circumstances but also because of divergent attitudes towards 'sovietisation'.

The roughest Soviet treatment was reserved for Poland. Traditionally anti-Russian, the Poles had seen their country invaded by both Germans and Soviets in September 1939. The Soviets were held responsible by most Poles for the murder of 15,000 captured Polish officers in the spring of 1940. Polish communists had also fared badly. Most of the leadership was executed during the Soviet purges, having been found guilty of Trotskyism and other heinous crimes. Then there was the westward shift of Poland's frontiers and the dislocation this entailed. All in all, Poland proved to be the most difficult country in which to find bourgeois politicians willing to cooperate with the Soviet Union. The discovery of some 4,000 bodies of Polish officers in the Katyn forest in early 1943 by the Germans (who blamed the massacre on the Soviets) led to a request by the Polish government-in-exile in London, headed by General Sikorski, for an inquiry to be undertaken by the International Red Cross. Previous to this Sikorski's government had refused to discuss changes in the pre-war Polish frontiers. Stalin seized the opportunity to terminate the Polish–Soviet agreement of 1941 and to break off diplomatic relations with the London Poles. Nevertheless, Stalin still hoped to find among them some politicians who would be willing to break the stalemate, since a future Polish government composed entirely of communists would be very weak. There were Polish émigrés in Moscow with their own organisation, and in Poland itself Wladyslaw Gomulka and fellow communists set up the National Homeland Council in January 1944 without Stalin's prior approval.

Stalin hoped that a broadly based provisional government could be established in Poland, but Stanislaw Mikolajczyk, Sikorski's successor, proved just as obdurate on the frontier question. However, the establishment of the second front in France in June 1944 made it likely that the Red Army would dominate Poland, and in view of some positive American remarks about the Homeland Council, Stalin formed a minority government – the Lublin committee – and imposed this on Poland on 22 July 1944. Although a minority, the Polish communists were not willing to follow Moscow's directives slavishly. For instance, they argued strongly in favour of the western Neisse as Poland's western frontier instead of the Oder, which Stalin had proposed.

The leaders of the non-communist Polish underground in Warsaw were unaware of the change in Soviet policy, and on 1 August 1944 they launched an uprising designed to secure them a position of influence in the post-war government. Stalin branded them as 'adventurers' and refused them military assistance. He even prevented American and British planes from flying in aid until September, by which time it was too late to save the insurgents. The Red Army was then able to take Warsaw without much trouble. In the rubble of the capital lay the hopes of non-communists for a major say in post-war Polish development. Along with the hopes died many of the social class which would have most effectively resisted the sovietisation of their country. The Lublin committee moved quickly in the wake of the Red Army to re-establish its authority and in January 1945 it was officially recognised by the Soviets as the provisional Polish government.

Soviet experience with the Czechoslovak government-in-exile in London was quite different. The Czechoslovaks lacked the suspiciousness about Soviet motives which so influenced Soviet–Polish relations, and many of the Czechoslovaks were openly anti-Western. The origins of Polish hostility lay in historical experience. Russia had partitioned and ruled part of Poland for over a hundred years before 1918 – an experience spared the Czechoslovaks. Their critical attitude to the West flowed from the Munich agreement of 1938 which had in effect handed their country over to Nazi Germany. Since the West had failed Czechoslovakia in its hour of need a new protector against a resurgent Germany had to be found. It was believed that the USSR would fit the bill very well. Eduard Beneš, a former President and head of the government-in-exile, played an important role in shaping Czechoslovakia's post-war life. He was willing to concede primacy to Soviet interests and abandoned plans to promote a Polish-Czechoslovak federation after liberation when the Soviets made clear their opposition. He took it upon himself to visit Moscow in December 1943 and to sign a treaty of friendship, alliance and mutual assistance. This guaranteed the communists a position of primary importance in the post-war government and in the shaping of the nation even before the war was over and before the communists had contested an election. At the last election in 1935 they had secured a mere 10 per cent of the vote. The communists actually refused the position of Prime Minister but claimed the ministries of the interior, defence, agriculture, propaganda and education.

Beneš urged the Soviet government to eliminate 'feudalism' in Poland and Hungary and sought Soviet support for the expulsion of the Germans from the Sudetenland and for the elimination of the Slovak fascists. He also agreed that the Agrarian party should be banned, thus permitting the communists to take the lead in rural politics and to apportion the rich land of the Sudetenland among their supporters. When Stalin hinted that the USSR was interested in what later became known as Sub-Carpathian Ukraine, Beneš led him to believe that no objection would be raised if it were annexed. This was an important concession, since it afforded the Soviet Union a direct frontier with Hungary. It must have been very gratifying for Stalin to observe how forthcoming Beneš was in promoting Soviet interests in his country. When the National Front government was established in March 1945, Czech and Slovak communists enjoyed a position of influence out of all proportion to the support they enjoyed among the population. After liberation, Soviet and US troops left Czechoslovakia; there was no need for Stalin to drag his feet over withdrawal, since its government was among the most pro-Soviet in the region. In Hungary the Soviets tried to reach agreement with Admiral Horthy, which would have involved the country changing sides and fighting its former ally, Germany. Horthy hesitated and even tried to surrender but was not decisive enough. Instead, the Arrow Cross, the local fascists, took over, and held Hungary to its pro-German course. As the Red Army advanced, however, a coalition government, consisting of members of the Smallholders' party, the National Peasants' party, socialists and communists, came into being in late December 1944 at Debrecen. The old political system and political class had been destroyed by the German and Soviet occupations so the opportunity existed for a new departure. The Soviets insisted on the resurrection of the old parties and so the fear of bolshevisation passed in 1945. The rural nature of the country contributed to the popularity of the Smallholders' party, and when elections were held in Budapest in October 1945 it won an absolute majority, even garnering the votes of the middle classes. In the national election which followed in November 1945 the Smallholders, much to their surprise and embarrassment – the local joke had it that it was as if the party leader had won a lion in a lottery and was afraid to take it home – polled just over 57 per cent of the votes, with the communists only claiming 17 per cent. The Smallholders were an uneasy coalition of interests, so the communists began to pick it to pieces. This process, referred to as 'salami tactics' by the communist leader, Matyas Rakosi, proved very successful.

In Romania, Marshal Antonescu headed a pro-German authoritarian regime which had sent combatant troops to fight against the Soviet Union and had gained control of Soviet territory up to Odessa. A coup carried out by King Michael and some of his officers, with the support of opposition politicians and communist-led armed civilian units, removed Antonescu on 23 August 1944 as the Red Army was penetrating Moldavia. The armistice agreement of 12 September 1944 and the Stalin-Churchill percentages agreement gave the Soviets a dominant say in the shaping of the new Romania. In October 1944 the communists established a National Democratic Front with the social democrats, and this organisation, aided directly and indirectly by the Soviets, gradually acquired greater and greater influence. The government could not control land seizures by peasants and therefore resigned, to be replaced by a new cabinet on 4 November 1944, which included a number of communists and left-wing social democrats. However, in January 1945, the Soviet representatives in the Allied Control Commission denounced the Prime Minister, Radescu, as a traitor and declared the anti-communist opposition to be fascist. Soviet pressure, combined with the wrecking tactics of Romanian communists, made it impossible for the government to maintain its authority, and on 28 February 1945 Andrei Vyshinsky, speaking for Stalin, presented King Michael with a two-hour ultimatum to name a new Prime Minister. The man acceptable to Moscow was Dr Petru Groza, of the tiny Ploughmen's Front. He was a rich landowner but in reality a fellow traveller. The real authority in the land was the Red Army which supported the communists, and the latter attracted more and more adherents as power beckoned.

Bulgaria was at war with the Western powers but not with the Soviet Union. The Soviets hoped that they could come to an agreement with the Bulgarians and refused to channel Anglo-American requests for a cease-fire to Sofia. The Romanian coup of August 1944 and King Michael's order that his army should allow passage to the Red Army to pursue the retreating Germans transformed the situation in Bulgaria. The USSR declared war on Bulgaria on 5 September 1944. The communist-led Fatherland Front staged a *coup d'état* on 9 September and communist partisans moved into Sofia. The traditionally pro-Soviet population then welcomed the entry of the Red Army. By mid-1945 the Fatherland Front was securely in the hands of the Communist party. The opposition was not as harshly treated as in Romania, however, since the new Bulgarian government was actively seeking Western recognition.

In Yugoslavia Soviet influence was more limited, due to the fact that Josip Broz Tito and his partisan movement had played the largest part in the liberation of the country. Soviet troops did not tarry long in Belgrade and elsewhere since they were needed for the advance into Hungary and Austria, a factor which acquired greater significance as time passed. In Albania the communists liberated the country themselves and proclaimed a provisional government in May 1944, following the Yugoslav example. The Albanian Communist party was a section of the Yugoslav, and Stalin appeared quite content to allow Tito to supervise developments there. A Soviet mission entered Albania in July 1944 but was not very active. Yugoslavia's plan was to form a Balkan union comprising itself, Albania and Bulgaria, but Stalin remained non-committal about this project.

In Finland the Soviet position was quite strong. When Finland (which had fought on the German side) left the war in September 1944 it accepted the provisions of the Treaty of Moscow of 1940. An Allied Control Commission, dominated by the Soviets, was established. The Communist party was legalised and the country settled down to pay off the burden of reparations. The Prime Minister, Paasikivi, conducted a policy which accommodated Soviet interests. The main reason why the Communist party failed to win a large following was that it was poorly led.

Hence by the end of hostilities in May 1945 the Soviets had neutralised most of the anti-Soviet forces in their sphere of influence. Just what would happen after the euphoria of liberation wore off, as social and political strife increased, remained uncertain. An even more difficult factor to assess was the Western reaction to the increasingly pro-Soviet orientation of the region.

WESTERN AND SOUTHERN EUROPE

If Soviet policy in eastern and south-eastern Europe was offensive, in the rest of Europe, regarded as the American sphere of influence, it was defensive. Its goal there was to erect barriers to the advance of American capitalism, and to this end communists were enjoined to resurrect the tactics of the popular front of the 1930s. This meant participating in all organisations which stressed national development and gaining as much influence as possible over political developments. Anti-Americanism was to be fostered, but this was not to include preparation for or attempts to seize power. The reconstruction of the war-ravaged economies was a primary goal, and, although strikes and protest movements were to be supported, they were not to be allowed to threaten economic chaos. The Soviets accepted that in the foreseeable future the regimes would remain bourgeois and every effort was therefore to be made to encourage them to adopt independent and neutral policies.

In France, the communists (PCF) used the power and influence they had built up during their years in the resistance to revitalise the economy by advocating greater labour productivity. Participating in government, they ignored socialist plans for the nationalisation of large-scale industry, economic planning and co-determination. They accepted the portfolios of ministries involved in the economy and pursued a policy of holding down wages while output increased. When this led to strikes, the communist-dominated trade union, the CGT, came out against the strikers. The provisional government, headed by Charles de Gaulle, concluded a friendship treaty with the Soviet Union in December 1944, and Maurice Thorez returned from exile in Moscow to lead the communists. His French citizenship was returned to him in 1945. The communists sided with the government in demanding the internationalisation of the Ruhr, separation of the Rhineland and Saar from Germany, and the payment of huge reparations. Even in colonial matters the PCF supported the government's policy of binding the dependent territories more closely to the motherland. As de Gaulle later wrote, Thorez's main concern was the promotion of communist interests, but on many occasions he rendered the French republic a service.

The role played by Thorez in France was taken in Italy by Palmiro Togliatti. In Italy, as in France, the communists (PCI) were the third most significant force, after the socialists and the Christian democrats. Hence they entered coalition governments whose aim was the re-building of the market economy. Indigenous communists were more radical than the exiles, however, and in January 1944, in Bari, communists joined other radicals in calling for the abdication of the king and the immediate transfer of power to the resistance. However, Togliatti's return from Moscow had a moderating influence and he announced a limited programme: a government of national unity, the convocation of a Constituent Assembly, and an uncompromising struggle against fascists and Germans. The PCI was prepared to subordinate all other issues to the war effort; it would postpone all debate about the future of the monarchy and meanwhile would collaborate with the other parties in Marshal Badoglio's royal government. The communists therefore stood by as the partisans in the north were disarmed in early 1944 and their local councils dissolved in the course of 1945. The PCI, illegal since 1926, had more in common with liberals, socialists and Christian democrats than, for example, in France. The PCI had never been as thoroughly bolshevised as the PCF and this had strengthened its commitment to democratic ideals. Yet its liberal attitudes accorded well with the interest of Moscow in 1945.

In Belgium, communists had played their part in the resistance and joined the first post-liberation cabinet but their influence quickly waned. In Greece, when the communists launched the 'second round' of their insurrection in December 1944, British troops were used to put it down. The communists received some aid through Yugoslavia and Albania but it was never sufficient to ensure victory. Stalin appeared to be quite content to let them fight it out with the British. If the latter won it meant he was keeping his side of the bargain; if the communists won it could not be blamed on Soviet involvement. In China, the Soviet government recognised Chiang Kai-shek, the Kuomintang leader, as head of state and Prime Minister, even though Chiang was the mortal enemy of the Communist party of China led by Mao Zedong, and had been responsible for bloody massacres of many of its members. Moscow's attitude was determined by its desire for a united front in order to combat American influence.

The Soviets agreed to the establishment of the United Nations Organisation – much to the satisfaction of the Americans, who did not want the UN to be seen as just another anti-Soviet institution. In the course of 1944 the Soviet government established diplomatic relations with countries in the Middle East – Egypt, Syria, Lebanon and Iraq – and attempted to use the presence of Soviet troops in Iran to political effect. In June 1945, Moscow demanded the lease of a base in the Straits and the transfer of two territories, Kars and Ardagan, ceded by Lenin, in 1922, to Kemal Ataturk. The 1936 Montreux Convention prohibited the passage of Soviet warships through the Straits, without permission from Turkey. Stalin raised the revision of the convention several times with Roosevelt and Churchill. At the Yalta conference the Western leaders conceded that a revision was necessary. Instead of negotiating a deal, Stalin issued his ultimatum to Turkey, in June 1945. The logic behind this move eluded Western policy-makers and has still to be explained. By so doing, Stalin aroused fears in the West that he was bent on imperial expansion. This was one of the factors which led the US President to launch the Truman Doctrine, in 1947. (Molotov, out of office, conceded that Stalin had been arrogant and had overplayed his hand (Zubok and Pleshakov 1996: 93).)

GERMANY

Germany presented an acute problem for the Soviet Union. Neither the tactics applied in eastern nor in western Europe were relevant to the situation there. The USSR needed to cooperate with the Western powers so as to ensure that German militarism never again reared its head, but not at the price of allowing American capital free play. A thoroughgoing social and economic transformation of the country was desirable, but how was this to be achieved? The methods adopted in eastern and south-eastern Europe would just not do; they ran the risk of concentrating resentment at miserable post-war conditions against the USSR, which in turn could only benefit the Americans.

The tactic adopted, therefore, was to proceed with the transformation of the Soviet zone once it had been discovered that residual support for Nazism was weak. The Soviets had no clearly thought-out plan for the future of Germany and indeed could not have had unless the Red Army had been able to occupy the whole country. Given the uncertainty until early 1945 about whether the Soviet Union would actually have a physical presence in Germany, Stalin and his advisers weighed up many options. Because they overestimated the strength of internal German resistance to Hitler, the Soviets called on all Germans to overthrow the national socialist regime, but as 1944 progressed – with the lack of any popular response to the attempt to assassinate Hitler on 20 July 1944 – it gradually became clear that this would not happen.

Various projects for the dismemberment of Germany were entertained. Besides the territories which were to be given to other countries, the Rhineland could either become a separate state or protectorate, while Bavaria could become independent; proposals along these lines were put to Eden in December 1941. At Tehran in November 1943 Stalin showed some sympathy for Roosevelt's plan to divide Germany into five states. At Yalta he asked for concrete suggestions about the dismemberment of Germany, without himself advancing any Soviet proposals. He made clear that he wanted the western Neisse recognised as the western frontier of Poland. He also announced that the USSR needed reparations worth $10,000 million from Germany, and that the other victims of German aggression should collectively receive a further $10,000 million. Little, however, came of the plans to dismember and weaken Germany economically. Churchill, especially, was aware that hasty agreements could engender future strife, and he did not want a repetition of Versailles. As soon as the Red Army was over the German border, members of the National Committee for a Free Germany – set up in the Soviet Union in 1943 and composed of exiled communists and prisoners-of-war who had been 'turned' in anti-fascist schools – began to establish their control of local administration. In March 1945 Stalin came out strongly against dismembering Germany (apart from the eastern territories taken by Poland and the USSR) and after the end of hostilities he made it clear that he knew how to distinguish between fascism and the German people. The process of democratisation was set in motion in the Soviet zone even before the Potsdam Conference, but there was no way in which the Soviets could push through a similar programme in the western zones. As they developed a policy in their own zone, it acquired its own momentum. From September 1945 onwards, the unexpected strength of the social democrats in the Soviet zone led to a policy of fusing the social democratic and communist parties. This took place in April 1946 and resulted in the Socialist Unity Party (SED) coming into being. By then the die had been cast and there was no going back. This, in turn, made it impossible to adopt one policy for the whole of Germany.

In broad terms, Stalin knew what his priorities were in Europe. Eastern and south-eastern Europe should fall within the Soviet sphere of interest, thereby meeting Moscow's security needs. Germany was the key to Europe and Stalin entertained hopes that the whole of Germany would go socialist, in the Soviet meaning of the word, sometime in the future. This was the main reason why he strongly opposed any attempt to dismember Germany. In the meantime, the Soviet Union would try to fashion a model socialist state in its zone. Western Europe was within the American sphere of influence and socialism could not be overtly promoted in the short term. Stalin thought he was entitled to eastern and south-eastern Europe but the Americans gradually began to see Soviet behaviour as a breach of faith. Even more ominously, they thought that Moscow had designs on much more than that region. Stalin did not handle the situation very well and it was very clear that trust between the former allies was fast evaporating. Why had Stalin become so difficult to deal with? The answer was simple: the atomic bomb. The Americans had it and he did not. He and his advisers failed completely to grasp the significance of the bomb before it was first deployed. His spies provided him with all the information he needed to judge its impact. The euphoria of victory over Germany faded very quickly as he realised that his conventional (non-nuclear) superiority in Europe and elsewhere could be nullified by a few atomic bombs. He told those who would be responsible for building the bomb: 'Hiroshima has shaken the whole world. The balance has been broken. Build the bomb – it will remove a great danger from us' (Zubok and Pleshakov 1996: 40; Holloway 1979: 41). Lavrenty Beria was put in overall charge. In characteristic fashion, he informed the scientists that if they failed they could not count on continuing breathing. The American bomb appears to be the fundamental reason why Stalin was determined to hold on to everything he had and to prevent the expansion of American influence into eastern and south-eastern Europe. Roosevelt treated him as an equal but Truman was certainly not following in his predecessor's footsteps.

Stalin's decision to launch a massive rearmament programme, the consequence of Hiroshima, was to transform Soviet industry and bring into being a formidable military-industrial complex. The Russians had to compete with the Americans and huge efforts were expended to catch up and surpass American achievements. The Soviet scientific community – at least those engaged in pure and applied science and technology – now assumed a leading role in the intellectual community. Huge investments meant huge sacrifices from the Soviet population. Consumption would have to wait. Eventually over three quarters of the scientific budget and the same proportion of scientists were devoted to defence. The scientists were concentrated in the USSR Academy of Sciences (Russian universities were and are not centres of leading research) and it acquired an enviable reputation at home and abroad. However in creating this scientific Leviathan, Stalin was offering a hostage to fortune. Henceforth the military economy took precedence over the civilian economy with the result that the latter remained inefficient and often scientifically backward. The most talented gravitated to the military economy. The defence burden was eventually to play a major role in the demise of the Soviet Union in 1991. On reflection, it was a shocking waste of talent and resources to plough most of Soviet wealth into the military-industrial complex. After all, one cannot eat a tank or a rocket.

CHAPTER THREE

CONFLICTS DURING THE WAR

On the face of it there were many reasons why the United States and the USSR should have been eager to cooperate both during and after the war. Only together could they defeat Germany; afterwards the USSR would need American capital and goods, and this in turn would ease the problem of over-production which would face the American economy at the end of hostilities. Neither power wanted to become embroiled in future wars, so there was considerable American understanding, especially from Roosevelt, for the Soviet determination not to tolerate anti-Soviet regimes in eastern and south-eastern Europe. The war was promoting the expansion of the US economy but the destruction of the Soviet economy. Washington thought that because it was rich, the Russians were bound to come asking for credits. Politically the two countries were equals but economically they were far from equal.

THE QUESTION OF THE SECOND FRONT

In one of his first messages to Churchill, Stalin, on 18 July 1941, asked the British to launch a second front in France and another in the Arctic. The question of a second front in Europe was to bedevil relations between the Allies during the war. Great Britain and the United States agreed that such a move was advisable; it would take some of the burden off the Red Army, it would allow the Western powers to influence directly events on the European mainland, it would lessen any temptation Stalin might have to negotiate a unilateral peace with Germany (just as Soviet Russia had done in March 1918), and it would reduce Stalin's suspiciousness by showing that the Western powers were not content to leave the actual fighting to the Soviets.

In May 1942 Molotov extracted a promise from Roosevelt in Washington to aim at a second front in Europe in 1942. The British favoured an invasion of north Africa rather than northern Europe but they were overruled. However, Roosevelt's good intentions could not be transformed into actions, for his military advisers made it clear that such an operation was out of the question in 1942; at the very earliest it could take place in 1943. The Americans therefore compromised, and proposed that small contingents of men should be landed on the French coast in late 1942, but the British opposed this as too risky. (The aim of these landings was to gain experience and to test German strength. The troops would be withdrawn after attaining their goal.) Roosevelt was then won over by Churchill to the view that the first Allied invasion should take place in north Africa, and it fell to the British Prime Minister to give this information to Stalin in Moscow in August 1942. The news caused the Soviet Prime Minister to lose his temper in front of a Western statesman – a rare occurrence – and he bitterly enquired if British troops were afraid of fighting Germans.

Early 1943 proved too optimistic a date for an assault on German-occupied France. It took Anglo-American forces until May 1943 to force the Germans out of Tunisia. Then Churchill and Roosevelt agreed in Casablanca to invade Sicily, as a way of knocking Italy out of the war. Serious planning for 'Overlord', the attack on northern France, only got under way in early 1944. William C. Bullitt had already proposed launching Allied troops into the Balkans and eastern Europe, later to be echoed by Churchill who saw such a move as striking at the 'soft underbelly' of the Axis powers. However, Roosevelt did not accept this argument, and took the view that strategy should be based on military considerations only; political objectives could take precedence only after the war had been won.

The delay in launching the second front fuelled Soviet suspicions about Anglo-American motives. However, a second front in 1942 or 1943 would most likely have failed, and in any case the Allies did what they could to sustain the USSR. Roosevelt provided the Red Army with about 10 million tonnes of war matériel between June 1941 and June 1944 – without tying any strings to the transfer – but even this may not have been enough to convince Stalin that the Anglo-Americans were willing to make as many sacrifices as his own people were. In early 1943 Stalin began renewed efforts to secure a separate peace with Germany, and only in September 1943, after the Germans had failed to make a positive response, did he set out to improve relations with the West. The fear that the Western powers might reach an agreement with Hitler behind his back lingered on until early 1945.

American military leaders were quite explicit about the need for the Soviet alliance. A memorandum of September 1943 states that neither the war against Germany nor that against Japan could be won without Soviet help; this would inevitably mean that Soviet influence in central and eastern Europe would greatly increase. As it turned out, the US Army was able to defeat Germany and Japan with less than half the troops originally thought necessary. After D-Day, 6 June 1944, there were only 90 German divisions in France and Italy to oppose the Anglo-American forces, compared with 250 German divisions on the eastern front.

US CAPITAL FOR THE SOVIET UNION?

Hopes were high during the war that the United States and the USSR would reach some mutually beneficial commercial agreement once hostilities ceased. Large American credits would permit the Soviet Union to import vitally needed equipment. The USSR would not be in a position to export industrial or agricultural goods, but it was a treasure trove of unexploited mineral reserves. Eric Johnston, the president of the American Chamber of Commerce, spent eight weeks in the Soviet Union during the summer of 1944 and was able to inspect any enterprise he wished. Stalin, in a long conversation with him, underlined the USSR's interest in importing heavy industrial products and exporting raw materials. Johnston received an enthusiastic response when he returned home and over 700 American firms declared that they were eager to sell to the Soviets. Banks began to form a consortium to finance US–Soviet trade, and moves were made to remove the ban, imposed in 1943, on loans to the USSR. Henry Morgenthau, secretary of the Treasury, proposed a credit of $10 billion and optimists spoke of annual exports of $1 billion–$2 billion. However, there were dissenting voices. The oil and coal industries did not relish the prospect of Soviet competition; doubts were raised about the Soviet Union's capacity to balance imports and exports; and George Kennan feared that the Soviets would exploit their huge purchasing power to the detriment of American industry. However, Averell Harriman, the United States ambassador in Moscow from October 1943, was very enthusiastic about doing business and President Roosevelt saw credits as a way of making up for the delays in launching the second front. Anastas Mikoyan, the very astute commissar for foreign trade, immediately asked for a credit of $1 billion over 25 years, with repayments to begin after 17 years at 1.25 per cent interest. Mikoyan could hardly have expected the Americans to accept such a proposal, for given the rate of inflation it would have resembled something like a Christmas present, but it was an opening bid and revealed that there were some sharp business minds in the Kremlin.

Little came of it, due to two factors. Congress would not commit itself to post-war credits while the war was still on; and the reserves of the Export-Import Bank were almost exhausted. Roosevelt therefore decided to make use of the Lend-Lease arrangements and encouraged the Soviets to put in orders for equipment which could be used for post-war reconstruction. Credits could be arranged at 3.375 per cent. Negotiations got under way, but in September 1944 the Soviet government broke them off, the rate of interest being the sticking point. Molotov then informed Harriman, on 3 January 1945, that the USSR would buy industrial equipment worth $6 billion if a 30-year loan at 2.25 per cent – with repayments to begin after 10 years – could be agreed. However, the climate for such an arrangement in Washington had become more frosty. Congress was now unwilling to extend Lend-Lease beyond the end of hostilities, and the voices demanding Soviet political concessions had become much louder and more influential. Congress, for its part, wanted to tie the credits to Soviet cooperation in other fields. Roosevelt therefore decided to delay his response to the Soviet request, but he informed the Soviet Union that the reason was that the loan would involve time-consuming legislative procedures. It soon became clear to Moscow, however, that Washington placed a low priority on increased trade, and any hope that Roosevelt had harboured that a loan could be used as bait for Soviet concessions elsewhere vanished.

CONFLICT OVER GERMANY

Although the United States and the USSR had a mutual interest in solving the German question, no agreement about post-war Europe or the future of Germany could be reached, and this was an important factor in the exacerbation of relations.

It was, however, the British government which made the early running, and it proposed on 1 July 1943 that a United Nations Commission for Europe should be established to supervise the liberated countries and those to be administered by the victors. More precise proposals were made by Anthony Eden in Moscow in October 1943, when he advocated the setting up of a European Advisory Commission (EAC) whose terms of reference were to include all problems which the Big Three wanted elaborated – including the peace settlement. When the EAC met for the first time in January 1944, in London, the British delegation presented its plans for three occupation zones and joint responsibility for Berlin.

It was in the interests of the Soviet Union, as long as there was no second front in Europe and while the Wehrmacht was still on Soviet soil, to spin out negotiations, for there was just no way of predicting the constellation of forces at the end of hostilities. As for the Americans, they decided that their representative, John G. Winant, should not be given authority to decide on the exact conditions of German surrender or on how a defeated Germany was to be administered. The main reason for this attitude was that the Roosevelt administration – like the Soviets – had no clear conception of what was to happen to Germany after the war. The Americans also refused to discuss reparations in the EAC. This thorny question was only considered, for the first time, at Yalta in February 1945, when Stalin asked for $20 billion for the Soviet Union and Germany's victims. Churchill opposed this, out of fear that, if granted, it would produce a rapid increase in Soviet economic strength. In the end Roosevelt accepted the sum as a basis for future discussions, but the Soviets failed to extract any hard-and-fast promises about reparations before the ending of the war. The division of Germany into occupation zones was agreed in principle but the possibility of dismembering Germany was not excluded. No firm agreement was reached on Poland's western frontier

[*Doc. 9*]. A major reason for the Americans' indecisiveness at Yalta was that they had not prepared themselves sufficiently well. They had not attempted to work out what the USSR's policy towards Germany might be, nor how this could be squared with American policy.

THE PROBLEM OF EASTERN AND SOUTH-EASTERN EUROPE

The most important source of conflict between the United States and the USSR concerned the post-war arrangements for this region. In contrast to its attitude towards Germany, the US administration had a very good idea of what it wanted here. The State Department was very keen that the principles of the Atlantic Charter should be applied [*Doc. 4*]; that self-determination should be enacted and the region integrated into the grand design of a universal market economy. Minority conflicts, which had contributed so much to the destruction of the Versailles system, had to be avoided, but the United States did not wish to become embroiled in the area; strife could be mediated through the agency of the United Nations. The goals of such an organisation had to be alluring to the American public, who, it has to be remembered, had rejected the idea of a world peace organisation after the First World War. Roosevelt floated the image of the United States, Great Britain, the Soviet Union and China acting as 'four policemen' who 'would maintain sufficient armed force to impose peace' [Yergin 1980: 45]. The idea had its weaknesses – for instance, China was unable to impose peace at home, let alone step outside its frontiers to quell conflict. Also the cooperation of the USSR was seen as vital to its implementation. It was taken for granted by President Roosevelt and the State Department that free elections in eastern and south-eastern Europe and the formation of governments which would maintain friendly relations with the Soviet Union were compatible goals. Washington wanted both democratic regimes in the region and Soviet friendship, and ended up with neither.

As a universalist and an adherent of Wilsonian principles, Roosevelt wanted to delay the discussions about territorial disputes until after the war and to avoid all talk about spheres of influence, if possible. When the British government, in February 1942, pressed Roosevelt to accept Soviet territorial demands in principle, he refused, and requested that the Soviet government should wait until the post-war peace conference. Again, in May 1942, he would not countenance territorial changes being written into the Anglo-Soviet treaty. In May 1944 Eden suggested to Molotov that the Soviet Union should take the lead in Romania while Great Britain did the same in Greece. Churchill persuaded Roosevelt to go along with this, but his Secretary of State was not present and Roosevelt did not minute the conversation. Churchill's percentages deal in October 1944 [*Doc. 7*] was not endorsed by the Americans. Because Roosevelt would not openly commit himself to accepting Soviet territorial claims, Stalin acted unilaterally to enforce his viewpoint. The Beneš agreement, the breaking-off of diplomatic relations with the London Poles, the surrender terms presented to Bulgaria, Romania and Hungary, the refusal to help the insurgents during the Warsaw uprising and the recognition of the Lublin committee as the provisional Polish government, were all unilateral acts, exhibiting little concern for Western wishes.

The inevitable result of these *démarches* was that the influence of the opponents of Roosevelt's policy of seeking close cooperation with the USSR increased. The intractable problem of Poland weighed heavily on Roosevelt's mind. The 7 million Polish Americans used every avenue to press their case for an independent, democratic post-war Poland, and in Michigan the chief Republican speaker of foreign affairs, Senator Vandenberg, who was dependent on Polish votes, declared that the Senate would not agree to the United States joining the UN if the provisions of the Atlantic Charter [*Doc. 4*] were not respected. Other eastern and south-eastern European minorities had also to be placated. Roosevelt attempted to convince the governments-in-exile that it was in their interests to come to some arrangement with the Soviet Union which would save face all round, but he failed in his objective – the Poles, for instance, would not negotiate on frontier changes. However, Stalin showed himself at the Yalta Conference to be more understanding and agreed to the publication of a 'Declaration on Liberated Europe' [*Doc. 10*] which embodied the principles of the Atlantic Charter [*Doc. 4*]. This document was replete with fine phrases and envisaged regimes in which all democratic elements would be represented; free elections were also promised. Stalin once confided to Anthony Eden that he regarded a declaration as 'algebra' but an agreement as 'practical arithmetic'. He did not wish to decry algebra but he preferred 'practical arithmetic' [*Doc. 5*]. The Yalta declaration on liberated Europe [*Doc. 10*], in his eyes, was pure algebra. Instead of the Lublin committee and the London Poles having equal representation in the government, as Churchill and Roosevelt wanted, some 'democratic leaders' were to be added to widen its base. Instead of free elections under Allied supervision, the Polish government itself was to organise them. Nevertheless, Roosevelt believed that a new era had dawned, and he informed Congress on 1 March 1945 that the foundation for a lasting peace, based on the just principles of the Atlantic Charter [*Doc. 4*], had now been laid. This struck a responsive chord; spring had arrived after a difficult winter. Yergin refers to it as 'Roosevelt weather' [Yergin 1980: 66]; optimism had really taken over.

The USSR committed itself at Yalta to enter the war against Japan two or three months after the termination of the European war and to participate actively in preparations for setting up the United Nations Organisation. As a tangible reward for their cooperation, the Soviets were to receive southern Sakhalin, the southern Kurile islands, and agree to the internationalisation of Dairen, a lease on Port Arthur and Sino-Soviet control of the Chinese eastern and the south Manchurian railways. The Anglo-Americans were strikingly forthcoming in the Far East in contrast to eastern Europe. France, at Great Britain's instigation, joined the Allied Control Council in Germany, thus weighting it further to the advantage of the West. Roosevelt's foreign policy can be seen as consisting of two parts: one for internal and the other for external consumption. A ground-swell away from isolation and towards universalism gradually overtook the American public from 1942 onwards. This made it necessary for Roosevelt to speak the language of pure Wilsonianism at home – the old power blocs were to go, spheres of influence were to be a thing of the past, national self-determination would prevail, liberal capitalism would penetrate to all corners of the globe. However, he was well aware that this was incompatible with the realities of power politics. His external policy was informed by the need to secure Soviet cooperation, and this meant, in practice, working towards a great power consortium and involved wheeling and dealing with Stalin. The two elements of his foreign policy were mutually exclusive, but he hoped that somehow (he was an inveterate optimist) solutions could be found which would permit symbiosis to come about. Such a relationship depended on mutual trust and it is probable that only Roosevelt on the American side could have engendered this trust. The Soviets were genuinely interested in a workable relationship with the United States; they wanted the acceptance of spheres of influence, and American technology. Yalta was a step forward but it was not the milestone which some Americans took it to be. Each side interpreted the agreement after its own fashion; if the declaration on liberated Europe [*Doc. 10*] was algebra to Stalin, it was no use the Americans claiming it was practical arithmetic. The inherent contradictions of US foreign policy were bound to surface and it was the German problem which occasioned this.

CHAPTER FOUR

1945: THE TURNING-POINT

The Grand Alliance did not survive the end of hostilities. Once its *raison d'être* no longer existed it came apart at the seams, despite the fact that fine words had circulated at Yalta about cooperation producing a rich harvest of mutual benefit. Within a year of that meeting Churchill had delivered his iron curtain speech [*Doc. 19*], alleging that a barrier had descended from Stettin in the Baltic to Trieste in the Adriatic. Meanwhile Molotov had vented his spleen on the Anglo-Americans [*Doc. 23*] by talking of insatiable imperialists and war-hungry groups of adventurers. Disillusion was almost complete.

Even before the end of hostilities a major row developed between the Soviet Union and the United States which revealed how little mutual trust existed. When SS General Karl Wolff arrived in Berne in early March 1945 to discuss a possible surrender of his troops in northern Italy with American and British representatives, the Soviets demanded a seat at the negotiating table. The Americans refused, on the grounds that the deliberations had nothing to do with a separate peace in western Europe and were merely of local military significance. The Soviets thereupon accused the West of duplicity, claiming that an agreement had been reached which would allow American and British troops to penetrate as far east as possible while at the same time permitting the Germans to strengthen their forces on the eastern front. This impugned Roosevelt's integrity and he was stung to reply. 'Frankly, I cannot avoid a feeling of bitter resentment towards your informers, whoever they are, for such vile misrepresentation of my actions or those of my trusted subordinates' [Churchill 1954: 447–8].

EASTERN AND SOUTH-EASTERN EUROPE

Soviet activities in the area liberated or occupied by the Red Army caused first misgivings and then offence in London and Washington. Part of the problem was that Moscow believed that it had been recognised as part of its sphere of influence. (At the Potsdam conference, Bulgaria was quietly handed over to Stalin by the Allies. He found it difficult to grasp why the West was so upset by Soviet actions in eastern and south-eastern Europe. One of the reasons for the friction was that the decision-makers who had tacitly acknowledged Soviet primacy in the region were no longer there. Roosevelt was dead and Churchill out of office. The new men, Truman and Attlee, were much less accommodating.)

Anti-communists were everywhere under threat in the region; indeed, many were liquidated. In Romania, in February 1945, Vyshinsky had brutally forced King Michael to remove one government and install another, which accelerated communist influence. In Poland the Provisional Government declared Pomerania, Upper and Lower Silesia and its part of east Prussia to be part of Poland, even while the Yalta Conference was taking place. Although the Western Allies had kept open the question of whether the Oder-Neisse line was to be the western frontier of Poland, four Polish woiwodships were established on former German territory on 14 March 1945 and most of the Germans still living there were expelled. In Moscow, Molotov and the British and American ambassadors wrangled over the restructuring of the Polish Provisional Government but had reached no agreement by late March. Then, on 21 April 1945, the Soviets concluded a treaty of friendship with the Provisional Government which recognised Polish territorial claims. The Western response was to refuse Poland admission to the consultative meeting of the United Nations.

KOREA

In Korea, as in Manchuria and northern China, the United States was keen to contain Soviet influence. During the war Roosevelt had supported the concept of a four-power trusteeship for the peninsula in an effort to ensure that the Soviet Union did not expand its influence over it. Were it to do so, Russia would then strengthen the economic resources of the Soviet Far East and occupy a dominating strategic position in relation both to China and Japan. At Potsdam the Americans attempted to avoid discussion of the application of the trusteeship to Korea. However, Korea was too important to Moscow, and when the Soviet Union declared war on Japan its forces penetrated Korea as well as Manchuria. Stalin agreed that the Americans could accept the surrender of Japanese forces in the south, and the United States then proposed the 38th parallel as the dividing line. This was accepted by the Kremlin despite the fact that the whole of Korea politically was within its grasp. Koreans did not favour trusteeship and wanted liberation after 40 years of oppressive Japanese occupation. To stem the pro-communist tide in the south, the Americans were obliged to accept the strongly anti-Soviet Syngman Rhee and Koreans who had collaborated with the Japanese. At the Moscow Council of Foreign Ministers conference in December 1945 Byrnes proposed trusteeship for Korea and Molotov accepted. However, virulent south Korean resistance led to Truman losing interest in the idea. The right in south Korea would never accept trusteeship, and that was the constituency on which the United States had to rely in order to stem the communist takeover of the whole of Korea.

SOUTH-EAST ASIA

In south-east Asia, as in Korea, US aspirations were diametrically opposed to the forces of nationalism and revolution. Facing defeat, Japanese forces relinquished power to Asians. Indonesia declared independence from the Netherlands. In Vietnam Ho Chi Minh proclaimed the formation of the democratic republic of Vietnam, independent of French control. Roosevelt had favoured trusteeship for the region, but Churchill convinced him that the colonial powers, Britain, France and the Netherlands, should be reinstated. Otherwise a communist tide could make the region pro-Soviet. At Potsdam Truman agreed that Britain should accept the surrender of Japanese forces south of the 16th parallel in Indochina and throughout south-east Asia. The Nationalist Chinese would assume responsibility for the Japanese in northern Indochina.

Only in Japan did the United States reserve for itself the lead role in dealing with the Japanese. Elsewhere Washington accepted the restoration of the old order. After the Japanese surrender Ho Chi Minh appealed to the Americans to protect Vietnam against Chinese looting and deny aid to the French. Washington did not respond. The United States hoped the European powers would follow the example of the Americans in the Philippines, which were to be granted independence in 1946.

THE SOVIET UNION IN A NEW LIGHT

Soviet behaviour in eastern and south-eastern Europe led the Americans to view the Soviets differently, and this change can be analysed on four levels [Loth 1980: 110–16]:

1 For the first time a whole range of Americans, from ordinary soldiers to top-level politicians, actually came into contact with Soviet citizens and their quite different attitudes and way of life. Many were led to ascribe these differences to the impact of Asia on Russian and Soviet culture. Averell Harriman spoke in April 1945 of the possibility of Europe being invaded by barbarians [*Doc. 12*], and maintained that Hitler's greatest crime had been to open the gates of Europe to the Asian hordes. General George Patton thought that Soviet officers behaved like recently civilised Mongolian bandits. On the British side there was also the same sense of shock. There were several fracas between British and Soviet troops over Soviet maltreatment of German civilians, especially women. An apple of discord was the wholesale rape of German women

by Soviet troops and personnel. Those raped included Ukrainian and Polish women who had been brought to Germany to engage in forced labour. The total number of those raped may have exceeded two million.

2 Astonishment and resentment at Soviet behaviour, both personal and political, strengthened the influence of the proponents of the 'Riga axioms' both in Congress and throughout the nation. It also added weight to Republican criticism, under way since 1944, of Roosevelt's foreign policy. Disappointed at the meagre results of the Yalta agreement, the critics demanded that the USSR should fulfil its commitments in accordance with the American interpretation of them. Senator Vandenberg emerged as a powerful spokesman for these critics at the founding meeting of the United Nations. He looked at the Soviet Union through the lens of Poland and did not like what he saw. The meeting became acrimonious and Alexander Cadogan, permanent under-secretary at the British Foreign Office, who had come to the conclusion at Yalta that Stalin was a great man, now wrote: 'How can we work with these animals?' [Dilks 1971: 739]. Vandenberg's diary was equally frank: 'I don't know if this is Frisco or Munich. We must stand by our guns . . . This is the point at which to . . . *win* and *end this appeasement of the Reds before it is too late*' [Loth 1980: 100].

3 American diplomats began to adopt the interpretation placed on the Yalta agreement by the US public, and the beliefs of the 'Riga' school of thought – which accused Roosevelt of lacking political acumen in dealing with the Soviets – gained wide currency. Diplomats who were universalists and who hoped that world affairs could be managed through a world peace organisation had to concede some disappointment but were not prepared to abandon their hopes of arranging a deal with the Soviets which would secure a non-communist future for eastern and south-eastern Europe. However, the contradiction between Roosevelt's internal and external foreign policies – Wilsonianism at home and a Great Power consortium abroad – now surfaced. Just as they had underestimated Soviet security needs in eastern and south-eastern Europe, the Americans now proceeded to overestimate the Soviet will to expand. The domino theory appeared – if one country falls under Soviet influence its neighbour will not be far behind – and Harriman in April 1945 declared before members of the State Department that Soviet plans to establish satellites constituted a major threat [*Doc. 12*]. Once they had established them they would then set out to take over countries contiguous to them. Soviet demands for military bases in the Straits and a mandate in Libya seemed to provide substantial proof of the accuracy of this domino theory. Joseph C. Grew, the Under Secretary of State, saw what was happening in eastern and south-eastern Europe as the harbinger of what would eventually happen throughout the rest of the world if the United States did not act to prevent it. He even regarded a war with the Soviet Union as inevitable. Henry Stimson, Secretary for War, warned

Harry Truman – who had succeeded to the presidency after Roosevelt's death on 12 April 1945 – that the mounting economic chaos in western and central Europe would lead to political revolution and communist infiltration. By the summer of 1945 the voices advocating the 'fulfilment' of the Yalta agreement, no more concessions to the Soviets, and the stabilisation of all countries in which there were no Soviet troops, dominated US policy-making.

4 The death of Roosevelt and the accession to power of Truman – a self-confessed amateur in foreign affairs – upset the balance between the internal and external components of American foreign policy. Although Truman was a Wilsonian he quickly adopted a 'realistic' approach, and in order to assert his authority he became very decisive. He had pledged to continue Roosevelt's foreign policy but it was so complex that arguably only Roosevelt himself could have done that. Truman quickly adopted the view that the USSR needed the United States more than vice versa. In negotiations he did not expect to get 100 per cent of what he wanted but he felt that on 'important matters' the Americans 'should be able to get 85 per cent' [Truman 1955: 81–2]. At his first meeting with Molotov on 23 April 1945 he put his cards on the table. In future, the Soviets would have to keep to their agreements, relations could no longer be 'on the basis of a one-way street'. Molotov turned white but managed, through his usual stutter, to reply: 'I have never been talked to like this in my life.' Truman sharply retorted: 'Carry out your agreements and you won't get talked to like that' [Truman 1955: 82]. Molotov then left Washington for the UN conference in San Francisco where he was very abusive. Presumably the Soviets had decided that they would show themselves as tough as the Americans; if the Americans were not prepared for compromise, then neither were they.

COOPERATION AND PRESSURE

Although the Americans had changed their view of the Soviet Union it did not follow that policy towards Moscow would also be drastically altered. Truman and James F. Byrnes, his wily Secretary of State, wanted to hold the line in Europe and if possible push the Soviets back. However, they continued to hope that a deal could be done with Moscow which would satisfy the needs of both sides. After all, the only other option was to re-arm for eventual war. The American public was keen on an international role but was not willing to make the necessary sacrifices. 'Bring the boys home' was a rallying call that few could resist. The public, however, was unaware of the true nature of US–Soviet relations, for the administration had not as yet brought all the conflicts out into the open.

The American administration refused to accept the Soviet interpretation of Yalta, yet at the same time was not willing to use force to ensure that its own interpretation prevailed. In an attempt to overcome this impasse Harry Hopkins travelled to Moscow at the end of May 1945 [*Doc. 13*] bearing the honeyed words of cooperation on his breath, and achieved a compromise solution on Poland. Agreement was reached with Stalin on the names of four additional politicians, from among the London Poles and the resistance, who would join the Lublin committee in a new cabinet. This was completed at the end of June 1945. No guarantee of free elections or a pluralistic democracy could be secured in Poland or elsewhere.

Tension between Britain and the United States increased in 1944 when the American Joint Chiefs of Staff concluded that the likelihood of a war against Russia or against Britain was about equal. Truman advised Churchill that they should repair to Potsdam separately so as not to give the impression to Stalin that they were ganging up on him. Truman enquired if Churchill would object if he had a private meeting with Stalin before the conference got under way. Churchill protested, sensing that America and Russia might strike a deal over Britain's head and inimical to it. Despite his protests, however, the first meeting of the Big Two took place in Babelsberg, outside Berlin, on 17 July 1945. To Churchill's further irritation Truman unilaterally recognised Poland's new government. Presented with this *fait accompli* Churchill had to concede. The State Department wanted the President to oppose Britain's plan for a western European bloc because it contained features which 'would place additional restrictions on trade, run counter to the principles of free access to foreign markets and raw materials'. At the meeting Truman assured Stalin that they would have no difficulty in 'reaching agreement on the matters which would be before them'. The President went further, and said that he proposed to 'deal directly with Stalin as a friend'. Stalin was just as forthcoming and averred that the Soviet Union 'would always try to meet the views of the United States'. Truman thought he had the measure of Stalin: 'I can deal with Stalin. He is honest – but smart as hell' [Moskin 2002: 203].

Stalin and Molotov then presented a shopping list: decide on German reparations, liquidate the Polish government in exile in London, accept Soviet trusteeship over former Italian colonies (primarily Libya), break off relations with Spain to 'permit the Spanish people to select a government of their choice', replace the Montreux Convention on the Straits with Russian control, and finally, in cooperation with Turkey, conclude a Soviet-Turkish alliance treaty which would return to the Soviet Union territory which had been 'torn from Soviet Armenia and Soviet Georgia' in 1921.

Truman soon wiped the smile of expectancy off Stalin's face. He flatly refused to countenance Soviet control over former Italian colonies and was not forthcoming on anything else. Despite having conceded diplomatic recognition of the communist-dominated Polish government he declined to recognise the governments of Romania and Bulgaria. Byrnes listed violations of the Yalta Declaration on Liberated Europe. It seemed that the United States was insisting on national self-determination in these states and in the same breath declaring that freely elected governments would, of course, be friendly to the Soviet Union. Stalin must have found all this rather confusing, since he was under the impression that the Americans had already conceded eastern and south-eastern Europe as a Soviet sphere of influence.

However, towards the end of the Potsdam Conference the Americans decided that a bit of horsetrading was in order. Byrnes proposed that in addition to the reparations the Soviets took from their zone they would be entitled to a certain percentage of available capital equipment from the western zones of Germany. Hitherto the Americans had been trying to restrict the amount of territory Poland could take from Germany, but now Byrnes was prepared to accept all annexations up to the western Neisse. Previously Stalin had linked progress on a peace treaty for Italy to recognition of Romania and Bulgaria. Now Byrnes placed a peace treaty for Italy at the top of the agenda for the Council of Foreign Ministers and agreed that diplomatic recognition of Romania, Bulgaria, Hungary and Finland should be prosecuted with diligence even before the conclusion of peace treaties with these states. Byrnes presented this deal on a take-it-or-leave-it basis. Stalin took it and praised Byrnes. It appeared that the Americans had discovered how to do business with the Soviets. However, this honeymoon only lasted until the failure of the conference of the Council of Foreign Ministers in London in September 1945.

Potsdam was Churchill's last fling, as the general election of July 1945 saw a sweeping victory for the Labour party, one of the planks of whose platform had been that a socialist government would find it easier to reach agreement with the USSR. This turned out to be a fundamentally false assumption. Clement Attlee replaced Churchill before the Potsdam Conference was over.

The Americans tried to pressurise the Soviets into making concessions by playing two of their supposed aces: their clear economic superiority and their monopoly of nuclear weapons (the first atomic bomb having exploded on 16 July 1945). Lend-Lease deliveries, except those destined for use in the war against Japan, were halted on 11 May in so abrupt a fashion that ships on the high seas were recalled. Strong Soviet protests led to some deliveries being restored, but Truman wanted to underline Moscow's dependence on American economic power. On the question of German reparations, Truman decided they should be as low as possible, since Congress was quite determined that they should not be financed, as after the First World War, by the American taxpayer. In any case, the United States favoured the rapid recovery of the German market economy and this would not be aided by huge reparations from fixed assets and current production.

In January 1945 the Soviet government asked the Americans for a \$6 billion credit, but in the following July Congress passed a law putting a limit of \$1 billion on advances from the Export-Import Bank. Thereupon the Soviets, on 28 August, asked for a \$1 billion credit but the Americans let it be known during the preliminary negotiations that they expected political concessions in return. The Soviet request was then 'mislaid' by the administration – something Moscow could not bring itself to believe. The Americans had already prepared a list of concessions they wanted. A Congressional delegation led by William M. Colmer visited the Soviet Union in September 1945 and returned recommending that credits be extended to the USSR and the countries of eastern and south-eastern Europe only on condition that the Soviet government guaranteed American property, permitted the distribution of US films, books and newspapers, made freedom of religion and the press a reality and carried out genuinely free elections. It also emphasised the need for the terms of the Yalta agreement (as the Americans interpreted them) to be fulfilled.

The same tactics were employed by Byrnes in his attempt to make capital out of the US atomic monopoly. He never threatened to drop the atomic bomb on the Soviet Union, because the great majority of the American public would have opposed such a move in 1945. But he also rejected the advice of Henry Stimson, the Secretary for War, that the Soviets be offered an atomic partnership provided they made concessions in eastern and south-eastern Europe. Byrnes wanted to demonstrate to the Soviets the awesome nature of the new weapon in the hope that they would become more flexible. The Potsdam Conference was therefore delayed until 16 July 1945, the day of the test explosion, to achieve the maximum effect. The news that the atomic bomb was more destructive than expected reached Truman on 21 July and he then casually mentioned to Stalin that the United States had a new weapon of unprecedented destructive power. 'He was a changed man,' Churchill noted of Truman after the plenary session on 21 July. 'He told the Russians just where they got on and off and generally bossed this whole meeting' [Yergin 1980: 115]. Byrnes was imbued with the same spirit, and was convinced that the bomb would make his task easier. 'He looks to have the presence of the bomb in his hip pocket . . . as a great weapon,' wrote Stimson [Yergin 1980: 122]. The atomic bombs dropped on Hiroshima and Nagasaki brought the war against Japan to a swift end, but they did not frighten Moscow into concessions. The Americans were to learn that it is no use having a wonder weapon if the other side does not believe that it will be used against it. After all, would the United States really have considered dropping a bomb on Moscow in order to secure free elections in Bulgaria? Hence Byrnes signally failed to translate American economic power and its atomic monopoly into tangible benefits in eastern and south-eastern Europe. Since the United States would not provide credit, the Soviet Union stepped up the exploitation of its sphere of influence. The attempt by the United States to make capital out of its atomic monopoly brought home to Stalin the importance of nuclear power. Neither Stalin nor Molotov had fully grasped the strategic importance of the atomic bomb before Hiroshima despite the abundance of intelligence information from Western capitals available to them. Of course, the bomb was a potential, not an actual threat. Its long-term implications were more important than short-term considerations.

Repeated American and British attempts to penetrate eastern and south-eastern Europe raised the price the Soviets demanded for their cooperation. The 'impotence of omnipotence' [Gaddis 1972: 244] was brought home to the Americans after dollar and atomic diplomacy had failed. Byrnes was then forced to revert to Roosevelt's concept of the four policemen [America, Britain, Russia and China] running the world. This again posed the old dilemma about how to reconcile a realistic foreign policy abroad with an idealistic foreign policy at home.

At Potsdam some compromises were agreed. The West gave provisional recognition to Polish administration over ex-German territory, while the USSR cut back its reparation demands from Germany – all of this accepted existing realities [*Doc. 14*]. However, Soviet demands for the internationalisation of the Ruhr, access to the Straits, and a mandate over Libya were rejected, as were American proposals for the internationalisation of Europe's main water routes, something which would have included the Danube. Western requests for a greater say in eastern and south-eastern Europe were also turned aside, with the Soviet Union pointing to the domination of the West in Italy and Greece. Potsdam ended amicably enough, however, since all contentious issues were left open, on the understanding that they would be dealt with by the Council of Foreign Ministers, which was to meet regularly.

This Council met in London between 11 September and 2 October 1945 and saw Molotov propose peace treaties with Hungary, Romania and Bulgaria, which in effect confirmed the *status quo*. Byrnes tried to apply the Polish solution – widening the democratic base of the government – but Molotov was adamant. Deadlock ensued, and Byrnes, who wanted some sort of agreement, thought of conceding the Soviets their sphere of influence. He was restrained by John Foster Dulles, the leading Republican at the conference, who warned him that if he gave way he would denounce him publicly as an appeaser. The conference proved so devoid of positive achievement that it did not even issue a joint communiqué.

Byrnes was exasperated by the Soviet behaviour during the conference but in public he spoke about fully understanding the Soviet desire to achieve close and friendly relations with the states on its western frontier and respecting their special security needs there. In order to acquire an independent source of information on the Balkans, Byrnes sent Mark Ethridge, a well-known liberal journalist, and Cyril Black, a Princeton history professor, on an extensive fact-finding mission. Byrnes was hoping that their report would reveal that the situation there was not as bad as the diplomats and the 'Riga' people had painted it. They visited Romania, Bulgaria and Moscow and concluded that the Soviet Union was behaving like an 'imperialist power in the worst sense' [Yergin 1980: 143]. They were even more critical than the State Department officials who had been toning down their material knowing that Byrnes was rather sceptical. Byrnes did not publish the report of the unofficial emissaries, for he wanted to keep on trying, and at the Moscow Council of Foreign Ministers meeting in December 1945 some progress was made. The Soviets agreed that in Romania and Bulgaria two non-communists should join the government, and in return the Secretary of State indicated that he was willing to participate in the drafting of peace treaties with these states. He also invited the Soviets to cooperate in a UN control system of atomic weapons.

Byrnes gradually found it more and more difficult to convince the American public that his foreign policy was based on the principles of the Atlantic Charter [*Doc. 4*]. The Republicans and the 'realists' in the State Department regarded him as an appeaser and he was severely criticised in Congress. A poll revealed that the number of Americans who believed in the possibility of long-term cooperation with the USSR had dropped from 54 per cent in September 1945 to 34 per cent in February 1946. Byrnes dominated American foreign policy formation mainly because the President was still getting his bearings. His relations with his British colleague Ernest Bevin were not always good, due to the American's propensity to launch initiatives without first informing or consulting his British opposite number.

At the Moscow meeting of the Council of Foreign Ministers, called at Byrnes' behest, the Secretary of State made concessions to Moscow. If two non-communist ministers were added to the Romanian and Bulgarian governments those states would be recognised by the United States. Among other things he accepted Soviet participation in two organisations to supervise the occupation of Japan. (The Americans, guided by General Douglas MacArthur, had been coming round to the view that it was in their interests to exclude Russia from the occupation of mainland Japan. Moscow had been given southern Sakhalin and the Kurile islands as a reward for participation in the war against Japan. The Americans were doing in Japan what the Soviets were doing in Romania and Bulgaria – namely, imposing their own agenda.)

When Byrnes returned to Washington he was met by an irate President on 5 January 1946. The latter had just read the Ethridge report on Romania and Bulgaria which Byrnes had withheld from Truman until 2 January. In it Ethridge had warned that to concede a 'limited Soviet sphere of influence at the present time would be to invite its extension in the future'. The President complained that Byrnes had hardly bothered to keep him informed on the progress of negotiations and was annoyed at the concessions made. Truman, in the light of the Ethridge report, declared Romania and Bulgaria to be 'police states' [Yergin 1980: 160]. He stated he was not 'going to agree to the recognition of those governments until there are radical changes' [Yergin 1980: 161]. In Truman's mind there was no doubt that 'Russia intends an invasion of Turkey and the seizure of the Black Sea Straits to the Mediterranean. Unless Russia is faced with an iron fist and strong language another war was in the making' [Yergin 1980: 161]. He concluded: 'I do not think we should play compromise any longer . . . I'm tired of babying the Soviets' [Truman 1955: 185].

He therefore instructed Byrnes to make Moscow aware of the American position on Iran (the withdrawal of Soviet troops from northern Iran), to insist on the internationalisation of the Kiel canal, the Rhine-Danube waterways and the Black Sea Straits, and to maintain 'complete control of Japan and the Pacific'.

Byrnes' Moscow policy had, in effect, been stood on its head. Henceforth he was to be 'firm' in dealing with the Soviets; nevertheless he still hoped for an American-Soviet agreement. Until April 1946, when he resigned as Secretary of State, Byrnes carried out the new American policy towards the Soviet Union. If concessions were to be made, they were to come exclusively from the Soviet side. The change of mind about the USSR had finally resulted in a change of policy. Roosevelt's grand design was buried and the policy of containment surfaced. America pursued the policy of negotiations until March 1947 when George C. Marshall, Secretary of State, returned from another Moscow meeting of the Council of Foreign Ministers convinced that nothing could be gained and much lost by negotiating with the Russians. The wheel had turned full circle.

The events of 1945 reveal some of the fundamental reasons for the emergence of the Cold War.

1 In 1945 it was American policy which changed, not Soviet. The United States tried to resolve the conflicts which arose in its own interests, on the whole. This caused the USSR to concentrate on consolidating its position in eastern and south-eastern Europe, but Moscow sought until the autumn of 1947 to reach agreement with the United States.

2 The reason for the change in American policy was the behaviour of the USSR in eastern and south-eastern Europe. The Americans underestimated the security needs of the Soviet Union and hence only succeeded in strengthening its desire to bolshevise the region. The single most important factor which led to more aggressive Soviet behaviour in the region was the atomic bomb. It could nullify Soviet conventional (non-nuclear) superiority at a stroke. American public opinion misjudged the Soviet Union, but it has to be remembered that the United States had gone to war in Europe to protect small countries against Nazi tyranny. It could not write off some countries merely because the USSR wanted close and friendly relations with them – something which was not possible in most of them if free elections were held. The Soviets feared the march of capitalism which in turn would almost certainly be accompanied by American imperialism. Hence they bolted the door because they could not compete on equal terms.

3 The incompatibility of American and Soviet views had to surface sooner or later, but it was not pre-ordained that this should lead to a division of the world into blocs and that each side should feel threatened by the other. The

economic expansion of the United States was inevitable, but it was not inevitable that the export of American capital and goods would be accompanied by American imperialism. Once American troops had pulled out of western and southern Europe, and assuming that Washington did not fear that the area would fall under communist control, there would be no reason for the United States to dominate this region. The prospects for a socialist Europe – more social democratic than communist – were in fact very bright in 1945 and 1946.

4 The greater strength of the US political and economic system, compared with that of the USSR, afforded Washington greater opportunities to change the post-war world. Had they so desired the Americans could have recognised the Soviet sphere of influence in eastern and south-eastern Europe, drawn the Soviets into joint control of atomic weapons and contributed to the reconstruction of the Soviet economy – thus redressing some of the imbalance. American decision-makers misread Soviet security interests in eastern and south-eastern Europe as proof of Soviet expansionism and refused to cooperate. This in turn led the Soviets to see US policy as aggressive capitalist expansionism and to harden their own attitude in their sphere of influence. A vicious circle thus came into being and it could not be broken after 1945. The formation of blocs became more and more pronounced [Loth 1980: 152].

5 The plethora of views competing for primacy in the United States made it extremely difficult to elaborate a consistent policy. Washington was just not clear what its interests and policies should be at any given moment. This weakness was most marked when dealing with Germany, since there was no clear vision of its future. Given the confusion of views in the US administration, the Soviet government had a difficult task in judging whether American proposals were genuine or merely trial balloons. The crucial test they always applied was American willingness to allow them heavy reparations from Germany and other ex-enemy states. Molotov's personality contributed to the mistrust between the former allies. His minatory stutter and stonewalling tactics infuriated many. He was very successful in holding on to Soviet gains but utterly failed to charm the Americans into trusting the Soviet Union. That said, he was severely taken to task by Stalin on occasions for appearing to be too friendly towards the United States. Stalin very jealously guarded his prerogative as chief foreign power decision-maker and usually provided Molotov with very detailed guidelines. Hence the Western perception of Molotov as an obdurate negotiator [a less flattering sobriquet was 'dome headed zombie'] who was not willing to give an inch is not wholly correct. Had he had more leeway, he might have been more accommodating. This would only have been a tactic on his part as he was an imperialist to his finger tips. The motto: what we have we hold, certainly applied to him.

CHAPTER FIVE

DECISIONS WHICH LED TO DIVISION

The change in American policy towards the end of 1945 occurred at a time when few of the pressing post-war problems had been resolved. The future of Germany had hardly been discussed and the peace treaties with the ex-enemy states had not yet been negotiated. The state of the European economy was critical; hunger, disease, the millions of displaced persons and refugees, the enormous problems of switching from a wartime to a peacetime economy – all these led to falls in output, unemployment and increasing debt burdens. The war had transformed the old political pattern. The United States was now the leading world power. The weakness of the British economy had resulted in that country becoming a junior partner of the United States, while the USSR had expanded into eastern and south-eastern Europe. In western and southern Europe a vacuum had appeared. All these problems were now caught up in the growing American–Soviet conflict; or, to put it another way, these problems provided the material base for the expansion of the conflict.

CONTAINMENT

The doctrine of containment played a decisive role in American thinking about the developing East–West conflict. Its most articulate and persuasive progenitor was George F. Kennan, and its origins go back to the 'Riga axioms'. Convinced that there could be no meaningful or long-term cooperation with the Soviet Union, Kennan found the tide of public and government opinion flowing against him until the contradictions inherent in Roosevelt's grand design surfaced. He was always in favour of a 'fully fledged and realistic show-down with the Soviet Union' over eastern and south-eastern Europe. He told Charles Bohlen in February 1945 that if the West was not willing to 'go the whole hog' to block the USSR, the only alternative was to split Germany, partition Europe into two spheres and decide the 'line beyond which we cannot afford to permit the Russians to exercise unchallenged power or to take purely unilateral action'. Before Yalta he had favoured the division of the world into spheres of influence and a propaganda war against the USSR in the

United States. What made Kennan's analysis decisive was the decision by Freeman Matthews, head of the European division of the State Department, to choose him as the person to write a comprehensive appraisal of Soviet policy. Kennan's famous 'Long Telegram' of 22 February 1946 [*Doc. 18*] is one of the most important documents of the post-war era. The suspiciousness and aggressiveness of the Soviet leadership stemmed, according to Kennan, from 'basic inner Russian necessities' and not from any 'objective analysis of (the) situation beyond Russia's borders'. He pointed out that the root cause of the Kremlin's 'neurotic view of world affairs' was the traditional and instinctive Russian sense of insecurity. This led Soviet leaders to go over to the offensive 'in patient but deadly struggle for total destruction [of] rival power, never in compacts or compromises with it' [Yergin 1980: 189]. American concessions would not affect official Soviet aggressiveness.

> We have here a political force committed fanatically to the belief that with US there can be no permanent *modus vivendi*, that it is desirable and necessary that the internal harmony of our society be disrupted, our traditional way of life destroyed, the international authority of our state be broken if Soviet power is to be secure. [Yergin 1980: 169]

The Soviets would do all in their power to strengthen the socialist bloc and weaken the capitalist countries. Aided by communist parties directed by an underground general staff of world proportions and secretly coordinated from Moscow, they would seek to undermine the stronger Western powers and to topple all those governments, from Turkey to Switzerland and Great Britain, which resisted Soviet demands. The Western nations must therefore draw together in a more cohesive bloc, led by the United States.

Kennan's analysis placed overwhelming emphasis on the role of ideology in Soviet foreign policy formation. He also overestimated Moscow's ability to dominate and manipulate foreign communist parties, as well as the influence of these parties in countries lacking a Red Army presence. Despite his awareness of Soviet economic weakness he was deeply pessimistic about the prospects for liberal capitalism in Europe and elsewhere. The weight he afforded ideology in his analysis of Soviet intentions led him to accord an inflexibility and single-mindedness to Moscow's purposes which did not, in fact, exist. On the contrary, the USSR had revealed considerable suppleness in its policy. Kennan also omitted to draw a line between eastern and south-eastern Europe, on the one hand, and the rest of Europe on the other. Afterwards he was to complain that he had been misunderstood, that he had not predicted that the Soviet Union would launch an all-out offensive to expand the number of countries under communist rule. A year later Kennan adopted the term 'containment' to describe his thinking, but again, in 1946, he did not make clear that it implied the division of Germany and of Europe into respective spheres of influence.

Kennan's Long Telegram was a devastating blow to the hopes and aspirations of Yalta. It was not new; it was a pungently expressed, intellectually coherent restatement of the old 'Riga axioms'. It made Kennan influential, indeed famous, overnight. Byrnes thought the Long Telegram a 'splendid analysis'; Matthews considered it 'magnificent'. James Forrestal, the Secretary of the Navy, so liked it that he had hundreds of copies made and dispatched them everywhere. Kennan was recalled from the US embassy in Moscow in April 1946 to support his views by personal advocacy in the administration and throughout the country.

A media campaign was launched at the same time. Vandenberg articulated suspicion about Soviet intentions in the Senate; Byrnes made it clear that the United States would not tolerate any change in the *status quo* to its own disadvantage. Churchill, with President Truman present, delivered his 'iron curtain' speech [*Doc. 19*] at Fulton, Missouri, on 5 March 1946, and called for an American–British alliance to prevent Soviet expansion (but the US public gave the speech a cool reception; it was not ready yet for a 'special relationship'). The American administration leaked enough information to *Time* magazine for it to publish on 1 April 1946 a full-page article, including a map which showed Iran, Turkey and Manchuria 'infected' and Saudi Arabia, Egypt, Afghanistan and India 'exposed'. In *Life* magazine on 3 and 10 June 1946 John Foster Dulles warned against a *Pax Sovietica*, and called on Americans to show military resolve, to provide economic aid to the endangered regimes and to stand up to the Soviet Union.

Kennan's Long Telegram was the decisive factor in the Truman administration's change of course to a policy of firmness towards the USSR. When Clark Clifford and George Elsey, a White House aide, were asked by Truman in July 1946 to prepare a detailed analysis of Soviet–American relations, the replies they received from officials were almost all along the lines of the Long Telegram. Clifford's report, passed to the President on 24 September 1946, underlined the remarkable unanimity of views. There was general agreement that the very existence of the Soviet Union threatened the United States. America must therefore speak the language of military might and make the containment of the Soviet threat its primary aim throughout the world. 'Stern policies' should be adopted to protect American interests and those of small nations. Those countries outside the Soviet sphere of influence should be extended economic and political support in their struggle against Soviet penetration. Military support was not ruled out as a last resort, but economic aid, trade agreements and technical assistance would be a much more effective way of demonstrating the staying power of capitalism. Those who stressed the flexibility of the Soviet leaders and the possibility of reaching an agreement with them found their audience dwindling. The most significant voice was that of Henry Wallace, Secretary of Commerce. In a speech on 12 September 1946 he advocated the recognition of the Soviet sphere of influence in eastern and south-eastern Europe and warned that 'the tougher we get, the tougher the Russians will get' [*Doc. 22*]. Byrnes threatened resignation if Wallace did not go, and conservatives like Vandenberg applied all the pressure they could. Wallace had gone so far as to claim that the President agreed with the sentiments he had expressed in his speech, but the only effect of this was that Truman demanded Wallace's resignation. There was no place in the administration now for anyone who had doubts about the new course in foreign policy.

Why did the doctrine of containment spread like wildfire and exert such influence, given that it did not accurately reflect the realities of the time? There are five possible explanations [Loth 1980: 188–92].

1 Churchill's opinion that appeasement had prepared the way for Hitler and had permitted him to launch a world war was generally accepted. It was a short step from viewing Nazi Germany as totalitarian and expansionist to seeing the USSR in the same light. Both regimes had an internal need to expand and this was a direct threat to the national security of all other states. The West had deceived itself over Germany, it must not do the same over the Soviet Union.

2 Paradoxically, the increase in American power had not been accompanied by a feeling of security – rather the reverse. Having earlier been caught off its guard by the totalitarian regimes, the United States was acutely aware of the risks to its security. The enormous expansion of its influence throughout the world meant that the potentiality of conflict had also increased. The obsolescence of all existing weapons due to swift technological change forced constant reappraisals of weapons programmes and of national security.

3 Insecurity was increased due to fears of a recession after the war, fuelled by memories of the 1930s. Management and labour were seeking ways of avoiding another depression, and the state of health of the European market economies held out little hope. The Soviet sphere of influence in eastern and south-eastern Europe, and the widespread activities of communist parties, as well as the expected world-wide assault on the imperial powers by their colonial subjects, added more gloom. A possible solution, however, was the free flow of capital goods, entailing the elimination of tariff barriers and of all restrictive legislation.

4 Wartime mobilisation had been remarkably successful in expanding output and enriching the United States. What was now needed was a peacetime equivalent which would inspire and motivate the American people. Without deliberately setting out to do so, Kennan provided the necessary rationale. The world war could be replaced by the cold war, thus allowing the US economy to benefit.

5 The Second World War had given rise to a formidable military apparatus in the United States. The end of hostilities signalled the end of its *raison d'être*. It needed a powerful reason to reassert itself and this it discovered in the Soviet threat. The move to merge the army, air force and navy in one ministry at the end of the war led to them all fighting for their separate existence. Was it an accident that James Forrestal, Secretary of the Navy – the service most threatened by technical change – became one of the most militant proponents of the policy of containment?

CONTAINMENT UNDER WAY

Byrnes conducted American foreign policy in 1946 according to the 'Riga axioms' as articulated in the Long Telegram. Every effort was made to claw back some of the concessions already made and to ensure that the USSR did not expand its influence. The American delegation at all the conferences which Byrnes attended included vociferous Republicans who always adopted a 'hard' line towards the Soviets. Unlike the previous year, the conflicts of 1946 were played out in full view of the US public.

Iran turned out to be the first testing-ground for the new policy. British and Soviet troops had occupied Iran in 1941 to prevent a possible pact between that country and Hitler, and they were due to leave six months after the end of the hostilities, at the latest. The agreed deadline was 2 March 1946. The Soviets sought to strengthen their position in northern Iran by promoting the aspirations of non-Iranians there. By December 1945 Azerbaijani communists and their supporters were claiming the right to autonomy within the Iranian state. The United States wished to see both British and Soviet troops out of the country, so as to break the British oil monopoly and to prevent the Soviets moving towards the Persian Gulf. The Iranian government, at British instigation, appealed to the Security Council of the UN at the end of January 1946, fearing that the USSR would not withdraw its units on schedule. The Soviet troops did not leave on 2 March 1946 and some troops even moved into central Iran. Faced with another appeal to the Security Council, the USSR declared on 25 March that it would withdraw its troops within five or six weeks. Azerbaijan was granted some autonomy within Iran and a joint Soviet-Iranian oil company was to be formed. Faced with Anglo-American hostility the Soviets had backed down. Byrnes insisted that the matter be debated in the Security Council and on 27 March 1946 he characterised Soviet policy in Iran as imperialist. This was meant for the US public and was to demonstrate that Byrnes was no appeaser. The Iranians then proceeded to abolish Azerbaijani autonomy and to execute the leaders; while the agreement to establish a joint Soviet-Iranian oil company was not ratified by the Iranian parliament. On the face of it, containment had worked. Since it had proved successful in Iran it might prove successful elsewhere.

To explain the Soviet back-down, Stalin, on 8 May 1946, sent a letter to one of the Azerbaijani leaders. He stated that a revolutionary situation, comparable to that of 1905 and 1917 in Russia, did not exist in Iran. Had Soviet troops stayed in Iran it would have undermined the Soviet position in eastern Europe. The British would claim that if Soviet troops could stay in Iran, why should British troops not remain in Egypt, Syria, Indonesia and Greece, and American troops in China, Iceland and Denmark? So the Soviet Union had decided to withdraw its troops from Iran and China in order to promote colonial liberation and render the Soviet policy of liberation more justified and efficient [Zubok and Pleshakov 1996: 45]. One way of interpreting this letter would be to regard it as a post-facto rationalisation of Soviet policy. However, it can also be read as evidence that Stalin was not willing to risk a confrontation with the West and was not willing to support pro-Soviet revolutionaries if it involved conflict with the West.

At the meeting of the Council of Foreign Ministers which began in Paris in April 1946 Byrnes again practised the new approach. Practically every Soviet proposal was rejected: large reparations from all ex-enemy countries were out of the question; there was to be no four-power control over the Ruhr; Yugoslav claims on Trieste were brushed aside, as was the Soviet desire to take over the UN mandate in Libya. Byrnes went over to the offensive and belaboured Soviet behaviour in eastern and south-eastern Europe, demanding once again the internationalisation of Europe's waterways and the removal of all trade preferences. Vandenberg thought that Byrnes had 'stood up 100 per cent' to the Soviets. Dulles believed that the days of appeasement were over. The first round of discussions ended on 15 May without any semblance of agreement.

During the second round of negotiations, which lasted from 15 June to 12 July 1946, some progress, however, was made. The Soviets made concessions by agreeing that the future of Libya, the Italian colonies and overseas possessions should be decided by the UN General Assembly, while Trieste should become an autonomous city under UN control. However, Byrnes could not gain Soviet acceptance of his 'open door' policy – free access for American capital and goods to eastern and south-eastern Europe. Draft peace treaties were agreed, and these were debated between 29 July and 15 October 1946 by representatives of all 21 allied states who had fought the Axis powers. The discussions were held in public – on Byrnes' initiative – and everyone played to the gallery. The smaller nations seized the opportunity to argue their case and Soviet policy came in for some harsh criticism. Nevertheless, the delegates knew that in the final resort the foreign ministers would decide, and this they did in New York between 4 November and 12 December 1946, the peace treaties being very similar to the original foreign ministers' drafts.

While Byrnes was in Paris a crisis in US–Soviet relations had developed elsewhere. On 7 August 1946 the Soviet Union, in a note, demanded that Turkey tear up the Montreux Convention of 1936 which provided it with considerable control over the passage of warships of the littoral states through the Straits. The USSR wished to have a major say in this and to erect joint Soviet-Turkish fortifications. Churchill had conceded in October 1944 that such a demand was reasonable and the Potsdam agreement had included a clause confirming the right of the Soviet Union to seek a revision of the Convention. However, the formal Soviet demand for a revision now came at a time when the US administration was determined to make no concessions to the USSR. Dean Acheson, Under Secretary of State, told President Truman that joint fortifications on the Straits would lead to Soviet control over Turkey and this in turn would extend to Greece and the entire Near and Middle East – which would then put the Soviet Union in a 'much stronger position to obtain its objectives in India and China'. The only way to hold the Soviets back was to make clear to them that the United States was 'prepared, if necessary, to meet aggression with force of arms' [Acheson 1970: 261]. A defensive war was now being contemplated to ensure that the domino theory did not become reality. This involved preparing for strategic strikes against the Soviet Union, including the use of atomic bombs. A sharp note of protest was sent to Moscow and the Turkish government was encouraged to stand firm. American warships were dispatched to the eastern Mediterranean and shortly afterwards Forrestal's proposal to station part of the US fleet permanently there was adopted. Containment had taken on a military aspect. Stalin, aware of war plans from his spies inside the American administration, retreated. Molotov, on reflection, judged that had Stalin not backed down, joint military aggression against the Soviet Union would have resulted (Zubok and Pleshakov 1996: 93). When Truman launched his policy of containment of communism in Greece and Turkey the following year, the Soviet response was quite mild. Stalin lived to regret his aggressive policy towards Turkey.

Another step towards containment was taken by Byrnes when he made a fundamental change in American attitudes towards international loans and credits. The aim now was to stabilise all economies outside the Soviet sphere of influence, thereby making them less susceptible to communist influence. The United States did not abandon its 'open door' policy towards the Soviet Union and its dependants – trade, after all, was trade – but credits were to be disbursed elsewhere. The State Department informed the Soviet Union on 21 February 1946 that negotiations on credits should include American claims for seized US property in liberated countries, a greater American say in the economic reconstruction of eastern and south-eastern European states, the question of the internationalisation of Europe's waterways, and agreement on Lend-Lease obligations, trade and shipping, and the removal of trade barriers. Such preconditions killed the Soviet passion for American money, and negotiations were broken off in June 1946.

The Export-Import Bank had amassed capital in anticipation of American credits for the Soviet Union. This money was largely used to help France overcome its economic difficulties. Leon Blum and Jean Monnet arrived in Washington in March 1946 and asked for huge credits. They pointed to the danger of the left gaining support if the economy did not recover. The American negotiators tried unsuccessfully to tie the expulsion of communist ministers from the French government to the loan. On 28 May 1946 a grand package was announced which not only reduced French war debts from $3.474 billion to $700 million but extended credits sufficient to cover three-quarters of the current French trade deficit of $1.8 billion.

Byrnes was quite clear about his priorities.

> The situation has so hardened that the time has now come, I am convinced, in the light of the attitude of the Soviet government and the neighbouring states which it dominates [that] we must help our friends in every way and refrain from assisting those who either through helplessness or for other reasons are opposing the principles for which we stand [US Department of State 1947: 59].

Negotiations with Czechoslovakia for the purchase of US army surplus stores, worth $50 million, were terminated after Byrnes had been outraged by the sight of the Czechoslovak delegation at the Paris Conference warmly applauding a diatribe by Andrei Vyshinsky against the United States. Support for the United Nations Relief and Rehabilitation Administration (UNRRA), for which the United States had been providing two-thirds of the funds but without gaining much influence over the disbursement of the money, was terminated at the end of 1946. Poland, Czechoslovakia and Hungary, which had received considerable aid from UNRRA, then applied to the World Bank for credits but were turned down. Instead, credits for and support of countries outside the Soviet sphere of influence were stepped up and amounted to $5.7 billion in 1946.

POLICY ON ATOMIC WEAPONS AND GERMANY

The two key problems which concerned the security of the United States and those countries outside the Soviet sphere of influence were atomic weapons and Germany. The decisions taken were conditioned by and contributed to the division of Germany, Europe and the world into two camps.

On the question of atomic weapons the Truman administration decided to accord priority to security. In the summer of 1945 Henry Stimson, Secretary for War, had advocated a partnership with the USSR in order to gain its cooperation, and he reiterated this advice in a memorandum to the President when he was on the point of retiring [*Doc. 16*]. After the failure of Byrnes' atomic diplomacy and the Council of Foreign Ministers meeting in London, the US government elaborated a policy whose aim was to test Soviet willingness to cooperate on atomic weapons. The goal was the internationalisation of such weapons. However, until a complete control system had been established,

Plate 1 Churchill, Truman and Stalin in Potsdam, 1945. Photo: U.S. Army, courtesy Harry S. Truman Library.

Plate 2 Stalin, Truman and Churchill in Potsdam, 1945. Photo: David King collection.

Plate 3 Stalin at the 19th Party Congress, October 1952. Photo: David King collection.

Plate 4 Vorushilov, Shkiryatov and Stalin at the 19th Party Congress, October 1952. Photo: David King collection.

the United States was to continue producing the wherewithal for the bombs without actually making any. The Soviets were presented with a choice: they could either trust the Americans and desist from developing their own atomic weapons, or they could start an expensive and risky atomic arms race. Bernard Baruch, the chief American negotiator, presented the US plan to the United Nations on 15 June 1946 [*Doc. 17*]. An International Atomic Energy Authority (IAEA) was to be established and it would gradually acquire complete control over raw materials and atomic plants throughout the world. Any country which infringed the rules would be punished and there would be no right of veto in the IAEA, unlike the UN Security Council. The original proposals were then altered by the Americans in their own favour by allowing Washington to build complete atomic bombs if it so desired. Further, the United States could retain its atomic capability long after the Soviets had provided the critical information about their raw materials and the level of research and development. Andrei Gromyko, Soviet ambassador to the UN, shortly afterwards turned the Baruch Plan down flat and called for the banning of the production and use of atomic weapons, followed by the destruction of all existing ones. A control system could be agreed sometime in the future. (As previously mentioned, the Soviets had decided to begin the building of their own atomic bomb in August 1945.) After months of debate the UN Atomic Energy Commission finally adopted the Baruch Plan on 30 December 1946, but the USSR prevented any further discussion by using its veto in the Security Council. The age of atomic weapons had begun. As far as Germany was concerned, in 1946, the United States began to interpret Soviet policy as an attempt to take over the whole of the country, and, faced with this prospect or the division of Germany into two spheres of influence, it chose the latter. Again George Kennan played a significant role in the formation of this policy. When asked for his opinion by Freeman Matthews, he wrote to the State Department on 6 March 1946 putting forward the argument that the Soviets would only allow a central German administration (which had been included in the Potsdam agreement but which the French government, supported by the French communists, had consistently vetoed) if they believed they could control it. Hence there were only two possibilities for US policy towards Germany: either to leave it as an entity highly susceptible to Soviet influence, or to bring the western zones together, cut them off from the east and integrate them in western Europe.

This amounted to a misreading of Soviet policy towards Germany. The Soviets had in fact set up central German agencies in their own zone before the Potsdam agreement had been signed, seeing them as the embryo of a future central German administration. It was the French who prevented this from becoming reality. It is, however, true that the Soviets did not have a clear-cut policy towards Germany. On the one hand they wanted their zone to proceed slowly towards socialism, but at the same time they almost stripped it naked.

Reparations caused considerable friction and there were many clashes between the Soviets and the east German politicians. The fusion of the communists (KPD) and the social democrats (SPD), in April 1946, to form the Socialist Unity Party (SED) negatively affected the image of the USSR throughout Germany. Most of the SPD leaders opposed the fusion but it may well have had the support of a majority among the rank and file. The fusion exacerbated relations between the KPD and the SPD in the western zones and led to the ending of cooperation. The fusion came at a time when the KPD had not yet recovered its pre-1933 strength in the western zones. Possibly about one-third of social democrats in the western zones favoured fusion with the communists so as to make the SED an all-German party. The Western Allies were appalled by this prospect and refused to license the proposed SED. They were aided in their anti-SED fight by the many SPD politicians who had left the Soviet zone.

Stalin did not want the division of Germany but his lack of diplomatic expertise gradually prised the two halves of Germany apart. Again, security took priority. It was better to hold on to what he had rather than to risk a neutral Germany falling into the American camp. As a Marxist, he believed that the whole of Germany would go socialist eventually. It might take 50 or more years but it was inevitable. To him, socialism meant Soviet-style socialism. In this, he was a Great Russian imperialist, fusing the advance of Soviet influence and power with the advance of socialism.

General Lucius Clay, the deputy US military governor in Berlin, did not agree with Kennan's analysis, and informed the State Department in April 1946 that the Soviets could not be faulted in the way they had carried out their obligations under the Potsdam agreement and had shown a desire for friendship and even some respect for the United States. Clay also did not believe the Soviets were planning any aggression.

Byrnes was not convinced that Kennan was right and decided to test the Soviet will to cooperate. At the Paris meeting of the Council of Foreign Ministers he put forward a proposal for a four-power pact to guarantee the demilitarisation of Germany for 25 years. Molotov did not reject the idea but asked that Soviet reparation requests be granted. This was unacceptable to the Americans, so nothing came of Byrnes' project.

In an effort to force the French to give up their vetoing of proposals to treat Germany as an integrated political unit, and at the same time to persuade the Soviets to treat it as an economic whole, Clay stopped all reparations deliveries from the American zone on 3 May 1946 until a general import and export plan was agreed for Germany. Byrnes went along with Clay's suggestion that an effort be made to create economic unity by linking up with the other occupying powers. The Soviets did not respond and the French made an ineffective counter-proposal, but on 27 July the British government agreed, and so Bizonia came into existence on 1 January 1947. On 6 September 1946 Byrnes delivered a major speech in Stuttgart, in which he proposed that German reconstruction begin immediately and that the Germans should 'now be given the primary responsibility for the running of their own affairs' [*Doc. 21*]. Although he did not make it clear, this obviously only applied to west Germany. He had by this time abandoned his hope of a united Germany outside the Soviet sphere of influence.

EASTERN AND SOUTH-EASTERN EUROPE

Just as the Americans were seeking to strengthen their position in all states outside the Soviet sphere of influence, so the Soviets were seeking to consolidate their power within this sphere. Stalin's speech in Moscow on 9 February 1946 set the tone for the Soviet future. Instead of concentrating on consumer goods and light industry as the population hoped, the Soviet leader praised the forced collectivisation and industrialisation of the 1930s. He spoke of three more Five-Year Plans being necessary to construct the heavy-industry base the USSR needed. This speech was misconstrued by the Americans, who took it to be the prelude to the Third World War; but in reality it showed how the Soviet Union was coming to terms with the exigencies of the Cold War.

An important factor in the policies of eastern and south-eastern Europe in 1946 was the hope that the United States would intervene on the side of the anti-communist forces. This led some democratic politicians to overplay their hand and to the communists becoming even more aggressive. In Poland, Stanislaw Mikolajczyk, deputy Prime Minister and chairman of the 600,000-strong Peasants' Party, found himself in greater and greater difficulties as violence against the government increased and opposition hardened throughout the country. He refused to join the democratic front, as requested by the communists and social democrats, and as a consequence the election scheduled for February 1946 was postponed and his party subjected to harassment, coercion and terror. The election eventually took place on 10 January 1947 and was manipulated by the communists – as they later freely admitted – so that the Peasant Party only won 28 of the 444 seats in the Sejm. The communists were now clearly the leading force in the country.

In Hungary, the Smallholders' Party (KGP), after their electoral victory in October 1945, provided the Prime Minister, Ferenc Nagy. A left bloc was set up by the communists, social democrats and national peasants within the coalition government on 5 March 1946, and it proceeded to instigate demonstrations against right-wing KGP deputies. The move was successful and the deputies in question had to leave the party. The bloc had demonstrated how the KGP could be broken up. Then the Soviet ambassador and the Soviet deputy chairman of the Allied Control Commission intervened on the side of the bloc to force more concessions out of the KGP. Thereupon the security forces, controlled by the communists, began to arrest KGP deputies on the trumped-up charge that they belonged to a counter-revolutionary organisation. By the summer of 1947 the KGP was demoralised and ripe for disintegration. Nagy was blackmailed into resigning (his young son was held hostage to ensure that he did), and new elections were called on 31 August 1947 which the communists duly won.

In Romania, E. Hatieganu, representing the National Peasants, and M. Romniceanu, representing the liberals, were added to the National Democratic Front government in January 1946 but as ministers without portfolio. Recognition of the government headed by Dr Petru Groza was duly accorded by the Western powers in February 1946. However, the two new ministers were shunned by their colleagues and they stopped collaborating in late summer 1946, although this did not affect Western recognition. Elections were held on 19 November 1946 – preceded by a venomous campaign – and gave the communists and their allies 372 seats out of a total of 414. Overt terror was unnecessary, for the central authorities falsified the results as they pleased. In less than a year after the elections the three main opposition parties had been liquidated. On 30 December 1947 King Michael abdicated and the People's Republic of Romania was proclaimed.

In Bulgaria, the Fatherland Front secured 90 per cent of the votes at the elections of 19 November 1945. It refused to admit opposition representatives to the government, despite the Moscow agreement. New elections on 27 October 1946 gave the Front 366 of the 465 seats in parliament and it then began, very successfully, to apply harassment and coercion against its main opponent, the Peasant Party.

The only exception to the pattern of harassment, arrest, coercion and fraud in the region was Czechoslovakia, since it was the only country in which there was a bourgeois democratic base for a pro-Soviet policy. In the free elections of 26 May 1946 the communists secured 38 per cent of the votes. Non-communist forces only experienced harassment from the summer of 1947 onwards when serious economic problems arose and the internal situation deteriorated.

CHAPTER SIX

THE TRUMAN DOCTRINE AND THE MARSHALL PLAN

The first year of containment brought the United States meagre results. The European economy was in such a critical state that there was no guarantee that the spread of communism could be stopped. American credits in 1946 had not produced the necessary upturn and Congress was in no mood to underwrite new, large loans. As for the American public, it had not yet fully embraced the belief that no agreement could be reached with the Soviets, and it was still lukewarm towards the doctrine of containment. All this changed in the course of 1947 as the Truman administration discovered the key to both problems: the Truman Doctrine and the Marshall Plan.

Although the Republicans demanded firmness in US foreign policy, they were not willing to bear the economic burden such a policy entailed. Congress had contested the $3.75 billion loan to Great Britain and the administration had great difficulty in getting it finally ratified in July 1946. The Republicans won the Congressional elections of November 1946 by promising to cut government expenditure and income tax by 20 per cent. When Truman placed his own budget for the year beginning 1 July 1947 before the new Congress, it sliced expenditure by a sixth and reduced the military allocation from $11.2 billion to $9 billion – something which General George C. Marshall (who had replaced Byrnes as Secretary of State) feared would have dire consequences in the occupied countries.

The situation in Europe was desperate. The 1945–6 loans were far too small to induce an upturn. France and Great Britain used up their credits much faster than expected, and when free convertibility of the pound sterling was introduced on 15 July 1947, as a condition of the loan, British reserves dropped $1.3 billion in four weeks. This led to the abandonment of convertibility on 20 August 1947, with only $400 million of the original $3.75 billion credit remaining. In 1947 the 16 countries which were later to receive Marshall Aid recorded a foreign trade deficit of $7.5 billion, while production was only 83 per cent of its pre-war level. The harvest was poor in 1946, and the severe winter of 1946–7 led to a shortage of coal, with transport difficulties in Germany, all contributing to a picture of gloom and despondency. Germany had been the linchpin of the European economy; thus it was vital to nurse it back to economic health.

There were two main obstacles. The first was the French veto on all proposals which would have led to Germany's being treated as a political or economic unit, since they wanted to force the separation of the Rhineland and the Ruhr from Germany and to benefit from a special relationship with them. The Americans feared that if they forced the French to back down it would increase anti-American feeling in France, something which could only benefit the communists. France would then be ripe for revolution. The second problem was the Soviet Union, and here the stumbling-block was reparations. At the fourth meeting of the Council of Foreign Ministers in Moscow, from 10 March to 24 April 1947, Molotov again proved obdurate on reparations. It appeared that they were seen as the touchstone of American willingness to cooperate with the USSR. Some progress was made on this difficult subject. In the absence of Bidault, the French Foreign Minister, the meeting decided to set up a central Germany agency, a German consultative council, and adopted a plan to establish a provisional German government step by step. All four foreign ministers agreed to carry through land reform in 1947 in their separate zones, as had already been done in the Soviet zone in 1945. All these agreements foundered on the rock of reparations. Clay was in favour of making concessions in order to save German unity, but Marshall would not concede one inch.

THE TRUMAN DOCTRINE

The solution to the problem of how to convince the American public that it was necessary to provide credits to threatened friendly governments was discovered by State Department officials during the debates concerning the British loan in early 1946. Arguments based on an 'open door' or 'one world' policy had little impact, but once Dean Acheson, Under Secretary of State, linked the loan to the struggle against communist influence in Great Britain the penny dropped. The US administration, in order to overcome the unwillingness of Congress and the people to provide foreign credits, had to link them to the fight against Soviet expansionism.

The first test was provided by the British statement of 21 February 1947 that all military and economic aid to Greece and Turkey would have to cease on 31 March, due to Britain's economic difficulties. Although Great Britain and the United States had already been sharing the cost, there could be little doubt that the US administration would take over the full burden. The situation in Greece and Turkey at that moment was not critical. The civil war was in its fourth year in Greece but the communists were not in sight of winning. In Turkey the government was obstinately refusing to make concessions on the Straits to the Soviets. Nevertheless, Acheson told Truman on 27 February 1947 that a

> highly possible Soviet breakthrough [in the Near East] might open up three continents to Soviet penetration. Like apples in a barrel infected by the corruption of one rotten one, the corruption of Greece would infect Iran and all to the East . . . Africa . . . Italy and France. . . . Not since Rome and Carthage had there been such a polarisation of power on this earth. [US Department of State 1947: 39]

Truman adopted this line of thinking in his address to both houses of Congress on 12 March 1947. He argued that a stark choice faced every nation. One way of life was 'based upon the will of the majority, and is distinguished by free institutions, representative government, free elections'. The other was based upon the 'will of a minority, forcibly imposed upon the majority'. He added: 'I believe that it must be the policy of the United States to support free peoples who are resisting attempted subjugation by armed minorities or by outside pressures' [*Doc. 24*]. He asked for $300 million for Greece and $100 million for Turkey. Congress provided the necessary funds but it was not handing the Truman administration a blank cheque. The Truman Doctrine, however, fitted the universalism and self-confidence in the American way of life like a glove.

The Greek civil war came to a bloody end in 1949 with the defeat of the communists, and Turkey remained within the Western camp. The strident anti-communism of the Truman Doctrine touched a responsive chord and it transformed the doctrine of containment into a national crusade.

THE MARSHALL PLAN

The unwillingness of the Republican majority in the US Congress and the inability of the British government to bear the burden of occupational costs (amounting to about £50 million in 1945 and £80 million in 1946), as well as the expense of propping up the German economy, provided two powerful arguments for General Clay in his struggle to revitalise the German economy. Ex-President Herbert Hoover recommended such action after an official visit in January–February 1947. German industry, especially heavy industry, should be freed from all restrictions so as to reduce the support paid by the American taxpayer and so to set on foot the economic reconstruction of Europe. Ernest Bevin warned that Great Britain could only afford to stay in Germany a short time longer and demanded a rapid rise in German steel production; otherwise the Labour government would dissolve Bizonia and use the Ruhr to finance the British zone. Marshall gave in; the solution to the intractable French and German problems had been forced on him. West Germany was to be developed irrespective of the consequences for German unity, and French opposition was reduced by making it clear that no provisional government for the whole of Germany was envisaged.

However, some answer to France's economic weakness had to be found. The originator of the idea to link the economic recovery of West Germany and France was John Foster Dulles. In a speech in New York on 17 January 1947 he put the future of Germany in the context of the economic unity of Europe rather than in the Potsdam view of Germany as an economic entity. He argued that small economic units in a divided Europe could not prosper; Europe had to unite so as to provide a market large enough to justify modern mass-production techniques. Walter Lippmann, an influential columnist, advocated a European economic union. A State, War, Navy Coordinating Committee was set up to examine the possibility of further foreign loans. The failure of the Council of Foreign Ministers meeting in Moscow in April 1947 to reach any agreement on Germany speeded up the process.

Three reasons suggest themselves to explain the attractiveness of the concept. In the first place, a multinational aid programme in Europe would permit a more rational use of US funds by aiding integration and the division of labour. Secondly, it promised to solve the French problem. France's desperate need for German reparations would be replaced by US credits, and the marrying of the French and German economies would reduce French fears of German economic power. Thirdly, by linking it to anti-communism the concept could be made very popular in the United States. Benefits, it was emphasised, would accrue to all sides; an expanding European market would take more US goods and a strong Europe would be a powerful bulwark against communist expansion.

Again Kennan played an influential role. In a memorandum of 23 May 1947 he underlined that the proposed programme should not be seen as something negative – to prevent Soviet expansion – but as something positive – to overcome European economic misery. The initiative was to come from several west European nations and the joint American-European programme was to include the whole of Europe, east and west.

The Marshall Plan was launched in a speech at Harvard University on 5 June 1947. 'Our policy is directed not against any country or doctrine but against hunger, poverty, desperation and chaos,' Marshall declared [*Doc. 25*]. American assistance was to provide a cure, not a palliative.

Marshall made it clear a week later that his proposals were to cover all countries 'west of Asia' and this expressly included the Soviet Union. The Marshall Plan had a political and an economic goal. Its political goal was to contain communism; its economic aim was to bring prosperity to Europe and thereby to provide export markets for the US economy. By inviting the countries of eastern and south-eastern Europe to participate he hoped to break the bonds which tied them to the Soviet Union. The whole of Europe would become economically interdependent. The market economy would be strengthened and the Soviet-style planned economy – not yet in operation in eastern and south-eastern Europe – would lose its attractiveness. Socialists and many others hoped that the Marshall Plan would allow Europe to grow together and prosper and in so doing to grow away from dependence on the Soviet Union and the United States. A third way would then open up between the communism of the USSR and the capitalism of the United States.

CHAPTER SEVEN

THE SOVIET RESPONSE

The Marshall Plan placed the Soviet Union in a predicament. On the one hand it wanted to prevent American political and economic dominance in Europe, but on the other it and its east and south-east European neighbours badly needed US capital and goods. If the Soviets rejected credits there was a risk that western and southern Europe would bloom and in so doing become rich and attractive not only to the rest of Europe but also to many other parts of the globe.

The initial, official Soviet response to the Plan was negative: *Pravda* described it, on 16 June 1947, as merely an extension of the Truman Doctrine involving interference in the internal affairs of other states. However, when Bevin and Georges Bidault, the French Foreign Minister, invited Molotov for discussions on 18 June 1947, the Soviet government accepted promptly, pointing out that it too favoured the rapid reconstruction of Europe.

Nikolai V. Novikov, Soviet ambassador in Washington DC, pointed out, on 24 June, in a telegram to Molotov, the political implications of the Plan. As he saw it, it aimed at creating a west European bloc against the Soviet Union. For the first time, the West had a coordinated policy and had left behind the haphazard actions of the past [Varsori and Calandri 2002: 277].

All three foreign ministers met in conference in Paris, beginning on 27 June 1947. Bevin and Bidault presented parallel suggestions to Molotov and Bevin adumbrated the setting up of a steering committee of interested European states which could work out a four-year programme for the reconstruction of the continent. The military governors would speak for Germany. Molotov agreed in principle but wanted Germany excluded since it fell within the competence of the Council of Foreign Ministers. Bevin and Bidault argued for a programme which would not infringe the sovereignty of any state or the development of its economy. This was unacceptable to Molotov so far as Germany was concerned, for the Soviet Union was still insisting on more reparations. Bevin and Bidault wanted to prevent the setting up of a committee on which the Soviet Union could employ delaying tactics indefinitely unless its point of view were accepted. The economic situation in France and Great

Britain was too precarious for them to allow this to happen. Bevin and Bidault agreed that it would be better to exclude the Soviets rather than have them as half-hearted members. Once they had taken this decision they deliberately exaggerated the differences between them and Molotov, so that, when the conference broke up, the responsibility for the division would devolve on the Soviets. In fact, Molotov did not commit himself either way; the final decision was taken in Moscow. Molotov received a telegram from Stalin on 1 July 1947 and after reading it 'did not say another word that day' [Acheson 1970: 234]. The following day he rejected the Anglo-French proposals as incompatible with the preservation of national sovereignty. The Soviets had clearly come to the conclusion that the risks of acceptance were greater than the risks of rejection.

Bevin and Bidault were relieved when Molotov departed, and under pressure from the left wing of the Labour party and the French Socialist party (SFIO) – both of which placed great emphasis on a common European recovery programme – they sought to involve the east and south-east European states in the plan. On 4 July 1947 the representatives of 22 European governments (only the Soviet Union and Spain were excluded) were invited to meet in Paris on the 12th to discuss participation. Most Western observers were surprised by the positive response from eastern and south-eastern Europe. The Czechoslovak government and Communist party decided to send a representative; the Polish Foreign Minister informed the US ambassador in Warsaw that Poland would send a delegation; the Hungarian government was unanimous in its decision to participate. Only the Yugoslavs and Romanians decided to seek Moscow's advice before reaching a decision, and even Bulgaria and Albania appeared to be interested in the invitation. Moscow now applied pressure. Since it had decided not to accept Marshall Plan money itself because of fear of US influence, it could not allow its neighbours to expand their contacts with the United States. On 5 July, Soviet ambassadors in east and south-eastern Europe received instructions from Moscow to transmit a negative evaluation of the Plan to the respective countries' foreign ministers. Belgrade was accorded special significance. The Soviet ambassador was to inform Tito that Moscow was pleased with his government's intention not to attend the meeting in Paris. However, it would be better to attend and prevent the Americans from pushing through their policy unanimously. The Yugoslavs should then walk out, taking with them as many delegations as possible. Stalin changed his mind on 7 July. The Yugoslavs and all the others, including the Finns, should boycott the conference. The reason was that Britain and France, the organisers of the meeting, would brook no opposition to their policies. Each state was to come up with its own reasons for being absent [Varsori and Calandri 2002: 284].

When Prime Minister Klement Gottwald and Foreign Minister Jan Masaryk were in Moscow on 8–9 July to discuss Czechoslovak participation, the Soviet Union made its displeasure very clear and even threatened to abrogate the

Czechoslovak–Soviet treaty of December 1943. Stalin said that Czechoslovakia's participation would permit the Western powers to use it as a tool against the Soviet Union. Neither the USSR nor its government was prepared to permit this. Masaryk was to remark when he returned to Prague that he had gone to Moscow as the Foreign Minister of a sovereign country but had returned as the lackey of the Soviet government. In the event the Soviets did not need to apply any pressure on the Czechoslovak government; it decided on its own not to send delegates to Paris. On 9 July the Bulgarian and Yugoslav governments announced that they would not attend; on 10 July Czechoslovakia and Hungary followed suit; on 11 July Romania, Albania, Poland and Finland opted out. It was clear to all that the doctrine of limited sovereignty now applied to the Soviet Union's allies. The decision of the USSR neither to participate in the Marshall Plan itself nor to allow its neighbours to do so meant that Moscow's policy of cooperating with the United States and of stabilising western and southern Europe – a policy which it had pursued since the end of the war – now lay in tatters. The Soviets' mistrust of American motives, and their deep pessimism about their ability to contain US influence in their own sphere of influence, led them to split Europe.

Bidault, like many other observers, was mystified by Molotov's behaviour. As he saw it, the Soviet Union had nothing to lose in joining the Marshall Plan and everything to gain. Once in, Moscow could have ensured that no one gain, had it so desired. By opting out, the Soviet Union made sure that it was certain to lose [Varsori and Calandri 2002: 281].

In failing to join the Marshall Plan, the Soviets missed a golden opportunity to influence the way Europe developed. The key to Europe was Germany and Britain and the US intended to promote the recovery of that country. Since Moscow had opted out, only west Germany would be developed. The gulf between east and west Germany opened up the day that Moscow walked away from the Marshall Plan. East Germans, with some justice, always complained that whereas they had to transfer capital to the Soviet Union, west Germany received capital from the United States. The absence of the Soviets permitted the rapid economic recovery of western and southern Europe, based on American credits. Keynesian economics could be applied, untrammelled by Russian interference. After all, Moscow's objective was to prevent the rebirth of strong capitalist economies. Presumably, Stalin and Molotov based their refusal to participate on the Marxist view that capitalist economies cannot work together successfully over the long term. Internal contradictions would lead to conflict, perhaps armed conflict. The Soviet dictator, as well as Molotov, failed lamentably to grasp the significance of Keynesian economics. He cut his empire off from American capital and technology and, in doing so, condemned it to technical and scientific backwardness. No wonder the American political right always looked upon the man in the Kremlin as their best friend. He could always be relied on to antagonise the US public and to harm the interests of the Soviet Union. The failure to join the IMF and the Marshall Plan and provoking the Berlin Blockade must go down as three of Stalin's most egregious diplomatic mistakes.

THE ROLE OF THE COMINFORM

Alternatives to the policy of cooperation with the Americans and stabilisation in western and southern Europe had been discussed in Moscow. One possibility was isolation, as Stalin mentioned to Averell Harriman in October 1945. Another was support for an all-out attempt by foreign communist parties to seize power. Yet another was an aggressive and uncompromising policy towards the 'great power capitalists, Great Britain and the United States' [Loth 1980: 178]. This would include the formation of a pan-Slav grouping, the consolidation of the existing strategic situation, the division of Germany into eastern and western parts, and 'offensive diplomacy towards the Anglo-American imperialist bloc' – as Stalin told Harold Laski, the Chairman of the Labour party and a leading left-winger, in 1946 [Loth 1980: 178]. Although the Western Allies agreed to implement the Marshall Plan, none of these alternative Soviet strategies was immediately put into effect. During the summer of 1947 the Soviet government remained uncertain about how to counter the new American initiative. Belgian, French and Italian communists waited in vain for instructions from Moscow on how they should react to the plan for west European recovery. They had to come to their own conclusions, and the French communists (PCF) welcomed it on condition that it was administered by the UN Economic Commission for Europe. The Central Committee of the PCF restated its positive approach as late as 4 September 1947.

By mid-September, however, the Soviet leadership had made up its mind on how to react to the Marshall Plan, and it invited the leaders of the communist parties of Poland, Czechoslovakia, Hungary, Romania, Bulgaria, Yugoslavia, France and Italy to a conference at Szklarska Poręba in Poland on 22 September 1947 at which a decision was taken to establish the Communist Information Bureau (Cominform). Zhdanov was the chief Soviet speaker at this conference and he divided the world into two antagonistic camps, with countries such as India and Indonesia outside. The United States, he claimed, was the chief power of the imperialist camp; it was bent on the strengthening of its own power and was preparing a new imperialist war. The Marshall Plan was the latest expression of American capital's desire to expand and its aim was the 'enslavement of Europe'. The 'anti-imperialist and democratic camp', led by the Soviet Union, had to fight resolutely against such an eventuality. Communists, especially in western and southern Europe, must therefore break with social democrats – seen as the tool of US imperialism – and unite all democratic and patriotic forces around them. The danger of a resurgent West Germany could be played up and this would make it easier to discipline the Soviet Union's neighbours.

It fell to the Yugoslav representatives, Edvard Kardelj and Milovan Djilas, to take the French and Italian parties to task for their 'unrevolutionary' post-war behaviour. They were upbraided for missing their chance in 1945 by concentrating on legitimacy and for acting in an opportunist manner by retaining their ministerial portfolios. All this was very unfair, but it was no defence to point out that such tactics had been favoured by Moscow. When the line changes the only policy for a communist party leadership was to change with it and condemn what was being condemned irrespective of its own feelings.

After the conference the communist parties abandoned their policy of stabilisation and gave unrest, resentment at low living standards and revolutionary ardour their head. One aim was to make the acceptance of the Marshall Plan impossible. In France a wave of strikes began on 18 November 1947. Two million workers downed tools, coal deliveries stopped, the transport network was subjected to sabotage and in Marseilles there were violent street battles between the security forces and strikers. The strikes collapsed on 9 December 1947, however, without achieving any tangible results, though in Italy they lasted throughout the winter of 1947–8.

The result of such deliberately fomented social unrest was to drive all non-communists together, and far from strengthening the communist parties it led to their isolation. It discredited the communists as coalition partners in government and led to their leaving office. The Cold War ceased to be merely an expression of international politics; it had become a reality in *internal* politics by the beginning of 1948. The communists returned to their ghettos and western and southern Europe moved to the right. Eastern and south-eastern Europe, on the other hand, moved to the left. The Soviet goal was the establishment of people's democracies and the introduction of planned economies along Soviet lines. Concepts such as the German and Hungarian roads to socialism were denounced. Henceforth there was to be only one road to socialism, the Soviet one. The task of the Cominform was merely propagandistic. It sought to glorify the achievements of the Soviet Union, to stress the decisive role played by the Red Army in the liberation of the area and the nastiness of the outside world. The Marshall Plan, therefore, ultimately led to the division of Europe and made the formation of blocs inevitable.

CZECHOSLOVAKIA

The situation in Czechoslovakia began to deteriorate during the summer of 1947. An economic crisis developed and there appeared little hope of obtaining outside assistance. A major difficulty for non-communist members of the government was that the results of reconstruction after 1945 did not accord with public expectations. Drought badly affected the 1947 harvest so that living standards dropped and the foreign trade deficit grew. The Czechoslovak government even approached the United States, hoping for help despite the fact that it had rejected the Marshall Plan, but Washington curtly refused.

The Communist party of Czechoslovakia – which had also been sharply criticised at Szklarska Poręba for its lack of revolutionary ardour – feared that social discontent could adversely affect its chances at the elections planned for early 1948. It therefore began to fill more and more key police posts with trusted comrades, to prepare trials against political opponents and to step up demonstrations against 'reaction'. This was possible since the Minister of the Interior was a communist. It then proposed measures which were calculated to improve its standing: payment of compensation for those who had been hit by the harvest failure; the nationalisation of all enterprises employing more than 50 workers; more land reforms and a reduction in the pay differentials of all state employees. The communists' coalition partners in the government reacted strongly against these proposals. When the Minister of the Interior replaced some more police leaders with his own nominees, Catholic, democratic and people's socialist ministers resigned on 20 February 1948, thinking they could force the government to dissolve and hold new elections. However, social democratic ministers did not resign in sympathy. As a riposte the communists organised huge demonstrations, and a general strike was called on 24 February. The following day President Beneš accepted the resignation of all non-communist ministers, but the Prime Minister, Gottwald, instead of dissolving parliament, formed a new National Front government on 29 February in which all the portfolios previously held by non-communists went to 'reliable' supporters of the communists. When the elections were eventually held, 237 of the 300 seats were won by communists or fellow travellers. Beneš lost the presidency and died shortly afterwards. The non-communist parties were dissolved. It was now inevitable that the economic difficulties would be dealt with by adopting Soviet methods and, in so doing, embracing the whole range of Soviet procedures in state and society.

THE EXPULSION OF TITO

Before the founding of the Cominform there was no more ardent Stalinist than Josip Broz Tito. The Yugoslav party had vehemently attacked the French and Italians at Szklarska Poręba and had enthusiastically followed the hard Soviet line in domestic and foreign policy. However, strains began to manifest themselves as the Soviets set out to plan the economic development of their satellites to meet not only internal but also Soviet needs. Yugoslavia did not wish to concentrate on heavy industry – as the Soviets insisted – and thereby to depress its people's living standards. It continued as before to diversify its economy, to increase consumer goods production, to expand trade with the West. In November and December 1947 Tito concluded treaties of friendship with Bulgaria, Romania and Hungary before similar treaties had been agreed with the Soviet Union. In January 1948 Georgi Dimitrov, the Bulgarian party leader, announced the formation of a customs union as a first step towards a Balkan Federation which was also to include Czechoslovakia and Poland.

Stalin then intervened and warned the Bulgarian and Yugoslav party leadership that the Soviet government could not tolerate relations which were not in its interests and to which it had not agreed. The Soviet leader claimed that the USSR had the right to interfere in the internal affairs of any people's democracy. Dimitrov gave way but Tito was more stubborn. Stalin thought he had only to 'wag his little finger' to remove Tito and to replace him with a more loyal party leader in Yugoslavia. On 18 and 19 March 1948 Stalin announced that all Soviet economic and military advisers would be withdrawn from Yugoslavia. However, the Yugoslavs remained loyal to Tito, and Stalin's supporters were arrested. A vitriolic correspondence ensued in which Tito repeatedly rejected the accusations made against him and stressed his loyalty to the Soviet Union and the socialist camp. This was of no avail, however, and on 28 June 1948 the Comintern expelled Yugoslavia on the grounds that Tito had fallen victim to 'bourgeois nationalism'. The other east and south-east European states then tore up their trade and friendship treaties with Yugoslavia and broke off diplomatic relations. They also announced an economic blockade and called on the Yugoslav people to remove the 'fascist Tito clique' and the 'hangman of the Yugoslav people'. A hunt was launched for Titoists throughout the people's democracies and this was often used to settle old political scores.

Without American support Yugoslavia would have collapsed and been reintegrated in the Soviet bloc. Fortunately for Tito, however, the United States overcame its aversion to Marxism and provided considerable financial assistance. Since Tito opposed Stalin he had to be helped; the Cold War now became a power struggle between East and West, with Washington willing to aid any state which opposed Moscow.

WAR, NEGOTIATIONS OR NEITHER

Despite the fact that the Cold War was on in earnest there were specialists who believed in early 1948 that Stalin was ready for a settlement with his capitalist opponents. One such expert was George Kennan, who thought that if the West held firm the Kremlin would negotiate. This depended on a revival of confidence in western Europe and the failure of communists to destabilise the region. If this happened a new situation would arise when the 'Russians will be prepared, for the first time since the surrender, to do business seriously with us about Germany and about Europe in general'. What would Moscow expect? 'What the Russians will want us to do will be to conclude with them a sphere-of-influence agreement similar to the one they concluded with the Germans in 1939.' It would then be up to Washington to explain to Moscow that this could not be done and to persuade the Soviets to 'reduce communist pressures . . . in Europe and the Middle East to the point where we can afford to withdraw all our armed forces from the continent and the Mediterranean and thereafter to acquiesce in a prolonged period of stability in Europe'. The Council of Foreign Ministers was not a suitable forum for these negotiations. They should be conducted face to face with Stalin by an American official who spoke Russian.

Other Washington officials were not so sanguine. In March 1948, one stated that Stalin had already 'come close to achieving what Hitler attempted in vain'. The US embassy in Moscow viewed the Soviet armed forces as 'capable of taking continental Europe and key areas of Asia within a few months', and assumed that the decision to resort or not to resort to military force was 'under constant review'. The most dangerous time would be when Western military strength had grown to a point where the Soviets perceived themselves at a disadvantage. This would be the situation in 'one or two years from now. . . . Immediate war' could then be expected. On 5 March 1948 General Lucius Clay cabled from Berlin that, whereas he had previously thought war was 10 years away, it could now break out with 'dramatic suddenness'. On 16 March the CIA advised the President that war was improbable only for the next 60 days. After that, all bets were off. On 17 March President Truman appeared before a joint session of Congress and requested the introduction of universal military training and selective service.

A third view emerged in Washington in late 1948: that the Russians were not ready either to strike or to settle, and that the Soviet threat was mainly political and hence should be contained by non-military means. Again the main inspiration was George Kennan, supported by Secretary of State Marshall. This approach was based on creating strength in the West rather than destroying Soviet strength. Kennan thought that Soviet power in Europe had reached a high point and henceforth would recede.

THE BERLIN BLOCKADE

The desire of the Western powers to see West Germany realise its economic potential – and in so doing to reduce occupation costs and to contribute to overall European development – led to much consultation and many proposals. At the meeting of the Council of Foreign Ministers in London in November–December 1947 Bevin and Marshall agreed on one last initiative to create an all-German state. If this failed, as expected, Bizonia would then be developed and a currency reform introduced. When the project for currency reform was discussed in the Allied Control Council, the Soviets opposed it. Representatives of the United States and other interested European states then met in London on 23 February 1948 and discussed the organisation of the three western occupation zones. They agreed on the 'London recommendations' on 7 June and proposed that the prime ministers of the West German *Länder* should immediately convene an assembly to draft a constitution. The French National Assembly passed the recommendations on 17 June, though only by a small majority – mainly because French demands for the internationalisation of the Ruhr had not been met and the balance between federal and central power in the future German state had been left in effect to the Germans to solve. On 18 June 1948 a currency reform in the three Western zones was announced and the Deutsche Mark replaced the Reichsmark.

In the summer and autumn of 1947 rumours had spread in east Germany about the introduction of a new zonal currency, the Soviet zone mark. This alarmed the Americans who feared that if this happened without a commensurate currency reform in the Western zones, the useless eastern marks would flood into western Germany and cause havoc. For instance, the activities of the western communists could be financed with these old notes. The US acted quickly and printed a new currency for the Western zones: the Deutsche Mark. It was all top secret and the notes were held ready for the day the Soviets would launch their currency reform in the east. As it turned out, the West went ahead with its reform and the Soviets were then forced to follow suit in the east. Berlin was a problem. Which currency should be valid there or should a new currency be printed for the German capital? The Americans solved the problem by printing a B on the Deutsche Mark notes. They had two tonnes of the new money ready – or 250 million marks. The Russians declared the currency illegal in East Berlin. Among other things they declared that anyone who accepted it was a traitor to German unity! This fuelled a black market and the exchange rate dropped to 30 east marks for one western mark [Parrish 1998: 165–7].

The Soviet Union tried various tactics to halt the formation of a separate West German state, but it discovered, just as the United States had done, that if the adversary believes it is immune from attack it can behave as it thinks fit within its sphere of influence. On 20 March 1948 the Soviet representative left the Allied Control Council and the Soviets began to put pressure on the West's weakest spot, West Berlin. Railway transport was subjected to much stricter controls, and when the Western powers extended their currency reform to West Berlin on 23 June 1948 the Soviets reacted quickly. The very next day they blockaded all links by land and cut off power and coal supplies. The new East German mark was then introduced in the Soviet zone and East Berlin. The goal of this blockade was to force the West to abandon its plans for a separate West German state. On the Soviet side it was a particularly inept piece of diplomacy, for it amounted to nothing less than blackmail; instead of halting integration plans it speeded up the formation of a West German state. At first the Western powers feared they would have to give in, and even envisaged Soviet interference with their plan to supply the two million West Berliners by air. Washington, in these early stages, was hypnotised by supposed Soviet strength and did not realise that Stalin would not risk a world war – one which the Soviet Union would almost certainly lose – simply in order to prevent the emergence of a West German state. General Clay did not share the prevailing view of Soviet strength and repeatedly asked for tanks to break through the barriers on the autobahns. Aneurin Bevan, a leading Labour left-winger, wanted to call the Soviet bluff by sending an armoured column along one of the blocked roads. To the public in western Europe and the United States it appeared that the USSR was trying to force the Western powers out of Berlin, as a prelude to seizing the rest of Germany. This made it almost impossible for the Americans to retreat from Berlin, as some had advised, and so strong was the wave of anti-communism unleashed by the Soviet move that earlier doubts about the advisability of establishing a separate West German state – first and foremost among the prime ministers of the *Länder* – were mostly dispelled. There appeared to be a stark choice for western and southern Europe: come together and survive or remain independent entities and sink. Their choice of a firm stand paid handsome dividends, for on 11 May 1949 the Soviets called off their blockade. All they had gained from the Western powers was agreement that the Council of Foreign Ministers should again convene.

A Parliamentary Council composed of representatives of all West German parties met from September 1948 to May 1949, and drew up a Basic Law for the new republic. The first parliament, the Bundestag, was elected in August 1949, and the first Federal government took office in September. The Soviets' answer was to promote the formation of the German Democratic Republic on 7 October 1949.

The Berlin Blockade increased the feeling of military insecurity in northern, western and southern Europe and there was pressure for a common military force to defend the region. This led to the drawing up of the North Atlantic Treaty – signed in Washington on 4 April 1949 – and eventually to the establishment of a common defence force, known as the North Atlantic Treaty Organisation (NATO). The Soviet Union, by way of rejoinder, established the Council for Mutual Economic Assistance (CMEA or Comecon) in 1949 and the Warsaw Pact, the Soviet Union's answer to NATO, in 1955. With the formation of the (west) European Economic Community in 1958 the division of Europe was complete.

PART THREE ASSESSMENT

CHAPTER EIGHT

WAS IT ALL INEVITABLE?

What was the Cold War about? When did it begin and when did it end? If the use of the term by the actors in the drama is adopted, then it began in 1947 and ended shortly after the Cuban Missile crisis of 1962. If the Cold War is understood to be the overt or covert antagonism which existed between the Soviet Union and the United States, between socialism and capitalism, between a collectivist, planned society and the pluralistic values of a market economy, then the Cold War began in October 1917 and ended with the collapse of the USSR in 1991. A more exact date would be 1989 when Gorbachev declared it to be over. On the other hand, if the Cold War is seen as the period during which the overt antagonism between Moscow and Washington dominated world affairs, then it began in 1943 and ended sometime in the 1960s or even as late as the end of the Vietnam War in 1975. During this whole period of Soviet–American confrontation a parallel process was under way – the formation of blocs. The division of Germany and the splitting of Europe, and indeed the world, into two camps, was a *fait accompli* by 1955. From then onwards the two major political groupings competed for spheres of influence. It was as if the scramble for colonies by the European powers in the nineteenth century had taken on a new lease of life. The new 'scramble', however, embraced the whole world, and there seemed to be no room for neutrals.

The analysis set out in the preceding pages has concentrated on the years 1941–9, with some attention being paid to the important pre-1941 era. The emphasis throughout has been on Soviet–American relations, as they dominated the world scene from 1943 onwards. Great Britain was important before that date but its economic weakness meant that it had to rely increasingly on the United States. This caused resentment in London; for example, the Conservative MP Robert Boothby likened the terms the Labour government had been forced to concede in return for the $3.75 billion American loan to those accepted at Munich. To him the government was selling the 'British Empire for a packet of cigarettes' [*Doc. 15*]. In fact, the British government had little choice, for without American aid the British economy would have collapsed.

The defeat of Germany and Japan, leaving a vacuum in central Europe and the Far East, meant that a new international order had to come into being. The two countries which had contributed most to the defeat of the Axis powers, the Soviet Union and the United States, were presented with a golden opportunity to reshape the political configuration of the globe. Never before had such a chance presented itself, never before had two powers so dominated the world. Their reactions to the rise of national socialist Germany had been different. The Soviet Union had indirectly aided the rise of Hitler, seeing him as the most extreme representative of finance capital, one who would so exacerbate social relations that he would eventually provoke a successful socialist revolution. But as German power increased, the Soviets became more alarmed. As the Soviet government was not ready for war it came to an agreement with Berlin in 1939, which in effect divided Europe into two spheres of influence, leaving the rest of the world until later. Stalin's success lulled him into a false sense of security, and the German invasion of the USSR on 22 June 1941 came as a shattering blow. On several occasions the USSR was within a hair's breadth of military defeat, and it was only in 1945 that Stalin could be sure that the Red Army would actually occupy some German soil. These events increased endemic Soviet feelings of insecurity. If the pact with Germany had not saved the Soviet Union from attack, could any future agreement with a comparable power ever be relied upon to guarantee legitimate Soviet security needs?

The United States reacted quite differently to the rise of Nazism. Washington did not regard Germany's increasing influence and power as a threat to US interests. Even when Hitler launched the Second World War in September 1939 with his attack on Poland the United States held back. Had American public opinion had its way it is unlikely that Great Britain would have received any Lend-Lease assistance before the United States was actually at war. America was willing to extend Lend-Lease aid to the USSR after June 1941, but it was the foolish German declaration of war on the United States on 11 December 1941 which drew the Americans into active participation in the European theatre; otherwise they would have concentrated their attention on winning the war against Japan in the Pacific.

The United States drew three lessons from its experience. The first was that appeasement does not pay; the Munich settlement of 1938 was a shining example of what to avoid. The second was that a totalitarian domestic policy produces a totalitarian foreign policy. If peace were to be preserved, following the defeat of the Nazis, Germany and the whole region previously under its influence would have to be won over to democracy, understood as American-style liberal capitalism. The third lesson was the need to extend the benefits of the open American society resting on a market economy in which protectionism, preference and tariffs had been removed. American foreign policy before 1941 had been isolationist. Had not the majority of the American people gratefully shaken off the dust of Europe from their feet? Since Europe was a mess it was important not to be sucked back into the maelstrom of conflict. Most Americans took a hard-headed attitude towards national security. If the US's security were not under threat, why should America become involved? There was no perceived threat emanating from Europe so the New World could cut itself adrift from the self-inflicted travails of the Old World.

Running parallel to this isolation was a streak of idealism. Rooted in Wilsonian ethics, it held that foreign policy had to be morally defensible. Not only had the United States to be right, it had to be seen to be right. It was a noble vision which eliminated spheres of influence and the use of force to settle disputes, and advocated the creation of a world authority to guarantee the security of all states and to mediate all international altercations. Although President Woodrow Wilson had failed to win over the American public to the support of this ideal, it lay deep in the consciousness of many American policy-makers.

President Roosevelt was a skilled expositor of the doctrine. The New Deal needed a touch of idealism in foreign policy to stimulate the American imagination during the days of debilitating struggle to right the economy. But Roosevelt was too much of a realist and pragmatist to believe that the rest of the world thought as America did. The United States could afford to be idealistic, for it was bordered in the north by Canada and in the south by Mexico, neither of which posed an economic, political or military threat. Europe's situation was totally different. The Soviet Union, for instance, had long been threatened on its western frontier, and the Soviet government, after its experience with Hitler, was determined to create a situation in which it would not be liable to attack from central and south-east Europe. Roosevelt appreciated this, and knew that after the defeat of Germany Soviet power could move into the vacuum created and might even extend to the Atlantic Ocean. He told Cardinal Spellman, in September 1943, that the European countries would have to undergo tremendous changes in order to adapt to the Soviet Union. He saw no point in the United States and Great Britain fighting the Soviets. They had been forced into a shotgun marriage during the war but he hoped that out of this would emerge a real and lasting partnership. Europeans would simply have to endure Russian domination, in the hope that in 10 or 20 years they would be capable of living well with the Russians. Hence he did not see the USSR as a threat to US security or even practising a foreign policy which was antagonistic to US interests. The world was large enough to accommodate both of them. He set out to reach an agreement with Stalin personally, even if aspects of it ran counter to the interests of his British allies. Especially at Yalta he made plain to Stalin his mistrust of Churchill whom he suspected of seeking to keep the British Empire intact after the war. Roosevelt saw Stalin as an anti-colonial ally and therefore tried to win the cooperation of the Soviet dictator in planning the new, post-war world. His principal assumption was that peace-keeping would be the responsibility of the United Nations, and he regarded it as essential that the USSR should play an active role in this organisation, for fear that it would otherwise degenerate into an anti-communist grouping.

What could Roosevelt offer Stalin to convince him that his offer of cooperation was genuine? The Soviet leader had two criteria against which to measure the fine words of the Americans: recognition of a Soviet sphere of influence in eastern and south-eastern Europe and if possible in those countries which bordered the USSR in the Middle East and Asia; and American acceptance of the Soviet demand for reparations from ex-enemy countries as well as American help in reconstructing the Soviet economy. Stalin's two main concerns, in short, were security and money. Returning to what Stalin told Eden about declarations being algebra but agreements being practical arithmetic (with the Soviet leader favouring the latter), it is clear that the Soviet Union was willing to make any declaration the Americans wanted but expected some tangible rewards.

However, Roosevelt could not openly accede to Soviet desires in eastern and south-eastern Europe, since such behaviour would have flown in the face of Wilsonian doctrine. Possessed of an infinitely resourceful mind, Roosevelt was always seeking ways of squaring the circle, of engaging in *Realpolitik* or power politics abroad while giving the impression at home that his foreign policy was pure Wilsonianism. Henry Stimson once declared that trying to follow Roosevelt's thinking was like chasing a vagrant beam of sunshine. In his own mind, Roosevelt was quite willing to concede the Soviets a sphere of influence, but the seven million Polish voters in America – to take only one example of a powerful minority pressure group – were quite determined that Poland should not fall under the shadow of the Soviet Union. On the economic side, if Lend-Lease had been extended and the Soviets had acquired huge credits to purchase surplus American stock, the Soviet government would not have been so concerned about reparations. Had Roosevelt lived it is possible that he could have agreed a form of words with Stalin which would have tacitly conceded the Soviet sphere of influence and set in train the recovery of the Soviet economy using the vast surpluses available in the United States. The American administration knew that the US public would not tolerate troops staying very long in Europe, or America footing the bill for Germany's or indeed Europe's recovery. The US taxpayer would expect a return on any American capital exported.

The year 1945 was a turning-point. Stalin could not bring himself to believe the honeyed words flowing from Washington and used practical arithmetic to gauge American goodwill. He had various options open to him: isolation; an aggressive policy (stopping short of war) against Great Britain and the United States; encouragement to foreign communist parties to seize power or at least to undermine the market economies in their respective countries; or cooperation, which would mean agreeing to maintain the *status quo* in western and southern Europe. In the event, Stalin chose cooperation, but he proceeded warily and with the greatest caution, looking to deeds, not words, as proof of American intentions. It has to be remembered that Western, including US, intervention between 1918 and 1920 had left a deep scar on the Bolshevik body politic. The Soviets took it for granted that, given the chance, the United States and the other capitalist powers would try to destroy the Soviet Union. Allied to this conviction was their ideological conviction that there could be no lasting settlement with the capitalist powers.

Molotov, in his old age, reveals insights into Soviet thinking about the US President:

> 'Roosevelt believed in dollars. Not that he believed in nothing else, but he considered America to be so rich, and we so poor and worn out, that we would surely come begging. "Then we'll kick their ass, but for now we have to keep them going." That's where they miscalculated. They weren't Marxists and we were. They woke up only when half of Europe had passed from them.' [Geddis 1998: 22]

Stalin must have cursed when he heard about the successful US testing of an atomic bomb. Gone was his conventional (non-nuclear) superiority. It changed his outlook on the world and strengthened his desire to cling on to as much territory as he could. Security was paramount in his mind. As a Great Russian imperialist he equated security with the acquisition of territory.

Roosevelt's death came at a critical moment in American–Soviet relations, for the inability or unwillingness of Great Britain and the United States to concede the Soviets a sphere in eastern and south-eastern Europe – something Stalin thought had already been accepted in principle by his wartime allies – led the USSR first to stabilise and then consolidate its position in that region. Yet every step in this direction provided ammunition in London and Washington for those who were having second thoughts about Soviet power and had little faith in Roosevelt's grand design. Clement Attlee, for instance, was already pessimistic about the future of East–West relations in 1945, and Ernest Bevin's suspicion of communists was well established. The British government was tied emotionally to eastern and south-eastern Europe. Speaking in the House of Commons on 20 August 1945 about the problems of Romania, Hungary, Bulgaria and Austria, Bevin stated that it was important to prevent the substitution of one form of totalitarianism for another. The difficulty which the Soviets faced was that there was only a popular basis for a close relationship with the USSR in one country in the region, Czechoslovakia. Bulgaria came a close second, but in some of the other countries – for example, Poland – there was downright hostility to such a relationship.

At this difficult and delicate moment for the development of post-war relationships there was a new American President, Harry Truman, who needed time to work out his own ideas and meanwhile afforded his Secretary of State, James F. Byrnes, considerable leeway in policy formation. Byrnes wanted

Soviet cooperation, but only on the basis that the US should be recognised as the stronger partner. His atomic diplomacy was not successful, and merely succeeded in convincing the Soviets that they should speed up their own atomic programme. Truman and Byrnes, indeed most politicians, overestimated the benefits which would accrue to the United States, in the short term, as a result of its atomic diplomacy. They also assumed that this monopoly would last a long time, despite warnings by scientists to the contrary. There was a feeling that when it came to sophisticated technology the Soviet Union could not match the United States. Yet in fact the USSR – helped by spies such as Klaus Fuchs – exploded its first atomic device in 1949. Even without the technological information it gained from spies, the Soviet Union would almost certainly have been able to construct the simpler type of atomic bomb by 1951. In fact, that year saw the successful test by the USSR of the more complex plutonium bomb. This rapid development of its own atomic capability, and the calculation that the United States would not actually use its atomic bombs, hardened Soviet attitudes. The longer Washington prevaricated over credits, the more suspicious Moscow became that America was not really interested in helping the Soviet Union. Byrnes' attempt to prise concessions out of the Soviets in eastern and south-eastern Europe in return for deliveries of surplus US stock forced Moscow to decide between security and credits. It chose security, for its fear of potentially hostile powers on its frontiers was greater than its desire for rapid economic recovery aided by US technology.

The Soviets' ignorance of the way in which American policy was made and their inexperience in international diplomacy multiplied their misconceptions. Likewise the Americans, although adept at elaborating their own proposals, were quite unprepared when they ran into Soviet objections. Washington never tried to see the problems from Moscow's point of view. Its sources of information in the Soviet Union were poor and it only had the haziest notion of policy discussions in the Kremlin. It took some time before the West realised that Stalin was not under enormous pressure from more hard-line colleagues in the communist Politburo. He was skilled at giving the impression that he had to make concessions to other politicians. It then dawned on Western policymakers that there was one decision-maker in the Kremlin and he brooked no opposition.

Moscow, on the other hand, was swimming in information about American and British official thinking. Donald Maclean at the British embassy in Washington, to name just one example, had access to top secret information and relayed it to the Soviet Union. In the light of the first-class information flow from London and Washington and elsewhere, and the genuine American desire in 1945 for cooperation based on mutual advantage, why did Stalin not make more of the opportunities offered? It may have been the acute awareness of Soviet economic weakness and American strength which led Stalin to adopt a safety-first policy. If the 'open world' economy came into being,

American influence might well replace that of the Soviets in the latter's sphere of influence. As the hope of American credits on terms acceptable to the Soviet Union receded, so the Soviet need for increased reparations mounted. Yet the increasingly acrimonious discussions on the problem of Germany (including reparations) merely strengthened the hand of those Americans who were committed to the 'Riga axioms'. American policy consequently became a self-fulfilling prophecy. The Soviets, it was argued, did not want an agreement since they were bent on expansion. Give them eastern and south-eastern Europe and they would then start asking for the countries to the west. Containment was the logical response to this. It was enunciated in February 1946 but only openly became official policy a year later, with the formulation of the Truman Doctrine and the Marshall Plan. These were necessary to construct the edifice of the Cold War, for they provided the United States with a world mission apparently based on Wilsonian idealism – yet one which, at the same time, promised to create the overseas markets necessary for the rapid expansion of the US economy.

Western fear of the Soviet Union played an important part in the origins of the Cold War. There were people such as General Clay and the journalist Isaac Deutscher who raised their voices against the prevailing wisdom, but in vain. They saw the Soviet Union for what it was, economically and militarily weak. Official misconceptions about the USSR's real strength mainly stemmed from ignorance of the Soviet Union, and here the Soviet obsession with secrecy was counter-productive.

In 1945 agreement could have been reached, but in 1946 it became much more difficult. One of the American proposals for post-war Germany was the pastoralisation of the country – a proposal associated with Henry Morgenthau, Secretary of the Treasury. It envisaged reducing German industry to a level which would make it impossible for Germany ever again to become a threat to its neighbours. This option was attractive if large reparations to the Soviet Union were deemed desirable, but no agreement on it could be reached at Potsdam. Truman, for one, was adamantly against it. The longer the powers haggled, the more pressing became the problem of what to do about the war-shattered German economy. In London and Washington there was increasing desire for a rapid revival of the German economy, since Great Britain was unable and the United States unwilling to sustain it for much longer. This was bound to raise concern in Moscow. In fact, it was in everyone's interests to reach an agreement on Germany, for once that had been achieved accord on other parts of the world could follow. Nevertheless, such was the importance of Germany to both sides that no one was willing to leave a vacuum. Each side feared that Germany would pass into the camp of its adversary. The Soviets assumed that the market economy would pull the country into the American orbit, while the Americans were apprehensive about the prospects of an all-German state going communist. France played a negative role throughout. It wanted a dismembered, divided Germany, and it needed reparations. Eventually, the only solution to the intractable European problem was to divide the continent into blocs and revitalise the Western economies as the surest way of resisting communism.

Mastny regards the Soviet Union's striving for power and influence far in excess of its reasonable security requirements as the primary source of the Cold War conflict. However, had Roosevelt made clear to Stalin the limits beyond which he could not stray, Stalin might have acted with more restraint. To Mastny, the West's failure to resist soon enough was an important secondary source of the Cold War. However Mastny accepts that Stalin favoured cooperation and did not want a Cold War. It was not in the Soviet Union's interests to engage in confrontation with America. However the Cold War did come about despite all Stalin's efforts to prevent it. The main reason was lack of trust on the Kremlin dictator's part. Another reason was that he made egregious mistakes such as the failure to join the IMF, World Bank and the Marshall Plan. The Berlin Blockade was probably the worst Soviet blunder.

Stalin was a very astute politician but was not omniscient. His main foreign policy adviser, Molotov, ruminated near the end of his life about 1945 and the opportunities which existed. Stalin, he argued, had not excluded the possibility of war with the capitalist states. 'World War I wrested one country (Russia) from capitalist slavery. World War II created a socialist system, and the third would finish off imperialism forever' [Gaddis 1998: 14]. Here, one is tempted to say that Stalin was committing the same error as in 1941. If war came it would be between capitalist states and the Soviet Union would ensure that it remained outside. When the capitalist states had exhausted themselves, the road would then be open for socialism as the only alternative. Moscow would then rule the world.

Gaddis changed his mind over time. In his early writings he emphasised national security interests but later stressed the role of ideas and images on the Soviet side. 'The "new" [post-1991] history is bringing us back to an old answer: that as long as Stalin was running the Soviet Union a Cold War was inevitable . . . The more we learn, the less sense it makes to distinguish Stalin's foreign policies from his domestic practices or even his personal behaviour' [Gaddis 1998: 292–3]. In other words, Stalin deployed the same tactics when dealing with internal dissent, economic decision-making, resolving conflicts among ministries, formulating ideology and so on as he did in international affairs. His goal was to acquire and maintain dominance in both.

Leffler sees the Cold War as the legacy of the Second World War [Leffler 1992: 26]. That conflict upset the international system, altered the balance of power in Europe, shattered colonial empires, restructured economic and social arrangements within nations, and bequeathed a legacy of fear that preordained a period of unusual anxiety and tension. Hence security became predominant. The national security policies of the Truman administration were an attempt to apply the lessons and cope with the legacies of the Second World War as much as they were an effort to contain the Soviet Union. The United States, by providing a security umbrella, acting as financial hegemon and promoting multilateral trade, helped stimulate unprecedented economic growth. Policy-makers also believed that the expansion of industrial power would drive a wedge between Russia and eastern Europe and wean the region away from Moscow. The Kremlin might eventually and gradually conform to international norms. Truman and his advisers believed the Cold War could be won. They were right.

Another way of looking at the origins of the Cold War is to concentrate on the economic weakness of Europe, the Middle East, south-east Asia and Japan. A major factor was the weakness of Great Britain. Instead of London becoming an effective ally of Washington in and after 1945, it rapidly became clear that Britain desperately needed US economic aid. This factor had an important impact on British thinking. London wanted to involve Washington more and more in European affairs. In the Middle East, British thinking was decisive. Britain was aware that it could not retain its control over the Egypt-Suez area without US military and economic help. It also needed protection for its extensive petroleum interests in the region. The Iranian crisis of early 1946 brought home to the United States the importance of bases in the Middle East. Washington accepted that British power had to be sustained in this region since this was in its own interests. In south-east Asia, the United States acceded to the wishes of the European colonial powers for the restoration of the old order.

In Germany, France vetoed all Allied attempts to treat Germany economically as a single unit. France's fear of a resurgent Germany dominated its thinking. In 1947, two-thirds of European trade was still on a bilateral basis. The inability of west Europeans to solve their own economic problems reduced their political self-confidence. Increasingly after 1945 they turned to the United States as their political, economic and military saviour. From a security point of view, western Europe was incapable of defending itself. Hence the strategy of containment of the Soviet threat owes its conception to the European, not the American, mind. Churchill and later Ernest Bevin worked indefatigably to weld the United States and western Europe together. The same pattern can be traced in Asia, where timorous allies clamoured for more and more American intervention in their region.

The Truman Doctrine, the Marshall Plan and, especially, the formation of NATO were articulated in the United States but were conceived in Europe. Had Germany and western Europe experienced a rapid economic transformation after 1945, much of Kennan's pessimism would not have arisen. The Americans became alarmed at the weakness of their allies and potential allies and exaggerated Soviet power. Geir Lundestad has coined the phrase 'empire by invitation' to explain the evolution of US global policy [Lundestad 1986: 55].

The Soviets were their own worst enemies. The despatches of US and British diplomats paint an unflattering picture of the Moscow leadership. A flavour of the view from the Kremlin (the British embassy overlooked the Kremlin) is provided by Frank Roberts, a brilliantly successful career diplomat. After observing the party Politburo at the opening session of the USSR Supreme Soviet, he reported on 30 April 1945:

> The Group at the back with M.I. Kalinin are enough to make one shudder and fill one with considerable apprehension regarding future Soviet policy. . . . They are all tough, fat, prosperous individuals who might equally have come to the top in any other ruthless, totalitarian society such as those we are defeating in Germany and Italy. Andrei Zhdanov in particular might be a plumper and perhaps more humane version of Hitler himself. Lavrenty P. Beria and George Malenkov . . . give the impression of being at worst perverts and sadists and at best reincarnations of medieval inquisitors justifying every action on the principle of the end justifying the means.

Not the type of gentlemen, if that is the right word, in whom one would place great trust!

The Cold War is over, with America the victor. The decisive factor was economic. Stalin must bear much of the blame for the Cold War because he had it within his power in 1945 to fashion a working relationship with the United States. Neither Stalin nor Truman wanted a Cold War. Perhaps in 1945 both the Soviet and American leaders were too confident that their own system would eventually win. However, in the short term, because of the depredations of war, both felt nervous about the other's ability to steal a march on them. Stalin, although essentially a *Realpolitiker*, was also influenced by Marxism. This held that an understanding with capitalist opponents would be transitory but useful until the next capitalist crisis broke out. This would place the Soviet Union in a good position to take maximum advantage of it. Given this, why did Stalin not take more risks to secure a working relationship? Ulam regards Stalin's domestic insecurity as the major reason. He needed to cut his empire off from the outside capitalist world. Contact with capitalists would run the risk of undermining his internal control [Ulam 1974: passim].

Could the Cold War have been ended earlier by deploying other policies? Was it necessary to build up such great strategic and conventional power? Everyone was aware that this increased risk-taking. Would Khrushchev or Brezhnev have become more amenable to American wishes without this relentless build-up? Khrushchev was appalled by the cost of the nuclear arms race and the dangers of it (epitomised in the Cuban missile crisis of 1962 when the world came perilously close to nuclear destruction). He wanted an accommodation with President John F. Kennedy but the latter's tragic death dashed any hopes that existed. This did not mean that Khrushchev had abandoned the goal of communism. Since it was inevitable why waste so many resources on useless weapons? After all, when one had enough nuclear weapons to wipe out the plant, what was the point of producing more?

Khrushchev's removal, in 1964, brought to power Leonid Brezhnev who lacked Khrushchev's innovative thinking. A Brezhnev goal was nuclear parity with the United States and this was achieved by the early 1970s. After that there was a furious arms race until 1985. By then the Soviet Union could no longer afford it and eventually it crippled the Soviet economy. All Soviet leaders understood the competition with capitalist powers to be economic. If Moscow could not raise labour productivity above that of the Americans or the Japanese, communism could not succeed. Kennan perceived that economic, not military, policy would be decisive. However, his counsel did not prevail, as America descended into anti-communist hysteria and McCarthyism. America had lost self-confidence. It was fortunate for the United States that at precisely that moment western Europe and Japan were beginning to recover their self-confidence, thanks to America's economic help. Eventually the Cold War benefited the West more than the East. That said, it was still a shocking waste of human and material resources.

DOCUMENTS

DOCUMENT 1 THE COLD WAR: AN ORTHODOX VIEW

The orthodox or traditional view of the origins of the Cold War is here presented by Arthur Schlesinger.

An analysis of the origins of the Cold War which leaves out these factors – the intransigence of Leninist ideology, the sinister dynamics of a totalitarian society, and the madness of Stalin – is obviously incomplete. It was these factors which made it hard for the West to accept the thesis that Russia was moved only by a desire to protect its security and would be satisfied by the control of Eastern Europe; it was these factors which charged the debate between universalism and spheres of influence with apocalyptic potentiality.

Leninism and totalitarianism created a structure of thought and behavior which made postwar collaboration between Russia and America – in any normal sense of civilized intercourse between national states – inherently impossible. The Soviet dictatorship of 1945 simply could not have survived such a collaboration. The difference between America and Russia in 1945 was that some Americans fundamentally believed that, over a long run, a *modus vivendi* with Russia was possible; while the Russians, so far as one can tell, believed in no more than a short-run *modus vivendi* with the United States.

Harriman and Kennan, this narrative has made clear, took the lead in warning Washington about the difficulties of short-run dealings with the Soviet Union. But both argued that, if the United States developed a rational policy and stuck to it, there would be, after long and rough passages, the prospect of eventual clearing. 'I am, as you know,' Harriman cabled Washington in early April, 'a most earnest advocate of the closest possible understanding with the Soviet Union so that what I am saying relates only to how best to attain such understanding.'

There is no corresponding evidence on the Russian side that anyone seriously sought a *modus vivendi* in these terms. Stalin's choice was whether his long-term ideological and national interests would be better served by a short-run truce with the West or by an immediate resumption of pressure. In October 1945 Stalin indicated to Harriman at Sochi that he planned to adopt the second course – that the Soviet Union was going isolationist. No doubt the succession of problems with the United States contributed to this decision, but the basic causes most probably lay elsewhere: in the developing situations in Eastern Europe, in Western Europe, and in the United States.

If the condition of Eastern Europe made unilateral action seem essential in the interests of Russian security, the condition of Western Europe and the United States offered new temptations for communist expansion. The point of no return came on July 2, 1947, when Molotov, after bringing 89 technical specialists with him to Paris and evincing initial interest in the project for European reconstruction, received the hot flash from the Kremlin, denounced the whole idea, and walked out of the conference. For the next fifteen years the Cold War raged unabated, passing out of historical ambiguity into the realm of good versus evil and breeding on both sides simplifications, stereotypes, and self-serving absolutes, often couched in interchangeable phrases. Under the pressure even America, for a deplorable decade, forsook its pragmatic and pluralist traditions, posed as God's appointed messenger to ignorant and sinful man, and followed the Soviet example in looking to a world remade in its own image.

In retrospect, if it is impossible to see the Cold War as a case of American aggression and Russian response, it is also hard to see it as a pure case of Russian aggression and American response.

Arthur J. Schlesinger, Jr 'Origins of the Cold War,' *Foreign Affairs* (46), 1 October 1967.

DOCUMENT 2 THE COLD WAR: A REVISIONIST VIEW

W.A. Williams, one of the key revisionist historians, here attacks the traditional view that the Soviet Union started the Cold War. He sees American universalism and the concomitant claim that it has the right to intervene anywhere as a major reason for the Cold War. He pays particular attention to the 'open-door' economic policy of the US government, seeing in it the seeds of conflict between the United States and the USSR in eastern and south-eastern Europe.

American leaders had internalized, and had come to *believe*, the theory, the necessity, and the morality of open-door expansion. Hence they seldom thought it necessary to explain or defend the approach. Instead, they *assumed* the premises and concerned themselves with exercising their freedom and power to deal with the necessities and the opportunities that were defined by such an outlook. As far as American leaders were concerned, the philosophy and practice of open-door expansion had become, in both its missionary and economic aspects, *the* view of the world. Those who did not recognize and accept that fact were considered not only wrong, but incapable of thinking correctly. . . .

Particularly after the atom bomb was created and used, the attitude of the United States left the Soviets with but one real option: either acquiesce in American proposals or be confronted with American power and hostility. It was the decision of the United States to employ its new and awesome power in keeping with the traditional Open Door Policy which crystallized the cold war. . . .

The real issue is rather the far more subtle one of which side committed its power to policies which hardened the natural and inherent tensions and propensities into bitter antagonisms and inflexible positions. Two general attitudes can be adopted in facing that issue. One is to assume, or take for granted, on the basis of emotion and official information, that the answer is obvious: Russia is to blame. That represents the easy, nationalistic solution to all questions about international affairs. That attitude also defines history as a stockpile of facts to be requisitioned on the basis of what is needed to prove a conclusion decided upon in advance . . . In undertaking such self-examination, the first and essential requirement is to acknowledge two primary facts which can never be blinked. *The first is that the United States had from 1944 to at least 1962 a vast preponderance of actual as well as potential power vis-à-vis the Soviet Union. . . .*

For power and responsibility go together in a direct and intimate relationship. Unless it tries all the alternatives that offer reasonable probabilities of success, a nation with the great relative supremacy enjoyed by the United States between 1944 and 1962 cannot with any real warrant or meaning claim that it has been *forced* to follow a certain approach or policy. Yet that is the American claim even though it did not explore several such alternatives.

Instead, and this is the second fact that cannot be dodged, the United States used or deployed its preponderance of power wholly within the assumptions and the tradition of the strategy of the Open Door Policy. The United States never formulated and offered the Soviet Union a settlement based on other, less grandiose, terms . . . The popular idea that Soviet leaders emerged from the war ready to do aggressive battle against the United States is simply not borne out by the evidence. . . .

In a similar way, it is a grave error to evaluate or interpret the diplomatic moves of 1945 and 1946 in an economic vacuum. This is true in three respects. First, a good many of them were specifically economic in character. Second, all of them were intimately bound up with Russia's concern to obtain either a loan from the United States or extensive reparations from Germany and its former allies in eastern Europe. And finally, the determination to apply the Open Door Policy to eastern Europe, which led directly to the policies of 'total diplomacy' and 'negotiation from strength' later made famous by Secretary of State Acheson, evolved concurrently with a deep concern over economic affairs in the United States . . . George F. Kennan's 1946–1947 explanation of Soviet behavior . . . spawned a vast literature which treated Stalin as no more than a psychotic and, on the other, an equally large body of comment which argued that the only effective way to deal with the Soviet Union was to apply the lessons learned from the experience with Hitler. When tested against known facts, rather than accepted on the basis of a syllogism, these interpretations and recommendations did not lack all validity. Even by their own logic, however, they pointed to ultimate failure. For, by creating in fact a real, avowed, and all-encompassing outside threat, action based upon such analysis and analogy lent substance to what Kennan originally defined as a hallucination in the minds of Soviet leaders. Having argued that they had to create imaginary foreign dangers in order to stay in power at home, Kennan concluded with a policy recommendation to create a very serious (and from the Soviet point of view, mortal) outside challenge to their authority.

William Appleman Williams, *The Tragedy of American Diplomacy*, rev. ed. (Delta Books, New York, 1962), pp. 206–9, 227, 266–7, 278–9.

DOCUMENT 3 THE COLD WAR: A POST-REVISIONIST VIEW

Melvyn P. Leffler finds that both sides contributed to the Cold War.

In 1946 and 1947 a tolerable configuration of power in Eurasia probably could not have been brought about without provoking the Soviets. The threats emanating from the post-war socio-economic dislocation and power vacuum were too great to allow for a policy of reassurance. Although unlikely, a sequence of events *might* have ended in Communist victories in France, Italy, and Greece, and *might* have led to an autonomous and revanchist Germany, and *might* have culminated in Soviet domination, however indirect, of major parts of western Eurasia. Prudent men could not take such risks when the leadership in the Kremlin was so totalitarian and repressive and when it possessed an ideology that appeared attractive to even larger numbers of people in the underdeveloped periphery. US officials intelligently decided to rebuild western Europe and to co-opt German and Japanese strength. These actions were of decisive importance in fueling the Cold War, but they were prudently conceived and skillfully implemented in cooperation with indigenous elites.

Although US actions necessarily engendered legitimate security apprehensions in the Soviet Union, the Russian response was neither so belligerent nor so daring as to have necessitated the huge buildup in strategic armaments, the stress on European conventional rearmament, and the endless struggles on the periphery. The Russians backed down in Berlin. Moreover their capacity to affect developments in the Third World was severely circumscribed by their limited power-projection capabilities and their economic backwardness.

Western Europe required security guarantees, not the extensive armaments that America wanted it to have. The Third World needed markets and capital and self-determination, not a reformed neo-colonial leadership bolstered by US military aid. . . .

The great achievement of the early Cold War years was that US officials helped forge a configuration of power in the industrial core of Eurasia that continues to safeguard vital US interests. . . . Western Europe is no longer weak and vulnerable; Germany and Japan are strong; Marxist-Leninist ideology and the Soviet model of development are discredited.

Melvyn P. Leffler A Preponderance of Power: National Security, the Truman Administration and the Cold War (Stanford University Press, Stanford, CA, 1992), pp. 516–18.

DOCUMENT 4 THE ATLANTIC CHARTER (14 AUGUST 1941)

President Franklin D. Roosevelt and Winston Churchill held a highly secret meeting on board a warship off Argentia, Newfoundland, from 9–12 August 1941 to discuss post-war peace objectives. Its outcome was this Charter.

Joint declaration of the President of the United States of America and the Prime Minister, Mr Churchill, representing His Majesty's Government in the United Kingdom, being met together, deem it right to make known certain common principles in the national policies of their respective countries on which they base their hopes for a better future for the world.

First, their countries seek no aggrandizement, territorial or other;

Second, they desire to see no territorial changes that do not accord with the freely expressed wishes of the peoples concerned;

Third, they respect the right of all peoples to choose the form of government under which they will live; and they wish to see sovereign rights and self government restored to those who have been forcibly deprived of them;

Fourth, they will endeavour, with due respect for their existing obligations, to further the enjoyment by all States, great or small, victor or vanquished, of access, on equal terms, to the trade and to the raw materials of the world which are needed for their economic prosperity;

Fifth, they desire to bring about the fullest collaboration between all nations in the economic field with the object of securing, for all, improved labor standards, economic advancement, and social security;

Sixth, after the final destruction of the Nazi tyranny, they hope to see established a peace which will afford to all nations the means of dwelling in safety within their own boundaries, and which will afford assurance that all men in all the lands may live out their lives in freedom from fear and want;

Seventh, such a peace should enable all men to traverse the high seas and oceans without hindrance;

Eighth, they believe that all of the nations of the world, for realistic as well as spiritual reasons, must come to the abandonment of the use of force. Since no future peace can be maintained if land, sea or air armaments continue to be employed by nations which threaten, or may threaten, aggression outside of their frontiers, they believe, pending the establishment of a wider and permanent system of general security, that the disarmament of such nations is essential. They will likewise aid and encourage all other practicable measures which will lighten for peace-loving peoples the crushing burden of armaments.

Reprinted in Walter LaFeber, *The Origins of the Cold War 1941–1947: A Historical Problem with Interpretation and Documents* (John Wiley, New York, 1971), pp. 32–3.

DOCUMENT 5 EDEN AND STALIN

In the wake of the Japanese attack on Pearl Harbor, Anthony Eden, British Foreign Secretary, flew to Moscow to discuss common Anglo-Soviet-American problems. He consulted with Stalin on 16 and 17 December 1941 and found him keen to settle the post-war frontiers, even though the German Wehrmacht was at the gates of Moscow.

Stalin's suggestions for this protocol showed me that the hope we had held in London, of being able to confine the discussion of frontiers to the general terms of the Atlantic Charter, had been vain. Russian ideas were already starkly definite. They changed little during the next three years, for their purpose was to secure the most tangible physical guarantees for Russia's future security.

Stalin proposed that Poland should expand westward at Germany's expense. Other occupied countries were to return to their old frontiers, Austria being restored, while the Rhineland and possibly Bavaria would be detached from Germany. The Soviet Union would regain her frontiers of 1941 with Finland and Roumania and would recover the Baltic States. Her frontier with Poland would be based on the Curzon line. [The Curzon line, proposed by the British at the Peace Conference of 1919–1920, was considerably west of the actual Russo-Polish boundary between 1921 and 1939; on the other hand, as a result of the Nazi-Soviet Pact of 1939, the new Russo-Polish boundary moved west of the Curzon line, thereby giving Russia large portions of Poland.] Stalin also wanted the right to establish bases in Finland and Roumania with a guarantee for the exits from the Baltic. The Soviet government would not object, he said, to Britain establishing bases in Denmark and Norway.

Stalin then put two questions. What were our views about reparation by Germany for the damage she had done, and how were we to keep peace and order in Europe after the war? He suggested a council of the victorious powers, with a military force at its disposal. The Soviet Union would have no objection if some European countries wished to federate.

I told Stalin that I agreed with much that he had said about post-war Europe. The British people were determined that every possible military measure should be taken to prevent Germany breaking the peace again. Exactly how this was to be done would have to be gone into carefully. There was no doubt that some kind of military control over Germany would be necessary and that Great Britain, the Soviet Union, and the United States, if they would help, would have to undertake it.

On the partition of Germany, I said, the British government had not taken a decision either way. There was no objection to it in principle. Nor had we closed our minds to a separate Bavaria or Rhineland; we were certainly in favour of an independent Austria . . . So far as reparations were concerned, I was sure, from our experience after the last war, that we should be against any money reparations; the restitution by Germany of goods taken away from occupied territories was another matter.

I then explained to Stalin that I could not agree to the secret protocol without reference to the Cabinet and added:

Even before Russia was attacked, Mr Roosevelt sent a message to us, asking us not to enter into any secret arrangement as to the post-war reorganization of Europe without first consulting him. This does not exclude our two countries from discussing a basis for the peace. . . .

Stalin: But there are many questions relating to the safety of our two countries which can be discussed between us.

Eden: We can discuss matters between us, but ultimately, for the purpose of the peace treaty, the Soviet Union, Great Britain, and the United States of America must all come in and agree with one another on the principal world affairs.

Stalin: I agree.

I then suggested that before we spoke of military plans, we ought to clear up a political point. Should we try to combine our two documents, or what course did Stalin propose?

Stalin: I think that what you have submitted is a kind of declaration, whereas ours are two agreements. A declaration I regard as algebra, but an agreement as practical arithmetic. I do not wish to decry algebra, but I prefer practical arithmetic.

Anthony Eden, *The Eden Memoirs, The Reckoning* (Cassell, London, 1965), pp. 334–5.

DOCUMENT 6 'THERE WILL NO LONGER BE NEED FOR SPHERES OF INFLUENCE'

Cordell Hull, US Secretary of State, took part in the Moscow conference of late October 1943. The central problem was Poland, though Hull said little on this subject. These extracts are from his report to Congress on 18 November 1943.

At the end of the war, each of the United Nations and each of the nations associated with them will have the same common interest in national security, in world order under law, in peace, in the full promotion of the political, economic, and social welfare of their respective peoples – in the principles and spirit of the Atlantic Charter and the Declaration by the United Nations. The future of these indispensable common interests depends absolutely upon international cooperation. Hence, each nation's own primary interest requires it to cooperate with the others.

These considerations led the Moscow Conference to adopt the four-nation declaration with which you are all familiar. I should like to comment briefly on its main provisions.

In that document, it was jointly declared by the United States, Great Britain, the Soviet Union, and China 'That their united action, pledged for the prosecution of the war against their respective enemies, will be continued for the organization and maintenance of peace and security.'

To this end, the four Governments declared that they 'recognize the necessity of establishing at the earliest practicable date a general international organization, based on the principle of the sovereign equality of all peace-loving states, and open to membership by all such states, large and small'. I should like to lay particular stress on this provision of the declaration. The principle of sovereign equality of all peace-loving states, irrespective of size and strength, as partners in a future system of general security will be the foundation stone upon which the future international organization will be constructed. . . .

The four Governments further agreed that, pending the inauguration in this manner of a permanent system of general security, 'they will consult with one another and as occasion requires with other members of the United Nations with a view to joint action on behalf of the community of nations' whenever such action may be necessary for the purpose of maintaining international peace and security.

Finally, as an important self-denying ordinance, they declared 'That after the termination of hostilities they will not employ their military forces within the territories of other states except for the purposes envisaged in this declaration and after joint consultation.'

Through this declaration, the Soviet Union, Great Britain, the United States, and China have laid the foundation for cooperative effort in the post-war world toward enabling all peace-loving nations, large and small, to live in peace and security. . . .

As the provisions of the four-nation declaration are carried into effect, there will no longer be need for spheres of influence, for alliances for balance of power, or any other of the special arrangements through which, in the unhappy past, the nations strove to safeguard their security or to promote their interests.

US Department of State Bulletin, IX, 20 November 1943. Reprinted in Walter LaFeber, *The Origins of the Cold War 1941–1947: A Historical Problem with Interpretation and Documents* (John Wiley, New York, 1971), pp. 41–2.

DOCUMENT 7 THE PERCENTAGES AGREEMENT

In early October 1944 Winston Churchill flew to Moscow to discuss with Stalin various post-war problems – especially who should have responsibility for overseeing eastern and south-eastern Europe. On 9 October 1944 they concluded the percentages agreement. Molotov amended the percentages on Bulgaria and Hungary the following day in favour of the USSR.

We alighted at Moscow on the afternoon on October 9, and were received very heartily and with full ceremonial by Molotov and many high Russian personages. This time we were lodged in Moscow itself, with every care and comfort. I had one small, perfectly appointed house, and Anthony another nearby. We were glad to dine alone together and rest. At ten o'clock that night we held our first important meeting in the Kremlin. . . .

The moment was apt for business, so I said, 'Let us settle about our affairs in the Balkans. Your armies are in Rumania and Bulgaria. We have interests, missions, and agents there. Don't let us get at cross-purposes in small ways. So far as Britain and Russia are concerned, how would it do for you to have ninety per cent predominance in Rumania, for us to have ninety per cent of the say in Greece, and go fifty-fifty about Yugoslavia?' While this was being translated I wrote out on a half-sheet of paper:

Rumania	
Russia	90%
The others	10%
Greece	
Great Britain	90%
(in accord with USA)	
Russia	10%
Yugoslavia	50–50%
Hungary	50–50%
Bulgaria	
Russia	75%
The others	25%

I pushed this across to Stalin, who had by then heard the translation. There was a slight pause. Then he took his blue pencil and made a large tick upon it, and passed it back to us. It was all settled in no more time than it takes to set down.

Of course we had long and anxiously considered our point, and were only dealing with immediate war-time arrangements. All larger questions were reserved on both sides for what we then hoped would be a peace table when the war was won.

After this there was a long silence. The pencilled paper lay in the centre of the table. At length I said, 'Might it not be though rather cynical if it seemed we had disposed of these issues, so fateful to millions of people, in such an offhand manner? Let us burn the paper.' 'No, you keep it,' said Stalin.

Winston Churchill, *Triumph and Tragedy* (Houghton Mifflin, Boston, MA, 1954), pp. 226–8.

DOCUMENT 8 DJILAS ON STALIN

Milovan Djilas became a member of the Politburo of the Communist Party of Yugoslavia in 1940, and when Germany occupied Yugoslavia in 1941 he joined the Partisans led by Tito. He headed a military mission to Moscow in 1944 and visited the Soviet capital again the following year. Note his assessment of Stalin's attitude to revolution.

Stalin presented his views on the distinctive nature of the war that was being waged: 'This war is not as in the past; whoever occupies a territory also imposes on it his own social system. Everyone impses his own system as far as his army has power to do so. It cannot be otherwise.'

He also pointed out, without going into long explanations, the meaning of his pan-Slavic policy. 'If the Slavs keep united and maintain solidarity, no one in the future will be able to move a finger. Not even a finger!' he repeated, emphasizing his thought by cleaving the air with his forefinger.

Someone expressed doubt that the Germans would be able to recuperate within fifty years. But Stalin was of a different opinion. 'No, they will recover, and very quickly. It is a highly developed industrial country with an extremely skilled and numerous working class and technical intelligentsia. Give them twelve to fifteen years and they'll be on their feet again. And this is why the unity of the Slavs is important. But even apart from this, if the unity of the Slavs exists, no one will dare move a finger.'

At one point he got up, hitched up his trousers as though he was about to wrestle or to box, and cried out emotionally, 'The war will soon be over. We shall recover in fifteen to twenty years, and then we'll have another go at it.'

There was something terrible in his words: a horrible war was still going on. Yet there was something impressive, too, about his realization of the paths he had to take, the inevitability that faced the world in which he lived and the movement that he headed. . . .

It is time something was said about Stalin's attitude to revolutions, and thus to the Yugoslav revolution. Because Moscow had always refrained at the crucial moment from supporting the Chinese, Spanish, and in many ways even the Yugoslav revolutions, the view prevailed, not without reason, that Stalin was generally against revolutions. This is, however, not entirely correct. His opposition was only conditional, and arose only when the revolution went beyond the interests of the Soviet state. He felt instinctively that the creation of revolutionary centres outside Moscow could endanger its supremacy in world Communism, and of course that is what actually happened. That is why he helped revolutions only up to a certain point – as long as he could control them – but he was always ready to leave them in the lurch whenever they slipped out of his grasp. I maintain that not even today is there any essential change in this respect in the policy of the Soviet Government.

In his own country Stalin had subjected all activities to his views and to his personality, so he could not behave differently outside. Having identified domestic progress and freedom with the interests and privileges of a political party, he could not act in foreign affairs other than as a dictator. And like everyone else he must be judged by his actual deeds. He became himself the slave of the despotism, the bureaucracy, the narrowness, and the servility that he imposed on his country.

It is indeed true that no one can destroy another's freedom without losing his own.

Milovan Djilas, *Conversations with Stalin* (Penguin, London, 1969), pp. 90–1, 103.

DOCUMENT 9 POLAND AT YALTA

Churchill, Roosevelt and Stalin discussed Poland at length at the Yalta Conference (6–11 February 1945). The crucial question was the composition of the Polish government. The declaration of 11 February 1945 appeared to concede much of what the West wanted. In the months which followed Churchill and Roosevelt/Truman argued bitterly with Stalin over the interpretation of this declaration.

6 February 1945

Marshal Stalin then gave the following summary of his views on the Polish question: Mr Churchill had said that for Great Britain the Polish question was one of honor and that he understood, but for the Russians it was a question both of honor and security. It was one of honor because Russia had many past grievances against Poland and desired to see them eliminated. It was a question of strategic security not only because Poland was a bordering country but because throughout history Poland had been the corridor for attack on Russia. We have to mention that during the last thirty years Germany twice has passed through this corridor. The reason for this was that Poland was weak. Russia wants a strong, independent and democratic Poland. . . . It is not only a question of honor for Russia, but one of life and death. . . .

11 February 1945

The following Declaration on Poland was agreed by the Conference:

'A new situation has been created in Poland as a result of her complete liberation by the Red Army. This calls for the establishment of a Polish Provisional Government which can be more broadly based than was possible before the recent liberation of the Western part of Poland. The Provisional Government which is now functioning in Poland should therefore be reorganized on a broader democratic basis with the inclusion of democratic leaders from Poland itself and from Poles abroad. This new Government should then be called the Polish Provisional Government of National Unity. . . .

This Polish Provisional Government of National Unity shall be pledged to the holding of free and unfettered elections as soon as possible on the basis of universal suffrage and secret ballot. In these elections all democratic and anti-Nazi parties shall have the right to take part and to put forward candidates. . . .

The three Heads of Government consider that the Eastern frontier of Poland should follow the Curzon Line with digressions from it in some regions of five to eight kilometres in favour of Poland. They recognize that Poland must receive substantial accessions of territory in the North and West. They feel that the opinion of the New Polish Provisional Government of National Unity should be sought in due course on the extent of these accessions and that the final delimitation of the Western frontier of Poland should thereafter await the Peace Conference.'

US Department of State, *Foreign Relations of the United States, The Conferences at Malta and Yalta, 1945*. Reprinted in Walter LaFeber, *The Origins of the Cold War 1941–1947: A Historical Problem with Interpretation and Documents* (John Wiley, New York, 1971), pp. 89, 93.

DOCUMENT 10 THE DECLARATION ON LIBERATED EUROPE

After the percentages agreement [Doc. 7] the Soviets afforded American and British representatives on the control commissions in Bulgaria, Romania and Hungary little scope. This document, agreed at the Yalta Conference (February 1945), makes an attempt to redress the balance in favour of the West.

The Premier of the Union of Soviet Socialist Republics, the Prime Minister of the United Kingdom and the President of the United States of America have consulted with each other in the common interests of the peoples of their countries and those of liberated Europe. They jointly declare their mutual agreement to concert during the temporary period of instability in liberated Europe the policies of their three governments in assisting the peoples liberated from the domination of Nazi Germany and the peoples of the former Axis satellite states of Europe to solve by democratic means their pressing political and economic problems.

The establishment of order in Europe and the re-building of national economic life must be achieved by processes which will enable the liberated peoples to destroy the last vestiges of Nazism and Fascism and to create democratic institutions of their own choice. This is a principle of the Atlantic Charter – the right of all peoples to choose the form of government under which they will live – the restoration of sovereign rights and self-government to those peoples who have been forcibly deprived of them by the aggressor nations.

To foster the conditions in which the liberated peoples may exercise these rights, the three governments will jointly assist the people in any European liberated state or former Axis satellite state in Europe where in their judgment conditions require (a) to establish conditions of internal peace; (b) to carry out emergency measures for the relief of distressed peoples; (c) to form interim governmental authorities broadly representative of all democratic elements in the population and pledged to the earliest possible establishment through free elections of governments responsive to the will of the people; and (d) to facilitate where necessary the holding of such elections.

The three governments will consult the other United Nations and provisional authorities or other governments in Europe when matters of direct interest to them are under consideration.

When, in the opinion of the three governments, conditions in any European liberated state or any former Axis satellite state in Europe make such action necessary, they will immediately consult together on the measures necessary to discharge the joint responsibilities set forth in this declaration.

By this declaration we reaffirm our faith in the principles of the Atlantic Charter, our pledge in the Declaration by the United Nations, and our determination to build in co-operation with other peace-loving nations world order under law, dedicated to peace, security, freedom and general well-being of all mankind.

In issuing this declaration, the Three Powers express the hope that the Provisional Government of the French Republic may be associated with them in the procedure suggested.

US Department of State, *Foreign Relations of the United States, The Conferences at Malta and Yalta, 1945*. Reprinted in Walter LaFeber, *The Origins of the Cold War 1941–1947: A Historical Problem with Interpretation and Documents* (John Wiley, New York, 1971), pp. 53–4.

DOCUMENT 11 ROOSEVELT TO STALIN ON POLAND

Roosevelt, in a letter to Stalin on 1 April 1945, expressed his concern at the latter's interpretation of the Yalta declaration on Poland. To Stalin it meant that the communists would stay in control, but to Roosevelt it meant that the communists would no longer dominate the government.

I cannot conceal from you the concern with which I view the development of events of mutual interest since our fruitful meeting at Yalta . . . So far there has been a discouraging lack of progress made in the carrying out, which the world expects, of the political decisions which we reached at the Conference, particularly those relating to the Polish question. I am frankly puzzled as to why this should be and must tell you that I do not fully understand in many respects the apparent indifferent attitude of your Government. Having understood each other so well at Yalta I am convinced that the three of us can and will clear away any obstacles which have developed since then. I intend, therefore, in this message to lay before you with complete frankness the problem as I see it. . . .

[The] part of our agreements at Yalta which has aroused the greatest popular interest and is the most urgent relates to the Polish question. You are aware of course that the Commission which we set up has made no progress. I feel this is due to the interpretation which your Government is placing upon the Crimean decisions. . . .

In the discussions that have taken place so far your Government appears to take the position that the new Polish Provisional Government of National Unity which we agreed should be formed should be little more than a continuation of the present Warsaw Government. I cannot reconcile this either with our agreement or our discussions. While it is true that the Lublin Government is to be reorganized and its members play a prominent role it is to be done in such a fashion as to bring into being a new Government. This point is clearly brought out in several places in the text of the agreement. I must make it quite plain to you that any such solution which would result in a thinly disguised continuance of the present Warsaw regime would be unacceptable and would cause the people of the United States to regard the Yalta agreement as having failed.

US Department of State, *Foreign Relations of the United States*, 1945, V. Reprinted in Walter LaFeber, *The Origins of the Cold War 1941–1947: A Historical Problem with Interpretation and Documents* (John Wiley, New York, 1971), pp. 94–5.

DOCUMENT 12 A 'BARBARIAN INVASION OF EUROPE'

Truman, although Vice-President, was not a member of Roosevelt's foreign policy group. After he became President, Truman called all his key advisers together to analyse East–West relations. One of the 'hardliners' was Averell Harriman, US ambassador to Moscow, who warned Truman on 20 April 1945 about the consequences for a country if it fell under Soviet control.

Ambassador Harriman said that in effect what we were faced with was a 'barbarian invasion of Europe', that Soviet control over any foreign country did not mean merely influence on their foreign relations but the extension of the Soviet system with secret police, extinction of freedom of speech, etc., and that we had to decide what should be our attitude in the face of these unpleasant facts. He added that he was not pessimistic and felt that we could arrive at a workable basis with the Russians but that this would require a reconsideration of our policy and the abandonment of the illusion that for the immediate future the Soviet Government was going to act in accordance with the principles which the rest of the world held to in international affairs. He said that obviously certain concessions in the give and take of negotiation would have to be made. The President said that he thoroughly understood this and said that we could not, of course, expect to get 100 per cent of what we wanted but that on important matters he felt that we should be able to get 85 per cent.

The Ambassador then outlined briefly the issues involved in the Polish question, explaining his belief that Stalin had discovered from the Lublin Poles that an honest execution of the Crimean [Yalta] decision would mean the end of Soviet-backed Lublin control over Poland since any real democratic leader such as Mikolajczyk would serve as a rallying point for 80 to 90 per cent of the Polish people against the Lublin Communists. . . .

He said he would like to inquire in this connection of the President how important he felt the Polish question was in relation to the San Francisco Conference [where the United Nations would be set in motion] and American participation in the world organization. The President replied immediately and decisively that in his considered opinion unless settlement of the Polish question was achieved along the lines of the Crimean decision that the treaty of American adherence to a world organization would not get through the Senate. He added that he intended to tell Molotov just this in words of one syllable.

US Department of State, *Foreign Relations of the United States*, Vol. V, Europe, Washington, 1967, p. 234.

DOCUMENT 13 SOVIET–AMERICAN DIFFERENCES

Prior to the Potsdam Conference, President Truman sent Harry Hopkins to Moscow (26 May–6 June 1945) to discuss some of the contentious issues. It was clear that the two sides interpreted the Declaration on Liberated Europe [Doc. 10] quite differently, for the Americans wanted trade ties with eastern and south-eastern Europe which the Soviets were not willing to concede. Poland and reparations were the main issues which caused the greatest discord.

Mr Hopkins stated that the United States would desire a Poland friendly to the Soviet Union and in fact desired to see friendly countries all along the Soviet borders.

Marshal Stalin replied if that be so we can easily come to terms in regard to Poland. . . .

Marshal Stalin said he would not attempt to use Soviet public opinion as a screen but would speak of the feeling that had been created in Soviet governmental circles as a result of recent moves on the part of the United States Government. He said these circles felt a certain alarm in regard to the attitude of the United States Government. It was their impression that the American attitude towards the Soviet Union had perceptibly cooled once it became obvious that Germany was defeated, and that it was as though the Americans were saying that the Russians were no longer needed. He said he would give the following examples: . . .

2. The question of the Reparations Commission. At Yalta it had been agreed that the three powers would sit on this Commission in Moscow and subsequently the United States Government had insisted that France should be represented on the same basis as the Soviet Union. This he felt was an insult to the Soviet Union in view of the fact that France had concluded a separate peace with Germany [in 1940] and had opened the frontier to the Germans. . . .

3. The attitude of the United States Government towards the Polish question. He said that at Yalta it had been agreed that the existing government was to be reconstructed and that anyone with common sense could see that this means that the present government [dominated by the Polish Communists] was to form the basis of the new. He said no other understanding of the Yalta Agreement was possible. Despite the fact that they were simple people the Russians should not be regarded as fools, which was a mistake the West frequently made, nor were they blind and could quite well see what was going on before their eyes. . . .

4. The manner in which Lend Lease had been curtailed. He said that if the United States was unable to supply the Soviet Union further under Lend Lease that was one thing but that the manner in which it had been done had been unfortunate and even brutal. For example, certain ships had been unloaded

and while it was true that this order had been cancelled the whole manner in which it had been done had caused concern to the Soviet Government. If the refusal to continue Lend Lease was designed as pressure on the Russians in order to soften them up then it was a fundamental mistake.

US Department of State, *Foreign Relations of the United States, The Conference of Berlin*, I. Reprinted in Walter LaFeber, *The Origins of the Cold War 1941–1947: A Historical Problem with Interpretation and Documents* (John Wiley, New York, 1971), pp. 62–4.

Truman had been briefed in detail about Stalin. Here are his first impressions.

Promptly a few minutes before twelve I looked up from the desk and there stood Stalin in the doorway. I got to my feet and advanced to meet him. He put out his hand and smiled. I did the same. We shook. I greeted Molotov and the interpreter and we sat down. After the usual polite remarks we got down to business. I told Stalin that I am no diplomat but usually said yes or no to questions after hearing all the arguments. It pleased him. I asked him if he had the agenda for the meeting. He said he had and that he had some more questions to present. I told him to fire away. He did and it is dynamite – but I have some dynamite too which I'm not exploding now. He wants to fire Franco [the Spanish dictator] to which I wouldn't object and divide up the Indian colonies and other mandates, some no doubt which the British have. Then he got on the Chinese situation, told us what agreements had been reached and what was in abeyance. Most of the big points are settled. He'll be in the Jap war on August 15. Fini Japs when that comes about.

We had lunch socially, put on a real show, drinking toasts to everyone then had pictures made in the back yard. I can deal with Stalin. He is honest – but smart as hell.

J. Robert Moskin, *Mr Truman's War: The Final Victories of World War II and the Birth of the Postwar World* (University of Kansas Press, Kansas, 2002), pp. 202–3.

DOCUMENT 14 REPARATIONS FROM GERMANY AS AGREED AT POTSDAM

The Potsdam Agreement (1 August 1945) mentioned no specific figure whereas at Yalta the Big Three had agreed to total reparations of $20,000 million, half going to the Soviet Union.

1. Reparation claims of the USSR shall be met by removals from the Zone of Germany occupied by the USSR and from appropriate German external assets.
2. The USSR undertakes to settle the reparation claims of Poland from its own share of reparations.

3. The reparation claims of the United States, the United Kingdom and other countries entitled to reparations shall be met from the western zones and from appropriate German external assets.
4. In addition to the reparations to be taken by the USSR from its own zone of occupation, the USSR shall receive additionally from the western zones:

Fifteen per cent of such usable and complete industrial capital equipment, in the first place from the metallurgical, chemical and machine manufacturing industries, as is unnecessary for the German peace economy and should be removed from the western zones of Germany, in exchange for an equivalent value of food, coal, potash, zinc, timber, clay products, petroleum products, and such other commodities as may be agreed upon.

Ten per cent of such industrial capital equipment as is unnecessary for the German peace economy and should be removed from the western zones, to be transferred to the Soviet Government on reparations account without payment or exchange of any kind in return.

US Department of State, *Foreign Relations of the United States, The Conference of Berlin*, II, Washington, 1960, pp. 1486–7.

DOCUMENT 15 'TO SELL THE BRITISH EMPIRE FOR A PACKET OF CIGARETTES'

A paper prepared for the War Cabinet on 14 August 1945 stated that Great Britain would be 'virtually bankrupt' in 1946–48 if US aid were not forthcoming. The Labour government obtained a loan in late 1945 but the terms were harsh. Churchill, now leader of the opposition, abstained in the vote, but Conservative MP Robert Boothby, always his own man, vented his anger.

Under the Bretton Woods Agreement, gold will purchase any currency. . . . Of 28 billion dollars of monetary gold in the world, 23 billion are in the vaults of Fort Knox. If we are going to make gold the basis of credit, in my estimation, we are handing over world economic power, outside the Soviet Union, finally and decisively to the United States. . . .

The third condition that we are now asked to swallow is the acceptance of the principle of non-discrimination in trade, involving the elimination of imperial preference and of quotas on imports. I do not think there is any need for me to dilate on this. I think if it is persisted in – and I hope it will not be – it will involve the break-up of the British Empire. . . . Nearly half our exports before the war went to the British Empire. . . .

Is there anything in the Agreement which obliges the United States of America, in any circumstances, to make cuts in her tariffs of a magnitude which would ensure a substantial importation of goods into the United States of America? Anyway, what is the value of the United States of America as a market to this country? Compare it with the value of the Empire market, which we are throwing away. . . .

I am going to speak bluntly, and say that there are two main objectives underlying the agreement which we are being asked to approve. The first is to get back as quickly as possible to the economic system of the 19th century – the system of *laissez faire* capitalism. The second is to break up, and prise open, the markets of the world for the benefit of the United States of America, who have an intense desire to get rid of their surplus products, which will be enormous, at almost any cost. . . .

I want now to put two propositions to the Chancellor of the Exchequer. The first is that multilateral trade and free convertibility, to which this Agreement admittedly commits us, are impractical in the modern world . . . The philosophy underlying the old Liberal doctrine of enlightened self-interest and the free-market economy depended for its success on the existence of empty spaces and continually expanding markets. The spaces are filling up. The era of uncontrolled capitalist expansion is drawing to a close . . . It is great optimism on their part if they place such reliance in the operation of free, knock-about Capitalism. I have no such confidence in the economic system of the United States of America. I think there may quite possibly be a slump there. And if there is, His Majesty's Government are, by these measures, depriving us of every weapon by which we might protect ourselves from its most dire consequences. . . .

There was a great chance, for a middle unit, standing between what . . . I call the knock-about Capitalism of the United States of America on the one hand, and the rigid, Socialist, closed economy of Russia on the other; free to expand, by multilateral agreement within that economy, between like-minded nations. That arrangement might have provided a balancing *bloc* which would have been of very great value in the world. I do not want to see the world divided into two, and only two, opposing systems. I think there is great danger in it. . . .

I never thought I should feel again as I felt at the time of the Munich Agreement, but I feel just the same as I did then. This is our economic Munich . . . I would not venture to dogmatize. But there is one mandate which his Majesty's Government never got from the people of this country, and that was to sell the British Empire for a packet of cigarettes.

Parliamentary Debates (Hansard), Fifth Series, Vol. 417, House of Commons, 12 December 1945, cols 459, 461, 463–9.

DOCUMENT 16 STIMSON PROPOSES AN ATOMIC AGREEMENT WITH THE USSR

In a memorandum to the President on 11 September 1945 Henry Stimson, Secretary for War but on the point of retiring, proposed that the United States should demonstrate its trust in the USSR by sharing with it the development of the atomic bomb. Stimson had favoured a hard-line attitude at Potsdam but its failure had led him to re-think his attitude to the Soviet Union.

Accordingly, unless the Soviets are voluntarily invited into the partnership upon a basis of cooperation and trust, we are going to maintain the Anglo-Saxon bloc over against the Soviets in the possession of this weapon. Such a condition will almost certainly stimulate feverish activity on the part of the Soviets toward the development of this bomb in what will in effect be a secret armament race of a rather desperate character. There is evidence to indicate that such activity may have already commenced. . . .

To put the matter concisely, I consider the problem of our satisfactory relations with Russia as not merely connected with but as virtually dominated by the problem of the atomic bomb. Except for the problem of the control of that bomb, those relations, while vitally important, might not be immediately pressing. The establishment of relations of mutual confidence between her and us could afford to await the slow progress of time. But with the discovery of the bomb, they become immediately emergent. These relations may be perhaps irretrievably embittered by the way in which we approach the solution of the bomb with Russia. For if we fail to approach them now and merely continue to negotiate with them, having this weapon rather ostentatiously on our hip, their suspicions and their distrust of our purposes and motives will increase. It will inspire them to greater efforts in all out effort to solve the problem. If the solution is achieved in that spirit, it is much less likely that we will ever get the kind of covenant we may desperately need in the future. This risk is, I believe, greater than the other, inasmuch as our objective must be to get the best kind of international bargain we can – one that has some chance of being kept and saving civilization not for five or for twenty years, but forever.

The chief lesson I have learned in a long life is that the only way you can make a man trustworthy is to trust him; and the surest way to make him untrustworthy is to distrust him and show your distrust. . . .

My idea of an approach to the Soviets would be a direct proposal after discussion with the British that we would be prepared in effect to enter an arrangement with the Russians, the general purpose of which would be to control and limit the use of the atomic bomb as an instrument of war and so far as possible to direct and encourage the development of atomic power for peaceful and humanitarian purposes. Such an approach might more specifically lead to the proposal that we would stop work on the further improvement in, or manufacture of, the bomb as a military weapon, provided the Russians and the British would agree to do likewise. It might also provide that we would be willing to impound what bombs we now have in the United States provided the Russians and the British would agree with us that in no event will they or we use a bomb as an instrument of war unless all three Governments agree to that use. We might also consider including in the arrangement a covenant with the UK [United Kingdom] and the Soviets providing for the exchange of benefits of future developments whereby atomic energy may be applied on a mutually satisfactory basis for commercial or humanitarian purposes.

US Department of State, *Foreign Relations of the United States*, 1945, Vol. II, *General: Political and Economic Matters*. Reprinted in Walter LaFeber, *The Origins of the Cold War 1941–1947: A Historical Problem with Interpretation and Documents* (John Wiley, New York, 1971), pp. 67–8.

DOCUMENT 17 THE BARUCH PLAN FOR THE CONTROL OF ATOMIC ENERGY

The only major progress made in Soviet–American relations in late 1945 to early 1946 was on the question of how to control atomic energy. On 27 December 1945 James F. Byrnes, Secretary of State, and V.M. Molotov, Soviet Foreign Minister, agreed to establish an Atomic Energy Commission in the United Nations. Bernard Baruch was the chief American negotiator. These are the American proposals.

The United States proposes the creation of an International Atomic Development Authority, to which should be entrusted all phases of the development and use of atomic energy, starting with the raw material and including

1. Managerial control or ownership of all atomic-energy activities potentially dangerous to world security.
2. Power to control, inspect, and license all other atomic activities.
3. The duty of fostering the beneficial uses of atomic energy.
4. Research and development responsibilities of an affirmative character intended to put the Authority in the forefront of atomic knowledge. . . .

When an adequate system for control of atomic energy, including the renunciation of the bomb as a weapon, has been agreed upon and put into effective operation and condign punishments set up for violations of the rules of control which are to be stigmatized as international crimes, we propose that

1. Manufacture of atomic bombs shall stop;
2. Existing bombs shall be disposed of pursuant to the terms of the treaty; and
3. The Authority shall be in possession of full information as to the know-how for the production of atomic energy. . . .

Now as to violations: in the agreement, penalties of as serious a nature as the nations may wish and as immediate and certain in their execution as possible should be fixed for

1. Illegal possession or use of an atomic bomb;
2. Illegal possession, or separation, of atomic material suitable for use in an atomic bomb;
3. Seizure of any plant or other property belonging to or licensed by the Authority;
4. Wilful interference with the activities of the Authority;
5. Creation or operation of dangerous projects in a manner contrary to, or in the absence of, a license granted by the international control body.

It would be a deception, to which I am unwilling to lend myself, were I not to say to you and to our peoples that the matter of punishment lies at the very heart of our present security system.

US Department of State Bulletin XIV, 23 June 1946. Reprinted in Walter LaFeber, *The Origins of the Cold War 1941–1947: A Historical Problem with Interpretation and Documents* (John Wiley, New York, 1971), pp. 73–4.

DOCUMENT 18 THE LONG TELEGRAM OF 22 FEBRUARY 1946

One of the key documents of the Cold War, written by Kennan in the US embassy in Moscow, and forwarded to Washington. Only a part of the telegram is reproduced here.

At the bottom of the Kremlin's neurotic view of world affairs is traditional and instinctive Russian sense of insecurity. Originally, this was insecurity of a peaceful agricultural people trying to live on vast exposed plain in neighborhood of fierce nomadic peoples. To this was added, as Russia came into contact with economically advanced West, fear of more competent, more powerful, more highly organized societies in that area. But this latter type of insecurity was one which afflicted rather Russian rulers than Russian people; for Russian rulers have invariably sensed that their rule was relatively archaic in form, fragile and artificial in its psychological foundation, unable to stand comparison for contact with political systems of Western countries. For this reason they have always feared foreign penetration, feared direct contact between Western world and their own, feared what would happen if Russians learned truth about world without or if foreigners learned truth about world within. And they have learned to seek security only in patient but deadly struggle for total destruction rival power, never in compacts and compromises with it.

It was no coincidence that Marxism, which had smoldered ineffectively for half a century in Western Europe, caught hold and blazed for first time in Russia. Only in this land which had never known a friendly neighbor or indeed any tolerant equilibrium of separate powers, either internal or international, could a doctrine thrive which viewed economic conflicts of society as insoluble by peaceful means. After establishment of Bolshevist regime, Marxist dogma, rendered even more truculent and intolerant by Lenin's interpretation, became a perfect vehicle for sense of insecurity with which Bolsheviks, even more than previous Russian rulers, were afflicted. In this dogma, with its basic altruism of purpose, they found justification for their instinctive fear of outside world, for the dictatorship without which they did not know how to rule, for cruelties they did not dare not to inflict, for sacrifices they felt bound to demand. In the name of Marxism they sacrificed every single ethical value in their methods and tactics. Today they cannot dispense with it. It is fig leaf of their moral and intellectual respectability. Without it they would stand before history, at best, as only the last of that long succession of cruel and wasteful Russian rulers who have relentlessly forced their country on to ever new heights of military power in order to guarantee external security for their internally weak regimes. This is why Soviet purposes must always be solemnly clothed in trappings of Marxism, and why no one should underrate the importance of dogma in Soviet affairs. Thus Soviet leaders are driven by necessities of their own past and present position to put forward a dogma which pictures the outside world as evil, hostile, and menacing, but as bearing within itself germs of creeping disease and destined to be wracked with growing internal convulsions until it is given final coup de grace by rising power of socialism and yields to new and better world. This thesis provides justification for that increase of military and police power in Russia state, for that isolation of Russian population from the outside world, and for that fluid and constant pressure to extend limits of Russian police power which are together the natural and instinctive urges of Russian rulers. Basically this is only the steady advance of uneasy Russian nationalism, a centuries-old movement in which conceptions of offense and defense are inextricably confused. But in new guise of international Marxism, with its honeyed promises to a desperate and wartorn outside world, it is more dangerous and insidious than ever before.

George F. Kennan, *Memoirs 1925–1950* (Bantam, New York, 1969), pp. 549–51.

DOCUMENT 19 CHURCHILL'S IRON CURTAIN SPEECH (5 MARCH 1946)

Winston Churchill, now Leader of the Opposition, was alarmed at the course of the Cold War and, in the presence of President Truman, called for a partnership between Great Britain and the United States to halt the Soviet colossus. Churchill was ahead of his time, however. Only a year later did his ideas become acceptable.

From Stettin in the Baltic to Trieste in the Adriatic, an iron curtain has descended across the continent. Behind that line lie all the capitals of the ancient states of central and eastern Europe. Warsaw, Berlin, Prague, Vienna, Budapest, Belgrade, Bucharest, and Sofia, all these famous cities and the populations around them lie in the Soviet sphere and all are subject, in one form or another, not only to Soviet influence but to a very high and increasing measure of control from Moscow. Athens, alone, with its immortal glories, is free to decide its future at an election under British, American, and French observation. . . .

However, in a great number of countries, far from the Russian frontiers and throughout the world, Communist fifth columns are established and work in complete unity and absolute obedience to the directions they receive from the Communist center. Except in the British Commonwealth, and in the United States, where communism is in its infancy, the Communist parties or fifth columns constitute a growing challenge and peril to Christian civilization. . . .

On the other hand, I repulse the idea that a new war is inevitable, still more that it is imminent. It is because I am so sure that our fortunes are in our own hands and that we hold the power to save the future, that I feel the duty to speak out now that I have an occasion to do so. I do not believe that Soviet Russia desires war. What they desire is the fruits of war and the indefinite expansion of their power and doctrines. . . .

From what I have seen of our Russian friends and allies during the war, I am convinced that there is nothing they admire so much as strength, and there is nothing for which they have less respect than for military weakness. For that reason the old doctrine of a balance of power is unsound. We cannot afford, if we can help it, to work on narrow margins, offering temptations to a trial of strength. If the western democracies stand together in strict adherence to the principles of the United Nations Charter, their influence for furthering these principles will be immense and no one is likely to molest them. If, however, they become divided or falter in their duty, and if these all-important years are allowed to slip away, then indeed catastrophe may overwhelm us all.

Congressional Record, 79th Congress, 2nd Session, A1146–7.

DOCUMENT 20 STALIN'S REPLY TO CHURCHILL'S SPEECH

Stalin's trenchant response to Churchill revealed his belief in Anglo-American collusion against the Soviet Union, his fear of Germany, and his conviction that eastern and south-eastern Europe was so vital to Soviet security that Soviet influence there should be seen as natural.

Question: What is your opinion of Mr Churchill's latest speech in the United States of America?

Answer: I regard it as a dangerous move, calculated to sow the seeds of dissension among the Allied states and impede their collaboration.

Question: Can it be considered that Mr Churchill's speech is prejudicial to the cause of peace and security?

Answer: Yes, unquestionably. As a matter of fact, Mr Churchill now takes the stand of the warmongers, and in this Mr Churchill is not alone. He has friends not only in Britain but in the United States of America as well.

A point to be noted is that in this respect Mr Churchill and his friends bear a striking resemblance to Hitler and his friends. Hitler began his work of unleashing war by proclaiming a race theory, declaring that only German-speaking people constituted a superior nation. Mr Churchill sets out to unleash war with a race theory, asserting that only English-speaking nations are superior nations, who are called upon to decide the destinies of the entire world. The German race theory led Hitler and his friends to the conclusion that the Germans, as the only superior nation, should rule over other nations. The English race theory leads Mr Churchill and his friends to the conclusion that the English-speaking nations, as the only superior nations, should rule over the rest of the nations of the world. . . .

The following circumstances should not be forgotten. The Germans made their invasion of the USSR through Finland, Poland, Rumania, Bulgaria, and Hungary. The Germans were able to make their invasion through these countries because, at the time, governments hostile to the Soviet Union existed in these countries. As a result of the German invasion the Soviet Union has lost irretrievably in the fighting against the Germans, and also through the German occupation and the deportation of Soviet citizens to German servitude, a total of about seven million people. In other words, the Soviet Union's loss of life has been several times greater than that of Britain and the United States of America put together. Possibly in some quarters an inclination is felt to forget about these colossal sacrifices of the Soviet people which secured the liberation of Europe from the Hitlerite yoke. But the Soviet Union cannot forget about them. And so what can there be surprising about the fact that the Soviet Union, anxious for its future safety, is trying to see to it that governments loyal in their attitude to the Soviet Union should exist in these countries? How can anyone, who has not taken leave of his senses, describe these peaceful aspirations of the Soviet Union as expansionist tendencies on the part of our state?

Pravda, 13 March 1946.

DOCUMENT 21 BYRNES' SPEECH AT STUTTGART (6 SEPTEMBER 1946)

Germany was divided economically as well as politically by the end of 1945. Byrnes proposed a treaty with the major powers to create a unified demilitarised Germany, but the Soviets turned it down. Great Britain and the United States agreed to merge their zones and the Americans decided to give Germans greater responsibility for their own affairs. Byrnes announced this at Stuttgart.

The carrying out of the Potsdam Agreement has . . . been obstructed by the failure of the Allied Control Council to take the necessary steps to enable the German economy to function as an economic unit. Essential central German administrative departments have not been established, although they are expressly required by the Potsdam Agreement. . . .

The United States is firmly of the belief that Germany should be administered as an economic unit and that zonal barriers should be completely obliterated so far as the economic life and activity in Germany are concerned.

The conditions which now exist in Germany make it impossible for industrial production to reach the levels which the occupying powers agreed were essential for a minimum German peacetime economy. Obviously, if the agreed levels of industry are to be reached, we cannot continue to restrict the free exchange of commodities, persons, and ideas throughout Germany. The barriers between the four zones of Germany are far more difficult to surmount than those between normal independent states.

The time has come when the zonal boundaries should be regarded as defining only the areas to be occupied for security purposes by the armed forces of the occupying powers and not as self-contained economic or political units.

That was the course of development envisaged by the Potsdam Agreement, and that is the course of development which the American Government intends to follow to the full limit of its authority. It has formally announced that it is its intention to unify the economy of its own zone with any or all of the other zones willing to participate in the unification.

So far only the British Government has agreed to let its zone participate. We deeply appreciate their cooperation. Of course, this policy of unification is not intended to exclude the governments not now willing to join. The unification will be open to them at any time they wish to join.

We favor the economic unification of Germany. If complete unification cannot be secured, we shall do everything in our power to secure the maximum possible unification. . . .

Similarly, there is urgent need for the setting up of a central German administrative agency for industry and foreign trade. . . .

Germany must be given a chance to export goods in order to import enough to make her economy self-sustaining. Germany is a part of Europe, and recovery in Europe, and particularly in the states adjoining Germany, will be slow indeed if Germany with her great resources of iron and coal is turned into a poorhouse. . . .

The Potsdam Agreement did not provide that there should never be a central German government; it merely provided that for the time being there should be no central German government. Certainly this only meant that no central government should be established until some sort of democracy was rooted in the soil of Germany and some sense of local responsibility developed. . . .

It is the view of the American Government that the German people throughout Germany, under proper safeguards, should now be given the primary responsibility for the running of their own affairs.

Department of State Bulletin, XV, 15 September 1946. Reprinted in Walter LaFeber, *The Origins of the Cold War 1941–1947: A Historical Problem with Interpretation and Documents* (John Wiley, New York, 1971), pp. 132–3.

DOCUMENT 22 'THE TOUGHER WE GET, THE TOUGHER THE RUSSIANS WILL GET'

Henry Wallace, US Secretary of Commerce, was appalled by Churchill's iron curtain speech. He favoured cooperation with the Soviet Union, and regarded the expansion of American trade abroad as vital if another depression was to be avoided. During the first half of 1946 he argued inside the administration for a volte face *in foreign policy. On 12 September 1946 he addressed a political rally in New York and made his worries public. Byrnes demanded that he resign. Wallace abandoned Truman and launched a campaign to defeat him at the Presidential election of 1948. It was Wallace who lost.*

In this connection, I want one thing clearly understood. I am neither anti-British nor pro-British – neither anti-Russian nor pro-Russian. And just two days ago, when President Truman read these words, he said that they represented the policy of his administration.

I plead for an America vigorously dedicated to peace – just as I plead for opportunities for the next generation throughout the world to enjoy the abundance which now, more than ever before, is the birthright of men.

To achieve lasting peace, we must study in detail how the Russian character was formed – by invasions of Tartars, Mongols, Germans, Poles, Swedes, and French; by the intervention of the British, French and Americans in Russian affairs from 1919 to 1921; by the geography of the huge Russian land mass situated strategically between Europe and Asia; and by the vitality derived from the rich Russian soil and the strenuous Russian climate. Add to all this the tremendous emotional power which Marxism and Leninism gives to the Russian leaders – and then we can realize that we are reckoning with a force which cannot be handled successfully by a 'Get tough with Russia' policy. 'Getting tough' never bought anything real and lasting – whether for schoolyard bullies or businessmen or world powers. The tougher we get, the tougher the Russians will get. . . .

We must not let our Russian policy be guided or influenced by those inside or outside the United States who want war with Russia. This does not mean appeasement.

We most earnestly want peace with Russia – but we want to be met half way. We want cooperation. And I believe that we can get cooperation once Russia understands that our primary objective is neither saving the British Empire nor purchasing oil in the Near East with the lives of American soldiers.

Vital Speeches of the Day, XII, 1 October 1946. Reprinted in Walter LaFeber, *The Origins of the Cold War 1941–1947: A Historical Problem with Interpretation and Documents* (John Wiley, New York, 1971), pp. 145–6.

DOCUMENT 23 MOLOTOV ON 'EQUAL OPPORTUNITY'

The Paris Peace Conference was discussing a peace treaty for Romania when on 10 October 1946 Molotov, the Soviet Foreign Minister, revealed his opinion of 'equal opportunity' or the 'open world' economy the United States was striving for. In so doing he overturned the principles of the Atlantic Charter and the Declaration on Liberated Europe.

We know that the United States made a very great effort in this war, in defence of its own interests and of our common aims, for which we are all very grateful to the United States. But for all that, it cannot be said that the United Sates is one of those states which suffered grave material damage in the second world war, which were ruined and weakened in this war. We are glad that this did not happen to our ally, although we ourselves have had to go through trying times, the consequences of which will take us long years to heal.

Now that you know the facts, place side by side Rumania, enfeebled by the war, or Yugoslavia, ruined by the German and Italian fascists, and the United States of America, whose wealth has grown immensely during the war, and you will clearly see what the implementation of the principle of 'equal opportunity' would mean in practice. Imagine, under these circumstances, that in this same Rumania or Yugloslavia, or in some other war-weakened state, you have this so-called 'equal opportunity' for, let us say, American capital – that is, the opportunity for it to penetrate unhindered into Rumanian industry, or Yugoslav industry and so forth; what, then, will remain of Rumania's national industry, or of Yugoslavia's national industry?

It is surely not so difficult to understand that if American capital were given a free hand in the small states ruined and enfeebled by the war, as the advocates of the principle of 'equal opportunity' desire, American capital would buy up the local industries, appropriate the more attractive Rumanian, Yugoslav and all other enterprises, and would become the master in these small states. Given such a situation, we would probably live to see the day when in your own country, on switching on the radio, you would be hearing not so much your own language as one American gramophone record after another or some piece or other of British propaganda. The time might come when in your own country, on going to the cinema, you would be seeing American films sold for foreign consumption – and not those of the better quality, but those manufactured in greater quantity, and circulated and imposed abroad by the agents of powerful firms and cinema companies which have grown particularly rich during the war.

Can anyone really fail to see that if, as a result of the application of the principle of so-called 'equal opportunity' in small states, unrestricted competition begins between the home products and the products poured out by the factories of the United States or Great Britain, nothing will remain of the sovereignty and independence of these states, especially considering the post-war conditions? Is it not clear that such unrestricted application of the principle of 'equal opportunity' in the given conditions would in practice mean the veritable economic enslavement of the small states and their subjugation to the rule and arbitrary will of strong and enriched foreign firms, banks and industrial companies? Is it not clear that if such 'principles of equality' are applied in international economic life, the smaller states will be governed by the orders, injunctions, instructions of strong foreign trusts and monopolies? Was this what we fought for when we battled the fascist invaders, the Hitlerite and Japanese imperialists?

V.M. Molotov, *Problems of Foreign Policy, Speeches and Statements, April 1945–November 1948*, Moscow, 1949, 215–16.

DOCUMENT 24 THE TRUMAN DOCTRINE

President Truman deliberately set out in this speech before Congress on 12 March 1947 to dramatise the Soviet threat so as to ensure that the aid requested for Greece and Turkey should be voted. He divided the world into two camps and called on the American people to take up their world mission.

At the present moment in world history nearly every nation must choose between alternative ways of life. The choice is too often not a free one.

One way of life is based upon the will of the majority, and is distinguished by free institutions, representative government, free elections, guarantees of individual liberty, freedom of speech and religion, and freedom from political oppression.

The second way of life is based upon the will of a minority forcibly imposed upon the majority. It relies upon terror and oppression, a controlled press and radio, fixed elections, and the suppression of personal freedoms.

I believe that it must be the policy of the United States to support free peoples who are resisting attempted subjugation by armed minorities or by outside pressures.

I believe that we must assist free peoples to work out their own identities in their own way. . . .

The seeds of totalitarian regimes are nurtured by misery and want. They spread and grow in the evil soil of poverty and strife. They reach their full growth when the hope of a people for a better life has died.

We must keep that hope alive.

The free peoples of the world look to us for support in maintaining their freedoms.

If we falter in our leadership, we may endanger the peace of the world – and we shall surely endanger the welfare of our own Nation.

Great responsibilities have been placed upon us by the swift movement of events.

I am confident that the Congress will face these responsibilities squarely.

Public Papers of the Presidents, Harry S Truman, 1947. Reprinted in Walter LaFeber, *The Origins of the Cold War 1941–1947: A Historical Problem with Interpretation and Documents* (John Wiley, New York, 1971), pp. 154–6.

DOCUMENT 25 THE MARSHALL PLAN

This Plan was launched in a speech by George C. Marshall, Secretary of State, at Harvard University on 5 June 1947. It was partly in response to European economic difficulties – Europe was importing twice as much as it was exporting to the United States – and partly to the American need to expand export markets. Europe wanted American goods but was chronically short of US dollars. Credits and aid therefore would have to be provided by the United States.

It is logical that the United States should do whatever it is able to do to assist in the return of normal economic health in the world, without which there can be no political stability and no assured peace. Our policy is directed not against any country or doctrine but against hunger, poverty, desperation and chaos. Its purpose should be the revival of a working economy in the world so as to permit the emergence of political and social conditions in which free institutions can exist. . . .

It is already evident that, before the United States Government can proceed much further in its efforts to alleviate the situation and help start the European world on its way to recovery, there must be some agreement among the countries of Europe as to the requirements of the situation and the part those countries themselves will take in order to give proper effect to whatever action might be undertaken by this Government. It would be neither fitting nor efficacious for this Government to undertake to draw up unilaterally a program designed to place Europe on its feet economically. This is the business of the Europeans. The initiative, I think, must come from Europe. The role of this country should consist of friendly aid in the drafting of a European program and of later support of such a program so far as it may be practical for us to do so. The program should be a joint one, agreed to by a number, if not all, European nations.

Department of State Bulletin, XVI, 15 June 1947, p. 1160.

DOCUMENT 26 THE MR X ARTICLE

George Kennan wrote this article, 'The Sources of Soviet Conduct', but published it in Foreign Affairs *under the pseudonym Mr X. It soon became clear who Mr X really was. Together with the Long Telegram, the Mr X article, of which this is an extract, articulates the doctrine of containment.*

It is clear that the main element of any United States policy towards the Soviet Union must be that of a longterm, patient but firm and vigilant containment of Russian expansive tendencies. . . . It is clear that the United States cannot expect in the foreseeable future to enjoy political intimacy with the Soviet regime. It must continue to regard the Soviet Union as a rival, not a partner, in the political arena. It must continue to expect that Soviet policies will reflect no abstract love of peace and stability, no real faith in the possibility of a permanent happy coexistence of the Socialist and capitalist worlds, but rather a cautious, persistent pressure towards the disruption and weakening of all rival influence and rival power.

Foreign Affairs, Vol. 25, No. 4, July 1947, pp. 580–1.

DOCUMENT 27 VYSHINSKY ON THE TRUMAN DOCTRINE AND THE MARSHALL PLAN

Initial Soviet reaction to the Marshall Plan was cautiously positive, but in July 1947 Molotov, the Soviet Foreign Minister, speaking at Paris on instructions from Stalin, turned down the offer of US credit. The other east and south-east European states were obliged to follow suit. Andrei Vyshinsky, deputy Foreign Minister and Soviet spokesman at the United Nations, delivered this verdict at the UN on 18 September 1947. It was predictably hostile.

The so-called Truman Doctrine and the Marshall Plan are particularly glaring examples of the manner in which the principles of the United Nations are violated, of the way in which the Organization is ignored.

As the experience of the past few months has shown, the proclamation of this doctrine meant that the United States Government has moved toward a direct renunciation of the principles of international collaboration and concerted action by the great Powers and toward attempts to impose its will on other independent states, while at the same time obviously using the economic resources distributed as relief to individual needy nations as an instrument of political pressure. This is clearly proved by the measures taken by the United States Government with regard to Greece and Turkey which ignore and bypass the United Nations as well as by the measures proposed under the so-called Marshall Plan in Europe. This policy conflicts sharply with the principles expressed by the General Assembly in its resolution of 11 December 1946, which declares that relief supplies to other countries 'should . . . at no time be used as a political weapon.'

As is now clear, the Marshall Plan constitutes in essence merely a variant of the Truman Doctrine adapted to the conditions of postwar Europe. In bringing forward this plan, the United States Government apparently counted on the cooperation of the Governments of the United Kingdom and France to confront the European countries in need of relief with the necessity of renouncing their inalienable right to dispose of their economic resources and to plan their national economy in their own way. The United States also counted on making all these countries directly dependent on the interests of American monopolies, which are striving to avert the approaching depression by an accelerated export of commodities and capital in Europe. . . .

It is becoming more and more evident to everyone that the implementation of the Marshall Plan will mean placing European countries under the economic and political control of the United States and direct interference by the latter in the internal affairs of those countries.

Moreover, this Plan is an attempt to split Europe into two camps and, with the help of the United Kingdom and France, to complete the formation of a *bloc* of several European countries hostile to the interests of the democratic countries of Eastern Europe and most particularly to the interests of the Soviet Union.

An important feature of this Plan is the attempt to confront the countries of Eastern Europe with a *bloc* of Western European States including Western Germany. The intention is to make use of Western Germany and German heavy industry (the Ruhr) as one of the most important economic bases for American expansion in Europe, in disregard of the national interests of the countries which suffered from German aggression.

United Nations, General Assembly, Official Records,
Plenary Meetings, 18 September 1947, pp. 86–8.

WHO'S WHO

Attlee, Clement (1883–1967) Took over from Churchill at Potsdam after the sweeping victory of the Labour party, in July 1945. Dry, unemotional and an academic socialist, Attlee was the antithesis of the mercurial, bon-vivant Churchill. He left dealing with Stalin to Ernest Bevin, his Foreign Secretary.

Beria, Lavrenty Pavlovich (1899–1953) Political gangster who was kind to his family. A fellow Georgian, he was Stalin's butcher in the Caucasus and succeeded Ezhov in 1939. He headed the Soviet atomic programme. He lost out to Khrushchev and others after Stalin's death and was executed.

Bevin, Ernest (1881–1951) Trade union leader who had to devote much time to outmanoeuvring communists. This gave him a natural aversion to Molotov and the Soviet communists. He strongly supported the US presence in Europe as a counterweight to the Soviet Union. His other main concern was promoting de-colonisation and consigning the British Empire to the past.

Budenny, Marshal Semen Mikhailovich (1883–1973) Became one of Stalin's favourite military men. A cavalry man, mechanised warfare in 1941 totally bewildered him. Stalin shunted him sideways. His intellect may have saved him during the purges.

Bulganin, Marshal Nikolai Aleksandrovich (1895–1975) Political marshal who occupied many high-ranking posts connected with defence and security. His task at the beginning of the war was to ensure that the military obeyed Stalin and implemented his orders. He was minister for the armed forces, 1947–9. Then he became deputy Prime Minister until Stalin's death. The fact that Stalin never became suspicious of his motives reveals his high political skill.

Byrnes, James F. (1879–1972) Important politician during the war and a Supreme Court judge. He stood down in favour of Truman as Vice President in 1944. Truman made him his Secretary of State and he was a strong defender of US interests.

Chuikov, Marshal Vasily Ivanovich (1900–82) Became famous at the battle of Stalingrad and afterwards occupied many high posts.

Churchill, Winston Spencer (1874–1965) Great wartime British Prime Minister who was a master of the spoken word but always played second fiddle to the Americans. He was also aware that the Red Army was strongest in Europe. His friendship with Roosevelt was very important for the war effort. Stalin and Churchill respected one another but the Soviet dictator won on points. One has to bear in mind that Churchill often had a weak hand to play. He began at Potsdam but was replaced by Clement Attlee, his wartime deputy Prime Minister, and leader of the Labour party, which won a landslide victory at the 1945 general election.

Eden, Anthony (Lord Avon) (1897–1977) Churchill's Foreign Secretary during most of the war. He was a man of principle who often found negotiations with the Russians difficult. He agreed a 20-year Anglo-Soviet alliance, in 1942. He was against making concessions to Stalin in eastern Europe. Churchill regarded him as his natural successor.

Gromyko, Andrei Andreevich (1909–89) Grim Grom (he always looked as if he had toothache) and Mr Nyet (No), Gromyko learnt his craft under Stalin. He was ambassador in Washington in 1943 and was present at Yalta and Potsdam. He headed the Soviet mission to the UN, 1946–8, and then became a deputy Foreign Minister. He had the best command of Russian among Soviet leaders and never revealed his acute sense of humour in public (Stalin liked his representatives to be serious).

Khrushchev, Nikita Sergeevich (1894–1971) Rumbustious, intelligent but uneducated party official who was entranced by Stalin. The spell was only broken after Stalin's death and he demolished his reputation in 1956. Khrushchev was party leader in Ukraine and Moscow and enthusiastically participated in the purges.

Konev, Marshal Ivan Stepanovich (1897–1973) One of the most successful Red Army commanders during the Great Fatherland War. Commander of the Kalinin Front, October 1941–December 1942. He commanded the Steppe Front, 1943–4 and became a Marshal of the Soviet Union in 1944. His front advanced to the Vistula and then Berlin. He continued to Torgau where he linked up with US forces. His forces then moved south and entered Prague in May 1945. He was first deputy People's Minister of Defence and commander of Soviet ground forces, 1946–50.

Lenin, Vladimir Ilich (1870–1924) One of the great political actors of the twentieth century in world politics. Inspired by the Enlightenment vision of a just, harmonious society, he brooked no opposition in his quest for revolution. Stalin was a key aide in 1917 and afterwards Lenin tried to smooth the acrimonious relationship between Stalin and Trotsky. In his Testament he warned the party against Stalin's inclination to abuse power. Stalin's associates rallied to his cause after Lenin's death and Trotsky fluffed his lines. Stalin never looked back and repaid his opponents with death.

Maisky, Ivan Mikhailovich (1884–1975) 'Pussy Face' Maisky was a very popular Soviet ambassador to the Court of St James, 1932–43. His main task in London was to press for a second front. He then became a deputy Foreign Minister. He was present at Yalta and Potsdam.

Malenkov, Georgy Maksimilianovich (1902–88) Skilled administrator, he played a key role during the war as a member of GKO. He was elected to the Politburo in 1946 and was also deputy Prime Minister. Stalin poked fun at his excess flab.

Marshall, General George (1880–1959) Appointed Chief of Staff of the US Army at the outbreak of war, in 1939, and only had 200,000 men. He was made chair of the Joint Chiefs of Staff Committee after Pearl Harbor to advise the President on strategy, a post he held throughout the war. The President kept him in Washington because he was so valuable to him. He accompanied Roosevelt to most international conferences. He became Secretary of State under Truman and drafted the Marshall Plan. He was almost unknowable (President Truman was not permitted to address him as George) but had a fine, impartial mind.

Molotov, Vyacheslav Mikhailovich (1890–1986) Ever faithful to Stalin, 'bootface' Molotov played a major role in foreign affairs and was greatly disliked in the West. His memoirs are somewhat disappointing and reveal little of Stalin's real thinking. He found the Khrushchev era soft because it was not Bolshevik enough, meaning not enough coercion was being used to mould the new society.

Rokossovsky, Marshal Konstantin Konstanovich (1896–1968) Proved himself an able commander during the Great Fatherland War during the battles of Moscow, Stalingrad and Kursk. He halted outside Warsaw, August 1944, and allowed the insurgents to be slaughtered by the Germans. After liberation he became Minister of Defence and deputy Prime Minister in Poland (he was of Polish origin). The Poles succeeded in having him recalled to Moscow in 1956.

Roosevelt, President Franklin Delano (1882–1945) Roosevelt had been President for nine years before the Japanese attacked Pearl Harbor. He had concentrated mainly on leading the US out of recession (New Deal). He was aware that Americans were opposed to involvement in the European war, 1939–41, but felt that it was in the US strategic interest that Britain and the Allies be saved from defeat. Lend-Lease was the result. He shared many of the war aims of Winston Churchill. The first fruit of this friendship was the Atlantic Charter. Despite the war in the Pacific he thought that Germany should be defeated first and Britain protected from defeat at all costs. Roosevelt, crippled by polio, appeared unfit to be a war leader but his fine intellect and resolve saw him through. He thought he understood Stalin but died before the war ended, leaving the difficult task of dealing with the Soviet leader to his successor, Harry Truman.

Sokolovsky, Marshal Vasily Danilovich (1897–1968) Successful military career saw him deputy Chief of the General Staff, February 1941. He was Marshal Konev's chief of staff on the Western Front, 1941–3. He was a commander at the battle of Kursk. In April 1945, he was appointed deputy commander of the 1st Belorussian Front, commanded by Marshal Zhukov, during the final assault on Berlin. He was commander of Soviet forces in (East) Germany, 1946–9, and was Chief of the General Staff, 1952–6.

Stalin, Iosef Vissarionovich (1878–1953) Brilliant but flawed politician who was one of the most important leaders of the twentieth century. He revealed matchless skill at political tactics and had a superb memory. He never forgot a slight. He relentlessly pursued the goal of making Soviet society socialist and the Soviet Union the leading country in the world. Although a Georgian he became an assimilated Great Russian and remorselessly suppressed non-Russian nationalism. He was willing to sacrifice anyone in the pursuit of moral-political unity (a harmonious society).

Timoshenko, Marshal Semen Konstantinovich (1895–1970) Occupied many top military posts during the Great Fatherland War but it was his friendship with Stalin, going back to the civil war, which saved him from retribution for failure. He was a cavalry man and replaced Voroshilov as Commissar for Defence, in May 1940, with special responsibility to reorganise the Red Army after defeat in the Winter War with Finland. He became commander of the Western Front when the Germans invaded and could do little to stem the tide. He was defeated by the Germans at Kharkov, May 1942. This cost him his command and he was transferred to the North-Western Front, his last operational command. He then moved to Stavka for the rest of the war.

Truman, President Harry S. (1884–1972) Senator from Missouri at the outbreak of the Second World War and saved the country millions of dollars with astute management of the defence programme. He was made Vice President in 1944 but was not drawn into decision-making, even though Roosevelt knew he was dying. He continued Roosevelt's policies towards the Soviet Union but spoke bluntly to

Molotov. He sought an understanding with Stalin but is seen as a Cold War President, giving his name to the Truman Doctrine. It promised aid to all countries under threat from communism.

Vasilevsky, Marshal Aleksandr Mikhailovich (1895–1977) Played a key role in the success of the Red Army during the Great Fatherland War. He was chief of staff during most of the war. Vasilevsky deputised for Stalin when the latter was attending the Yalta Conference, February 1945. In June 1945 he went to the Far East as commander-in-chief against the Japanese. In 1946, he again became Chief of the General Staff and deputy Minister of Defence. He was Minister of the Armed Forces, 1949–53.

Voroshilov, Marshal Klimenty Efremovich (1881–1969) Close to Stalin from the Civil War, he proved himself a great survivor. He was Commissar for Defence, 1934–40. He gave way to the more able Timoshenko, in May 1940, as part of the reorganisation of the Red Army. He then became a deputy chair of Sovnarkom and the chair of the defence committee. He was appointed to the GKO, responsible for the overall running of the war. He was put in command of the armies of the North-Western Front, but could do little to stem the German advance. He signed the armistice for the Allies with Hungary and headed the Allied (Soviet) Control Commission in Hungary, 1946–7. He was USSR deputy Prime Minister, 1946–53.

Vyshinsky, Andrei Yanuarevich (1883–1954) Venomous, merciless state prosecutor who gained world-wide notoriety for his courtroom behaviour during the great show trials. A former Menshevik, he always had to prove his loyalty to Stalin. He came out with the famous line, in closing for the prosecution, during the first great show trial: 'I demand that these mad dogs be shot, every last one of them!'. He was deputy Commissar for Foreign Affairs, 1940, and deputy chair of Sovnarkom, 1939–44. In 1949, he replaced Molotov as Minister of Foreign Affairs (he was reputed to have reported to Stalin over Molotov's head) and was permanent Soviet representative at the United Nations. He turned his venom on the United States, especially during the Korean War, 1950–3. In a memorable phrase, Leonard Schapiro described him as the nearest thing to a human rat he had ever seen!

Zhdanov, Andrei Aleksandrovich (1896–1948) Guardian of Stalinist cultural orthodoxy, from socialist realism to the xenophobia of the late 1940s, known as *the Zhdanovshchina*, he became a member of the Politburo, in 1939. In 1934, he laid down the rules for writers – socialist realism; all published work was to be didactic and optimistic. He led the defence of Leningrad, 1941–4. The leading light at the founding of the Communist Information Bureau (Cominform) at Szklarska Poręba, Poland, in September 1947. He died suddenly in 1948, probably naturally – he was a heavy drinker. Malenkov and Beria seized the opportunity to settle scores with the Leningrad leadership in what became known as the Leningrad Affair. This resulted in many officials being executed and many hundreds being dismissed.

Zhukov, Marshal Georgy Konstantinovich (1896–1974) Most prominent and successful Red Army commander during the Great Fatherland War. He defeated the Japanese at Khaikin-Gol, Mongolia, 1939. He was made Chief of the General Staff and deputy Commissar for Defence, January–July 1941. In October 1941, he replaced Voroshilov as commander of the northern sector and was personally responsible for the defence of Leningrad. He then moved to Moscow and became commander-in-chief of the entire Western Front. He was responsible for the defence of Stalingrad. He participated in the battle of Kursk and became commander of the 1st Belorussian Front, November 1944. His troops reached Berlin, in April 1945. He then became commander of Soviet occupation forces in Germany. Stalin was wary of his popularity and in April 1946 demoted him to commander of the Odessa military district. After Stalin's death, he returned to Moscow as deputy USSR Minister of Defence. A brilliant but rude and abrasive man, he was undoubtedly the leading military man of his generation.

GUIDE TO FURTHER READING

There are now enough books on the Cold War written by historians and international relations specialists to fill several libraries. This review can afford only a flavour of the multitudinous writings on offer. The best book to begin with is Odd Arne Westad (ed.), *Reviewing the Cold War Approaches, Interpretations, Theory* (Frank Cass, London, 2000). It is the product of a symposium which brought together many of the leading scholars in the field. The published contributions are the result of intense debate and many revisions.

The best summary of the orthodox school of thought is Arthur M. Schlesinger, Jr., 'Origins of the Cold War', *Foreign Affairs*, 46 (1967), pp. 22–52. Also instructive is Jerald Combs, *American Diplomatic History: two Centuries of Changing Interpretations* (University of California Press, Berkeley, CA, 1983. The most influential writers of this school are William H. McNeill, *America, Britain and Russia: Their Co-operation and Conflict, 1941–1946* (Oxford University Press, New York, 1953). This study has stood the test of time extremely well. Another influential text is Herbert Feis, *Churchill-Roosevelt-Stalin: The War They Waged and the Peace They Sought* (Princeton University Press, Princeton, NJ, 1957).

The leading lights of the revisionist school are William Appleman Williams, Thomas J. McCormick, Walter LaFeber and Lloyd C. Gardner. William Appleman Williams, *The Tragedy of American Diplomacy*, rev. ed. (Delta Books, New York, 1962); Thomas J. McCormick, *Half-Century: United States Foreign Policy in the Cold War* (Johns Hopkins University Press, Baltimore, MA, 1989); Walter LaFeber, *America, Russia and the Cold War 1945–1990*, 6th ed. (McGraw-Hill, New York, 1991); Lloyd C. Gardner, *Architects of Illusions: Men and Ideas in American Foreign Policy, 1941–1949* (Quadrangle, Chicago, 1970). See also Gar Alperowitz, *Atomic Diplomacy: Hiroshima and Potsdam, the Use of the Atomic Bomb and the American Confrontation with Soviet Power* (Vintage Books, New York, 1967); Donna Fleming, *The Cold War and Its Origins 1917–1960* (Doubleday, New York, 1961), 2 vols. Gabriel Kolko is an impressive writer. See especially Gabriel Kolko and Joyce Kolko, *The Limits of Power: The World and United States Foreign Policy, 1945–1954* (Harper & Row, New York, 1972).

John Lewis Gaddis, *The United States and the Origins of the Cold War, 1941–1947* (Columbia University Press, New York, 1972, reprinted 2000) can be regarded as the text which established post-revisionism. A stimulating, up-to-date statement of his position is John Lewis Gaddis, *We Now Know: Rethinking Cold War History* (Oxford University Press, New York, 1998). Other major writers of this persuasion are Melvyn P. Leffler, *A Preponderance of Power: National Security, the Truman Administration, and the Cold War* (Stanford University Press, Stanford, CA, 1992); Geir Lundestad, 'Empire by Invitation? The United States and Western Europe, 1945–1952, *Journal of Peace Research*, 23 (1986), pp. 263–77; Ibid., *'Empire' by Integration: the United States and European Integration, 1945–1997* (Oxford University Press, Oxford, 1998); Anders Stephanson, *Kennan and the Art of Foreign Policy* (Harvard University Press, Cambridge, MA, 1989). See also Melvyn P. Leffler, *The Specter of Communism: The United States and the Origins of the Cold War, 1917–1953* (Hill and Wang, New York, 1994). Daniel Yergin, *Shattered Peace: The Origins of the Cold War and the National Security State* (Penguin, London, 1980), is a splendid, left-of-centre post-revisionist analysis. A thoughtful analysis of the Cold War is Wilfred Loth, *Die Teilung der Welt. Geschichte des Kalten Krieges 1941–1945* (Deutsche Taschenbuch Verlag, Munich, 1980) No. 100, p. 146 in 2nd edn.

The best account of Britain's role is Sean Greenwood, *Britain and the Cold War 1945–1991* (Macmillan, Basingstoke, 2000). The memoirs of Churchill and Eden are revealing: Winston Churchill, *Triumph and Tragedy* (Houghton Mifflin, Boston, MA, 1954); Anthony Eden, *The Eden Memoirs, The Reckoning* (Cassell, London, 1965). See also David Dilks (ed.), The Diaries of Alexander Cadogan, 1938–1945 (Cassell, London, 1971).

Of special note in regions outside western and eastern Europe are: Michael M. Boll, *Cold War in the Balkans: American Foreign Policy and the Emergence of Communist Bulgaria, 1943–1947* (University Press of Kentucky, Lexington KY, 1984); Geir Lundestad, *America, Scandinavia, and the Cold War* (Universitetsforlaget, Oslo, 1980); Bruce R. Kuniholm, *The Origins of the Cold War in the Near East: Great Power Conflict and Diplomacy in Iran, Turkey, and Greece* (Princeton University Press, Princeton, NJ, 1980); William W. Stueck, *The Road to Confrontation: American Policy Towards China and Korea, 1947–1950* (University of North Carolina Press, Chapel Hill, NC, 1981). On American relations with Japan see: William R. Nester, *Power across the Pacific: A Diplomatic History of American Relations with Japan* (Macmillan, Basingstoke, 1996); worthy of note is: Walter LaFeber, *The Clash: A History of US-Japan Relations* (Norton, New York, 1997); Michael Schaller, *The American Occupation of Japan: The Origins of the Cold War in Asia* (Oxford University Press, New York, 1985); Andrew Rotter, *The Path to Vietnam: Origins of the American Commitment to Southeast Asia* (Cornell University Press, Ithaca, NY, 1987).

On the Soviet occupation of east Germany the primary text is: Norman M. Naimark, *The Russians in Germany: A History of the Soviet Zone of Occupation, 1945–1949* (Harvard University Press, Cambridge, MA, 1995). Also important is: Carolyn Eisenberg, *Drawing the Line: The American Decision to Divide Germany, 1944–1949* (Cambridge University Press, New York, 1996). The most incisive account of the Berlin Blockade is Thomas Parrish, *Berlin in the Balance: The Blockade, the Airlift, the First Major Battle of the Cold War* (Perseus Books, Reading, MA, 1998).

There has been a lively debate over the years about 'lost opportunities', meaning that windows of opportunity existed but this was not fully grasped or there was no desire to recognise that they existed. It follows, of course, that had they been taken everything would have turned out differently. A recent example of this argument is Deborah Larson, *The Anatomy of Mistrust* (Cornall University Press, Ithaca, NY, 1997). However, the overwhelming weight of recent scholarship does not flow in this direction. See, for example, the excellent study by Stein Bjornstad who is sceptical about the missed opportunities for German unification: Stein Bjornstad, *The Soviet Union and German Unification During Stalin's Last Years* (Institutt for forsvarsstudier, Oslo, 1998).

The view that Truman was willing to pay the price of a Cold War because he did not believe that the West could win a war with the Soviet Union comes through in the following: Francesca Gori and Silvio Pons, *The Soviet Union and Europe in the Cold War, 1943–1953* (Macmillan, Basingstoke, 1996); and David Reynolds, ed., *The Origins of the Cold War in Europe: International Perspectives* (Yale University Press,

New Haven, CT, 1994). See also Antonio Varsori and Elena Calandri, *The Failure of Peace in Europe, 1943–48* (Palgrave, Basingstoke, 2002).

There are some major histories of the Cold War from beginning to end: Richard Crockatt, *The Fifty Years War: The United States and the Soviet Union in World Politics, 1941–1991* (Routledge, London, 1995); J.P.D. Dunbabin, *The Cold War: The Great Powers and Their Allies* (Longman, Harlow, 1994), 2 vols; Ralph B. Levering, *The Cold War: A Post-Cold War History* (Harlan Davidson, Arlington Heights, IL, 1994); Ronald E. Powaski, *The Cold War: The United States, and the Soviet Union, 1917–1991* (Oxford University Press, New York, 1998); Martin Walker, *The Cold War: A History* (Henry Holt, New York, 1993).

A valuable documentary source is Walter LaFeber, ed., *The Origins of the Cold War 1941–1947: a Historical Problem with Interpretation and Documents* (John Wiley, New York, 1971). George Kennan, *Memoirs 1925–1950* (Bantam New York, 1969), is a major source.

On the Soviet side, the most important works are: Vladislav Zubok and Constantine Pleshakov, *Inside the Kremlin's Cold War: From Stalin to Khrushchev* (Harvard University Press, Cambridge, MA, 1996); and Vojtech Mastny, *The Cold War and Soviet Insecurity: The Stalin Years* (Oxford University Press, New York, 1996). Milovan Djilas, *Conversations With Stalin* (Harcourt, Brace & World, New York, 1962), makes fascinating reading. The book which affords the greatest insight into Stalin the man is Sergo Beria, *Beria My Father Inside Stalin's Kremlin* (Duckworth, London, 1999). On Moscow's relations with the Greek communists see: Peter J. Stavrakis, *Moscow and the Greek Communists, 1944–1949* (Cornell University Press, Ithaca, NY, 1989). An important subject is Stalin and the bomb. The classic text is David Holloway, *Stalin and the Bomb* (Yale University Press, New Haven, CT, 1994). Molotov's memoirs are worth consulting. Albert Resis, ed., *Molotov Remembers: Inside Kremlin Politics: Conversations with Felix Chuev* (Ivan R. Dee, Chicago, IL, 1993).

On eastern Europe see especially: Krystyna Kersten, *The Establishment of Communist Rule in Poland, 1943–1948* (University of California Press, Berkeley, CA, 1991); Norman Naimark and Leonid Gibianskii, *The Establishment of Communist Regimes in Eastern Europe, 1944–1949* (Westview Press, Boulder, CO, 1997); Odd Arne Westad, Sven Holtsmark and Iver B. Neumann, eds., *The Soviet Union in Eastern Europe, 1945–1989* (St Martin's Press, New York, 1994); also interesting is Martin McCauley, ed., *Communist Power in Europe, 1944–1949*, rev. ed. (Macmillan, Basingstoke, 1979). Worth perusing are: Geir Lundestad, *The American Non-Policy Towards Eastern Europe, 1943–1947: Universalism in an Area Not of Essential Interest to the United States* (Universitetsforlaget, Oslo, 1975); and ibid., *East, West, North, South: Major Developments in International Politics, 1945–1996* (Universitetsforlaget, Oslo, 1997).

On the Marshall Plan, the best book is: Michael J. Hogan, *The Marshall Plan: America, Britain and the Reconstruction of Western Europe, 1947–1952* (Cambridge University Press, New York, 1987).

On the American side there is a mass of material. Very enlightening are: Dean Acheson, *Present at the Creation. My Years in the State Department* (New American Library, New York, 1970); Robert H. Farrell, ed., *Off the Record: The Private Papers of Harry S. Truman* (Harper & Row, New York, 1980); Harry S. Truman, Memoirs: Years of Decision (Doubleday, New York, 1955); J. Robert Moskin, *Mr Truman's War: The Final Victories of World War II and the Birth of the Postwar World* (University Press of Kansas, Kansas, 2002); W. Averell Harriman and Elie Abel, *Special Envoy to*

Churchill and Stalin, 1941–1946 (Random House, New York, 1975); Robert L. Messer, *The End of an Alliance: James F. Byrnes, Roosevelt, Truman, and the Origins of the Cold War* (University of North Carolina Press, Chapel Hill, NC, 1982). A splendid analysis of Soviet foreign policy is Adam B. Ulam, Expansion and Coexistence: The History of Soviet Foreign Policy, 1917–1973, 2nd edn (Rinehart & Winston, New York, 1974).

An interesting left-of-centre analysis of the first and second Cold War is Fred Halliday, *The Making of the Second Cold War* (Verso, London, 1983).

The best fictional portrayal of Stalin is to be found in Robert Harris, *Archangel* (Arrow, London, 1998).

INDEX

SEMINAR STUDIES IN HISTORY

General Editors: Clive Emsley & Gordon Martel

The series was founded by Patrick Richardson in 1966. Between 1980 and 1996 Roger Lockyer edited the series before handing over to Clive Emsley (Professor of History at the Open University) and Gordon Martel (Professor of International History at the University of Northern British Columbia, Canada and Senior Research Fellow at De Montfort University).

MEDIEVAL ENGLAND

The Pre-Reformation Church in England 1400–1530 (Second edition)
Christopher Harper-Bill 0 582 28989 0

Lancastrians and Yorkists: The Wars of the Roses
David R Cook 0 582 35384 X

Family and Kinship in England 1450–1800
Will Coster 0 582 35717 9

TUDOR ENGLAND

Henry VII (Third edition)
Roger Lockyer & Andrew Thrush 0 582 20912 9

Henry VIII (Second edition)
M D Palmer 0 582 35437 4

Tudor Rebellions (Fourth edition)
Anthony Fletcher & Diarmaid MacCulloch 0 582 28990 4

The Reign of Mary I (Second edition)
Robert Tittler 0 582 06107 5

Early Tudor Parliaments 1485–1558
Michael A R Graves 0 582 03497 3

The English Reformation 1530–1570
W J Sheils 0 582 35398 X

Elizabethan Parliaments 1559–1601 (Second edition)
Michael A R Graves 0 582 29196 8

England and Europe 1485–1603 (Second edition)
Susan Doran 0 582 28991 2

The Church of England 1570–1640
Andrew Foster 0 582 35574 5

STUART BRITAIN

Social Change and Continuity: England 1550–1750 (Second edition)
Barry Coward 0 582 29442 8

James I (Second edition)
S J Houston 0 582 20911 0

The English Civil War 1640–1649
Martyn Bennett 0 582 35392 0

Charles I, 1625–1640
Brian Quintrell 0 582 00354 7

The English Republic 1649–1660 (Second edition)
Toby Barnard 0 582 08003 7

Radical Puritans in England 1550–1660
R J Acheson 0 582 35515 X

The Restoration and the England of Charles II (Second edition)
John Miller 0 582 29223 9

The Glorious Revolution (Second edition)
John Miller 0 582 29222 0

EARLY MODERN EUROPE

The Renaissance (Second edition)
Alison Brown 0 582 30781 3

The Emperor Charles V
Martyn Rady 0 582 35475 7

French Renaissance Monarchy: Francis I and Henry II (Second edition)
Robert Knecht 0 582 28707 3

The Protestant Reformation in Europe
Andrew Johnston 0 582 07020 1

The French Wars of Religion 1559–1598 (Second edition)
Robert Knecht 0 582 28533 X

Phillip II
Geoffrey Woodward 0 582 07232 8

The Thirty Years' War
Peter Limm 0 582 35373 4

Louis XIV
Peter Campbell 0 582 01770 X

Spain in the Seventeenth Century
Graham Darby 0 582 07234 4

Peter the Great
William Marshall 0 582 00355 5

EUROPE 1789–1918

Britain and the French Revolution
Clive Emsley 0 582 36961 4

Revolution and Terror in France 1789–1795 (Second edition)
D G Wright 0 582 00379 2

Napoleon and Europe
D G Wright 0 582 35457 9

The Abolition of Serfdom in Russia, 1762–1907
David Moon 0 582 29486 X

Nineteenth-Century Russia: Opposition to Autocracy
Derek Offord 0 582 35767 5

The Constitutional Monarchy in France 1814–48
Pamela Pilbeam 0 582 31210 8

The 1848 Revolutions (Second edition)
Peter Jones 0 582 06106 7

The Italian Risorgimento
M Clark 0 582 00353 9

Bismarck & Germany 1862–1890 (Second edition)
D G Williamson 0 582 29321 9

Imperial Germany 1890–1918
Ian Porter, Ian Armour and Roger Lockyer 0 582 03496 5

The Dissolution of the Austro-Hungarian Empire 1867–1918
(Second edition)
John W Mason 0 582 29466 5

Second Empire and Commune: France 1848–1871
(Second edition)
William H C Smith 0 582 28705 7

France 1870–1914 (Second edition)
Robert Gildea 0 582 29221 2

The Scramble for Africa (Second edition)
M E Chamberlain 0 582 36881 2

Late Imperial Russia 1890–1917
John F Hutchinson 0 582 32721 0

The First World War
Stuart Robson 0 582 31556 5

Austria, Prussia and Germany, 1806–1871
John Breuilly 0 582 43739 3

EUROPE SINCE 1918

The Russian Revolution (Second edition) *Anthony Wood*	0 582 35559 1
Lenin's Revolution: Russia, 1917–1921 *David Marples*	0 582 31917 X
Stalin and Stalinism (Third edition) *Martin McCauley*	0 582 27658 6
The Weimar Republic (Second edition) *John Hiden*	0 582 28706 5
The Inter-War Crisis 1919–1939 *Richard Overy*	0 582 35379 3
Fascism and the Right in Europe, 1919–1945 *Martin Blinkhorn*	0 582 07021 X
Spain's Civil War (Second edition) *Harry Browne*	0 582 28988 2
The Third Reich (Third edition) *D G Williamson*	0 582 20914 5
The Origins of the Second World War (Second edition) *R J Overy*	0 582 29085 6
The Second World War in Europe *Paul MacKenzie*	0 582 32692 3
The French at War, 1934–1944 *Nicholas Atkin*	0 582 36899 5
Anti-Semitism before the Holocaust *Albert S Lindemann*	0 582 36964 9
The Holocaust: The Third Reich and the Jews *David Engel*	0 582 32720 2
Germany from Defeat to Partition, 1945–1963 *D G Williamson*	0 582 29218 2
Britain and Europe since 1945 *Alex May*	0 582 30778 3
Eastern Europe 1945–1969: From Stalinism to Stagnation *Ben Fowkes*	0 582 32693 1
Eastern Europe since 1970 *Bülent Gökay*	0 582 32858 6
The Khrushchev Era, 1953–1964 *Martin McCauley*	0 582 27776 0

NINETEENTH-CENTURY BRITAIN

Britain before the Reform Acts: Politics and Society 1815–1832 *Eric J Evans*	0 582 00265 6
Parliamentary Reform in Britain c. 1770–1918 *Eric J Evans*	0 582 29467 3
Democracy and Reform 1815–1885 *D G Wright*	0 582 31400 3
Poverty and Poor Law Reform in Nineteenth-Century Britain, 1834–1914: From Chadwick to Booth *David Englander*	0 582 31554 9
The Birth of Industrial Britain: Economic Change, 1750–1850 *Kenneth Morgan*	0 582 29833 4
Chartism (Third edition) *Edward Royle*	0 582 29080 5
Peel and the Conservative Party 1830–1850 *Paul Adelman*	0 582 35557 5
Gladstone, Disraeli and later Victorian Politics (Third edition) *Paul Adelman*	0 582 29322 7
Britain and Ireland: From Home Rule to Independence *Jeremy Smith*	0 582 30193 9

TWENTIETH-CENTURY BRITAIN

The Rise of the Labour Party 1880–1945 (Third edition) *Paul Adelman*	0 582 29210 7
The Conservative Party and British Politics 1902–1951 *Stuart Ball*	0 582 08002 9
The Decline of the Liberal Party 1910–1931 (Second edition) *Paul Adelman*	0 582 27733 7
The British Women's Suffrage Campaign 1866–1928 *Harold L Smith*	0 582 29811 3
War & Society in Britain 1899–1948 *Rex Pope*	0 582 03531 7
The British Economy since 1914: A Study in Decline? *Rex Pope*	0 582 30194 7
Unemployment in Britain between the Wars *Stephen Constantine*	0 582 35232 0
The Attlee Governments 1945–1951 *Kevin Jefferys*	0 582 06105 9

The Conservative Governments 1951–1964
Andrew Boxer 0 582 20913 7

Britain under Thatcher
Anthony Seldon and Daniel Collings 0 582 31714 2

Britain and Empire, 1880–1945
Dane Kennedy 0 582 41493 8

INTERNATIONAL HISTORY

The Eastern Question 1774–1923 (Second edition)
A L Macfie 0 582 29195 X

India 1885–1947: The Unmaking of an Empire
Ian Copland 0 582 38173 8

The Origins of the First World War (Second edition)
Gordon Martel 0 582 28697 2

The United States and the First World War
Jennifer D Keene 0 582 35620 2

Anti-Semitism before the Holocaust
Albert S Lindemann 0 582 36964 9

The Origins of the Cold War, 1941–1949 (Third edition)
Martin McCauley 0 582 27659 4

Russia, America and the Cold War, 1949–1991
Martin McCauley 0 582 27936 4

The Arab–Israeli Conflict
Kirsten E Schulze 0 582 31646 4

The United Nations since 1945: Peacekeeping and the Cold War
Norrie MacQueen 0 582 35673 3

Decolonisation: The British Experience since 1945
Nicholas J White 0 582 29087 2

The Origins of the Vietnam War
Fredrik Logevall 0 582 31918 8

The Vietnam War
Mitchell Hall 0 582 32859 4

WORLD HISTORY

China in Transformation 1900–1949
Colin Mackerras 0 582 31209 4

Japan Faces the World, 1925–1952
Mary L Hanneman 0 582 36898 7

Japan in Transformation, 1952–2000
Jeff Kingston 0 582 41875 5

China since 1949
Linda Benson 0 582 35722 5

US HISTORY

American Abolitionists
Stanley Harrold 0 582 35738 1

The American Civil War, 1861–1865
Reid Mitchell 0 582 31973 0

America in the Progressive Era, 1890–1914
Lewis L Gould 0 582 35671 7

The United States and the First World War
Jennifer D Keene 0 582 35620 2

The Truman Years, 1945–1953
Mark S Byrnes 0 582 32904 3

The Korean War
Steven Hugh Lee 0 582 31988 9

The Origins of the Vietnam War
Fredrik Logevall 0 582 31918 8

The Vietnam War
Mitchell Hall 0 582 32859 4